THE BOOK OF LIFE

Biblical Answers to Existential Questions

Louvain Theological and Pastoral Monographs is a publishing venture whose purpose is to provide those involved in pastoral ministry throughout the world with studies inspired by Louvain's long tradition of theological excellence within the Roman Catholic tradition. The volumes selected for publication in the series are expected to express some of today's finest reflection on current theology and pastoral practice.

LOUVAIN THEOLOGICAL & PASTORAL MONOGRAPHS

—————————— 41 ——————————

THE BOOK OF LIFE

Biblical Answers to Existential Questions

by

Hans Ausloos & Bénédicte Lemmelijn

PEETERS
LEUVEN – PARIS – WALPOLE, MA

WILLIAM B. EERDMANS PUBLISHING COMPANY
GRAND RAPIDS, MICHIGAN/CAMBRIDGE, U.K.

2010

Original (but the English version has been revised and updated):
H. AUSLOOS & B. LEMMELIJN, De bijbel: een (g)oude(n) gids. Bijbelse antwoorden op
menselijke vragen (Leuven/Voorburg: Acco, 2005, ²2006) 192 p. –
ISBN 90-334-5955-8.

Translated by: David Kirchhoffer

Published jointly 2010
in Belgium by
Peeters Publishers
Bondgenotenlaan 153
3000 Leuven
and in the United States of America by
Wm. B. Eerdmans Publishing Company
2140 Oak Industrial Dr. N.E., Grand Rapids, Michigan 49505 /
P.O. Box 163 Cambridge CB3 9PU U.K.
www.eerdmans.com

Manufactured in Belgium

12 11 10 09 08   5 4 3 2 1

A catalogue record for this book is available from the Library of Congress

Eerdmans ISBN 978-0-8028-6574-8
Peeters ISBN 978-90-429-2296-9
D/2010/0602/14

TABLE OF CONTENTS

PART III
THE BIBLE: A BOOK OF LIFE

GENERAL INTRODUCTION

In a social context in which questions concerning religion, life's meaning, and philosophies of life are being pushed to the periphery, and yet, at the same time, perhaps as never before, still manage to enter into the public forum again and again, this book seeks to stimulate a critical, "adult" reflection on faith and religion in general, and on Christianity in particular. This will primarily be done in dialogue with the biblical, and more specifically the Old Testament, tradition that functions as its foundation.

In this book, we aim to make it clear that, throughout the ancient texts found in biblical literature, topical, fundamentally existential, human questions are raised that are not only still being asked today, but, moreover, for which there is still no final answer... This book does not pretend to give a final answer. Yet, it does aspire to begin, together with its readers, a process of reflection against the background of, and in dialogue with, an age-old reflection that is still worth pondering today.

This book consists of three larger parts. The first part briefly presents the starting point of every reflection on religion, faith and philosophy of life in a Christian context. In today's Western society, one indeed notes a crisis with regard to this issue. In two chapters, reference is made in this regard to its twofold cause: on one hand, the cultural-historical evolution of pre-modernity, via modernity, to post-modernity; and, on the other hand, the "strange" character of the biblical tradition itself, which functions as the foundation of the Judeo-Christian tradition.

In the second part, possible responses to this crisis are discussed. The first chapter discusses some "negative" reactions, reviewing mainly fundamentalism, and the tendency to historicise biblical narratives. The second chapter sketches the way in which a "positive" response can rise above this crisis of disenchantment in an enriching and critical approach. Here, light is first shed on the question of the Bible and historicity in order to then devote attention to the rise of historical-critical exegesis. Finally, we focus on the shift from a diachronic to a synchronic approach to the biblical text.

Against the background of the discussion of the negative and positive responses to the crisis that the Western, Judeo-Christian tradition has had deal with since the beginning of the twentieth century, the third and final part, in which the title of this book finds its origin, concretely directs our attention to some fundamental, existential, human questions that come up in the biblical tradition. After discussing the relationship between the Old and New Testaments, which concludes that the Old Testament must be given appropriate attention (Chapter one), we deal, in three chapters, with the way in which the biblical, and particularly the Old Testament, literature handles, thinks about, and arrives at aspects of an answer to essential questions. The second chapter of the third part speaks about the origin and goal of human existence against the background of the creation poem in Genesis 1:1–2:4. In the third chapter, the realisation of human coexistence is discussed, on the one hand from the point of view of the respect for life in the Decalogue in Exodus 20:1-17 and on the other, from the perspective of the question of social justice in the Old Testament concept of the jubilee year. Finally, the fourth chapter attends to God's relationship to the fortunes of human beings. Starting from three themes that, to this day, define and occupy human beings and society, namely, violence, suffering and love, it is shown how the literature of the Old Testament is connected to human existence, in all its attempts to find meaning, in an essential and true to life way.

For the name of God in the Old Testament, we have opted for
"YAHWEH." Faithful to the original Hebrew text, in which the name
of God is composed of the so-called tetragrammaton — the four
letters Y, H, W and H, we render the transcription of these consonants in small caps. In order to facilitate the pronunciation of the
name of God, we follow the Christian tradition which, perhaps in
imitation of the Jewish tradition, has, since time immemorial,
vocalised the name of God as Yahweh. Unless stated otherwise,
citations of biblical texts are taken from the *New Revised Standard
Version.*

The background to this book is a course titled "Religion, Meaning, and Philosophies of Life"[1] that the authors have taught for
some years at the Faculty of Arts (subfaculties of Languages and
Literature, Area Studies, History and Archaeology, Art History,
and Musicology), the Faculty of Psychology and Educational
Sciences (Department of Psychology), and the Faculty of Social
Sciences (Department of Social and Cultural Anthropology). In
developing the various parts of this publication, we drew upon the
courses "Introduction to the Study of the Old Testament," "Content
and Theologies of the Old Testament," "Pentateuch and Historical
Books," "Psalms and Wisdom Literature," and "Prophetic Books,"
which the authors teach at the Faculty of Theology. To all the
students who stimulated our reflection through countless fascinat-
ing and edifying discussions, we express our gratitude. Sincere
thanks are equally due to David Kirchhoffer, who translated the
original Dutch text with the utmost care. Finally, our heartfelt
thanks go to our *Doktorvater,* Prof. Dr. M. Vervenne, who opened
the door of Old Testament biblical studies to us quite a few years
ago and blazed the trail that we still follow today, with ever growing
interest.

---

[1] The Dutch name in fact is "Religie, Zingeving en Levensbeschouwing."

We dedicate this book to all the people who helped us to become who we are today: our parents, who like all parents dream with us and nourish great plans; our children, Matthias, Elke and Ruben, who like all children keep our feet firmly planted in reality and help us to realise that there are today — and usually immediately — many other things to be done.

PART I

FROM MYSTERY TO DISENCHANTMENT

CHAPTER ONE

FAITH AND CHRISTIANITY: SUBJECT TO TIME?

It sounds clichéd, and maybe it is a bit, but it still functions as the starting point of this book, and perhaps even of every conversation about theology today: Christian faith is, here and now, on a day in the twenty-first century, in a Western context, no longer a self-evident fact.[1] Even religion in general is no longer self-evident. Contemporary society, with its strong orientation towards technology and its tendency to investigate reality using the positive sciences, sees things as explicable and doable. The human being is deluded into thinking that he is autonomous, in control of everything. Christianity, which, as a religious-ethical system, determined politics and culture for ages and controlled and regulated everyday life, has been thrown into crisis in Western Europe.

The reactions to this are many and varied. Some people radically reject Christianity. Others are totally indifferent, an attitude that is perhaps more far-reaching than that of rejection, because it means that no further discussion is even necessary.

"Believing, what is that? I am baptised, have made my first communion. So, I've been through all the stages that belong to a Dutch Catholic education. But I have never had any affinity for Catholicism or any other religion for that matter. It happened to me, it belonged to my education and my youth, while I had the feeling that I would

---

[1] In this regard, see also "Geloof en samenleving vandaag," *Een zaaier ging het land op om te zaaien (Mc 4,3): Het jaar van de verkondiging*, Verklaringen van de bisschoppen van België. Nieuwe reeks, 29 (Brussels: LICAP, 2003) 8-13, in which this chapter finds its inspiration.

not go along with it any further... Therefore: God and I? Sorry, we don't know one another." [2] The Actor Leo Madder, in *Dag Allemaal,* 25 May 2003.

Others grasp at the straws they find in an un-nuanced and fundamentalistic endorsement of what is presented to them. Finally, there are, however, also people who, in this context, grow toward a new religious openness. Life's questions, at the meta-level, continue to present themselves and pressingly ask to be answered through a new and probing search. But religion and Christian faith no longer coincide.

"I call myself a religious atheist. I have no God and that gives me the advantage that I can dabble in all religions. Because I do indeed have a religious sensitivity." [3] Anthropologist Rik Pinxten in *De Standaard,* 17 September 2003.

The crisis described above is a consequence of a cultural-historical development. Pre-modern thought had no problem with religion. Christianity offered an answer to all questions; the Bible was considered to be a historical account. Before the rise of modernity, religious frames of reference, and particularly Christianity, had an almost self-evident importance in the functioning of both the individual's life and the social order. One could say that the culture was itself religious. Religion and culture were indissolubly bound to one another. Very concretely, this meant that philosophical

---

[2] Translated from the Dutch: *"Geloven, wat is dat? Ik ben gedoopt, heb mijn communie gedaan. Afijn, al die stadia doorlopen die horen bij een Hollandse katholieke opvoeding. Maar ik heb nooit enige affiniteit met het katholicisme of welk geloof dan ook gehad. Het overkwam me, het hoorde bij mijn opvoeding en mijn jeugd, terwijl ik het gevoel had dat ik er geen stap verder mee kwam... Dus: God en ik? Sorry, wij kennen elkaar niet."*

[3] Translated from the Dutch: *"Ik noem mezelf een religieuze atheïst. Ik heb geen God en dat geeft me het voordeel dat ik kan grasduinen bij alle religies. Want ik heb wel een religieus gevoel."*

thought, ethics, politics, art, literature and cultural social life were essentially defined by religious and/or Christian convictions. Everything was related to a particular way of seeing things: the traditional believer experienced a god who people encountered in all possible day-to-day things and moments. Human existence, nature, and the world were permeated with the presence of the divine. From this experience of reality, a seemingly self-evident answer flowed forth, to all questions of meaning: from where, to where, why, what for and what must I do? What is the meaning of existence? This answer was formulated and worked out in detail in the doctrines of religious institutions. The result was a stable world in which all knew their places and their tasks, and where, for every question, there was an answer near at hand.

With the arrival of modernity, the tower of certainty was shaken to its foundations. The paradigm of the positive sciences, then in its ascendancy, and the rationality that prevailed, deemed it necessary to explain the human being and the world in light of these new insights. In this regard, the "modern" method of approaching reality is especially marked by two processes, namely, on the one hand, differentiation on the structural level and, on the other, functional rationalisation.[4]

Differentiation on the structural level has to do with the fact that one no longer perceives reality as one, all-encompassing whole, but rather splits it up into distinct, autonomous sectors or spheres. In pre-modernity, religion served as the answer to all questions and problems. If one had toothache, one appealed to St. Apollonia. And for a "troublesome child," one sought the assistance of St. Rita. And even though the communion of saints may still play a role that

---

[4] See also Anton Van Harskamp, "Boze droom van het christendom? Verkenningen rond het fundamentalisme als idee en verschijnsel," *Tijdschrift voor Theologie* 33 (1993) 5-26, especially 8-10.

is not to be underestimated, one now has toothache treated by a dentist and has recourse to psychological counselling and/or therapy in cases of serious behavioural problems. In this framework, religion is also assigned its own domain. Religion becomes a matter that belongs especially, or even purely, to the private sphere and thus no longer exerts an all-encompassing influence on other domains in society. "Christendom" or *the* Christian society no longer exists. Functional rationalisation flows forth from the desire for safety and certainty. In response to a world, which pre-modern thought often experienced as threatening, modernity developed a permanent reflexivity that critically analyses nature and society and continuously devises new strategies and solutions, which nevertheless in their turn are seemingly immediately critically called into question in order to obtain a still firmer grip on reality. However, the result is that this constant pressure to change carries with it the paralysing and frightening feeling that "nothing is certain anymore," through which the original motive that drove functional rationalisation, namely, the desire for safety and certainty, is again undermined. This fact leads in turn to a renewed and stronger search for certainty. In this way, a typically modern thought process results in the opposite of what it aims to achieve. The practically dominant permanent criticism only brings the question of ultimate certainty more manifestly to the fore in the various (including the religious) structural domains of life.

In this modern context, religion became a primitive phenomenon that had supplied people with answers in a time when people "did not know better." Problem solved. Modern culture, which bore the standard of an explicit humanism and anthropocentricism, believed above all in the human being and the potential of human rationality. Science and technology took control of reality; (individual) freedom and emancipatory self-realisation became the core values.

And indeed, thanks to this development, humanity was better able to grasp reality. The human being is no longer totally subject to reality, but instead is able to alter the course of things, intervene in a transformative way and improve reality on the way to an ever increasing humanisation. The modern ideal is objective, measurable, controllable, and, therefore, "certain" knowledge. Knowledge that does not meet these criteria is branded subjective. It belongs to the domain of feelings and is distrusted. However, in this context, the world is narrowed down to the strictly observable. As a result, the religious vision of the world becomes problematic: belief in God's existence is dependent upon proof; proof that is not available. The human being is thus left to his own devices.

This new attitude also took root with regard to the foundation of Christianity — the Bible. Only that which was rationally explicable could be historically acceptable and only that which was historically demonstrable could contain truth and be of value. All the rest became excess baggage, stories, fairytales and myths. It is, incidentally, no coincidence that in theology, and more specifically in biblical studies, it was precisely during this period that the historical-critical method was developed and the tendency toward "demythologizing" (Bultmann) reigned supreme. Archaeology had to deliver proof of what had happened historically. Narratives for which no evidence could be retrieved were reduced to "tales." Biblical texts were atomised into verses, parts of verses and still smaller divisions and dissected based on their literary and redactional development — their present redactional layout, be it historical or otherwise. Diachronic analysis of the text became the only legitimate method.

Yet, history appears to have proven the folly of this mentality. Throughout the purification and disenchantment by modernity, the idea and the experience gradually grew that this rationalistic image of the human being and the world was deficient (cf. above where we have already pointed out the ambiguity of a relentlessly applied functional rationalisation). Modern culture was confronted with its own limitations. In its wake, political ideologies, with a vision of an achievable, ideal society, terrorised people to the extent that it became irrational. Social injustice manifested itself as a result of the fact that some had and could, while others had none and could not. Ecologically speaking, the wellbeing of the world and the human being is, in the context of the utilitarian functionalism of modernity, no longer guaranteed.

Above all, however, modernity realised that though it might know a great deal, there was still a great deal more that it did not know. There are questions for which no strictly scientific, positivist answer exists. The human being does not only want to survive, he does not even only want to live; he wants to know why he lives and even what comes after this life. The question of meaning, the unfathomable problem of suffering, the basis of values and norms, and the legitimisation of ethical forms of social living are not adequately answered by purely positivist discourse. Love, beauty and happiness, and also suffering and death, cannot be described in an objective rational way, let alone explained.

So, post-modernity once again raised the question of the binding factor, of the norm, of the surplus: religion. Religion has, from a historical perspective, always had to do with what goes beyond people: powers and forces that affect us, which we do not control, and upon which, to a great or lesser extent, we are nevertheless dependent (cf. sun worship); powers and forces that one calls "transcendent," i.e., things that go beyond the observable, describable, and constructible. The human experience of powerlessness and finiteness is also situated against this backdrop. This "primal consciousness," and the way it translates into an interest in the sacred, draws renewed attention in post-modernity. Holism, New Age, growing interest in how other religions deal with the "divine," interest in paranormal phenomena, in short, the search for the transcendent has, after the realisation of the limits of modernity, boomed. Religion as such, or at least "religion without god," thus appears not to be out of date.

The Latin word *religio* is, according to Cicero, derived from the Latin *re-legere*, which means to go over again, to reread; or to carefully ponder, to attentively read. According to Lactantius, it is derived from the Latin *re-ligare*, meaning to bind again, to rebind; or to strongly bind.[5] Then perhaps religion, as the attentive reading of what connects human beings and the transcendent, and continuously reconnects them, has indeed not yet finished its task. Nevertheless, it no longer proceeds in the form of the self-evident Christianity of pre-modernity. Christianity proclaims, in contrast to the general religious sensitivity, a God who, in the biblical tradition, does not coincide with reality, but who indeed personally enters into reality. With that, Christianity has *de facto* become one of the answers, one of the many different traditions that present themselves in the world that unfolds itself before us today. The monopoly is over. The challenge to critically rediscover Christianity, however, becomes ever greater.

[5] Herman-Emiel Mertens, *Schoonheid is uw naam* (Leuven: Acco, 1997) 34.

CHAPTER TWO

THE BIBLE: A "STRANGE" FOUNDATION

The cultural-historical shift, described above, from pre-modernity, via modernity, to post-modernity, is not the only cause of the people's estrangement from faith and Christianity. Christianity itself, and more specifically the Judeo-Christian tradition as presented in its "foundation," the Bible, is in fact, "strange." Holy Scripture, on which the tradition is based, is, concretely, a large number of books (Old and New Testament) with differing content, of diverse literary genres, written and edited by various authors and redactors over the course of several centuries. This all adds up to a text that strikes people in the twenty-first century as strange in many ways. And it is too. Consequently, biblical texts almost inevitably need to be mediated by exegesis.

In general, exegesis is defined as the discipline that concerns itself with the interpretation of the Bible. The term comes from the Greek verb ἐξηγέομαι (*ex-eigéomai*), which means "to lead out." In relation to texts, the word denotes "explaining" meaning. Hence, the substantive ἐξήγησις (*ex-eigeisis*) means "explanation" or "interpretation;" the term exegete, ἐξηγητής (*ex-eigeiteis*), refers to the person who practises exegesis, i.e., the "interpreter."

Within theological discourse, exegesis strives to explain biblical texts, those of the Old and New Testaments. Exegesis, however, is also a day-to-day activity. Indeed, day in and day out, people try to capture what is meant in what they hear, read or observe. And although people experience this as obvious and would seldom call the daily process of interpretation "exegesis," it is still essential for every form of communication. Traffic signs and symbols need to be interpreted; legal documents often require a complicated "exegesis" and their interpretation is usually the subject of discussions between lawyers; but also all forms of media beg for substantial interpretation by the reader, listener or viewer. In addition, when people communicate with one another, they are *de facto* constantly interpreting. Is a question a "genuine question" or is it instead rhetorical in nature? Is what someone is saying serious or is it meant to be an ironic joke? Does a text offer objective information or is it propaganda? Is that compliment meant to flatter in order to obtain something from a superior or is it heartfelt praise from a sincere friend? All these elements turn communication and interpretation into a complicated interplay of different factors. First, there is the subject: the speaker and the listener, or the writer and the reader. Then there is the form that is used to communicate, and finally there is the context in which the communication takes place.

When people speak to one another, in other words in verbal communication, mutual understanding is facilitated by the usually direct contact between parties. The body language or the intonation can, for example, explain a great deal. It is quite different when one is interpreting written documents, of which the Bible is an example. The writer of the text is usually not present, often not even known. The world in which he/she lives, which he/she experiences, is not necessarily the same as that of the reader. Moreover, the text itself can also represent various literary genres that must be understood in light of their purpose. In other words, there are primarily two factors that determine the correct comprehension and proper interpretation of a text, namely, first, the extent to which the writer and the reader (or if you prefer, the sender and receiver of the message) share the same lived experience, and, second, the extent to which the content and the style of the message are of a specific and/or specialised nature. This double complexity, which applies to every attempt to understand written communication, is expressed in various subfactors that also arise with regard to an adequate understanding of the Scriptures. From this it follows that the exegesis of a biblical passage — Old and New Testament — is in fact an especially complex affair, during which one must take various factors into account.[1]

1. Exegetes as "Outsiders"

No text from the Bible was originally addressed to today's readers. When the prophets denounced apostasy and injustice, and held out the prospect of the Babylonian threat, then they were addressing themselves to the Israelites of the first millennium BC. And neither are the so-called "Ten Commandments" addressed to people of the twenty-first century. Instead they are addressed to the Israelites, whom God had freed from slavery in Egypt (Exodus 20:2). As a result, today's readers of the Bible are in fact reading texts that were not primarily addressed to them. For that matter, there is no reader today who is part of the biblical authors' original social milieu. At first, it perhaps appears to be a theoretical problem. However, the simple example of a letter, which is read by someone other than the addressee, where it soon becomes apparent that this third person neither understands everything that is meant nor can interpret everything that is referred to, makes it clear that the problem is indeed also very concrete. In the same way, it is true for the reading of biblical texts.

---

[1] These elements are taken from John H. Hayes and Carl R. Holladay, *Biblical Exegesis: A Beginner's Handbook* (Atlanta, GA/London: SCM, 1982) 5-18.

2. Language Barrier

No Old Testament text is composed in a modern, living language. The books of the Old Testament are written in Hebrew, Greek, and Aramaic. Even for the Israeli who speaks Modern Hebrew or the Greek-speaking Greek, biblical Hebrew and Greek are foreign languages. Indeed, although there are numerous similarities, Modern Hebrew or Greek is not identical to biblical Hebrew or Greek. For readers who wish to read the Bible in its original form, language is thus a serious problem. Furthermore, it is difficult to retrieve the exact meaning of some Hebrew, Greek or Aramaic words when, for example, they only occur once in the Bible (so-called "*hapax legomena*").[2] Moreover, the language system of Hebrew differs markedly from that of non-Semitic languages, such as Dutch which is originally an Indo-European language variety.

In order to help overcome this language barrier, translations of Bible texts have been made since ancient times. However, the Italian saying "*Traduttore traditore*" or the French version "*Traduire, c'est trahir*" — translation is betrayal — is also very true for the Bible. The awareness of this limitation manifests itself in the many translations and revisions of translations that appear in a single language and that all strive toward rendering the original scriptural text as faithfully as possible. Consequently, one could say that the contemporary reader, when he interprets a biblical text on the basis of a translation, is actually squaring the interpretation or interpreting it to the power of two. First, the translation used is itself already

---

[2] See, in this respect also, Hans Ausloos and Bénédicte Lemmelijn, "Rendering Love: Hapax Legomena and the Characterisation of the Translation Technique of Song of Songs," *Translating a Translation. The LXX and its Modern Translations in the Context of Early Judaism*, ed. Hans Ausloos, Johann Cook, Florentino García Martínez, Bénédicte Lemmelijn and Marc Vervenne, Bibliotheca Ephemeridum Theologicarum Lovaniensium, 213 (Leuven/Paris/Dudley, MA: Peeters, 2008) 43-61.

an interpretation; then this reader, in turn, endeavours to interpret this interpretation again.

3. Cultural Chasm

Between the original writers and readers of the Scriptures and the readers of the twenty-first century, yawns an enormous cultural chasm. The culture in which the Old Testament texts came about is that of the ancient Near East. This culture was primarily patriarchal. The question of women's liberation never came up. The society was not global, but strongly concentrated in the local cities and their surrounding villages. Agriculture and stock farming were central, while industry was nonexistent. Slavery was generally accepted. The mortality rate was high and the average life-expectancy was low. The whole culture lived according to the rhythm of the seasons. There was no electricity and ICT. Medicine was not developed and religion was central to it. When a man died childless, a relation had to beget children by the surviving wife. Adultery was punished by the death penalty.

This cultural chasm implies that the biblical text, read by today's readers, often requires (historical-cultural) explanation. It is, for example, nearly impossible to talk sensibly about the right to vote if one has no notion of what "democracy" is. Similarly, one is no more capable of understanding or interpreting certain biblical texts, if one does not even know what they are about. After all, the text firstly contains explicit references to cultural givens that seem strange to us today. But then there are also implicit presuppositions that hinder the correct understanding of the text.

4. Chronological Gulf

The cultural chasm is inevitably linked to the many centuries that have passed since the biblical texts were composed. Anyone would agree that correctly understanding a newspaper article about an issue that was highly topical only a few decades ago is by no means easy for a reader today, considering that it requires at least an insight into the historical situation at that time. Well now, between the origin of the biblical texts and the age in which today's reader finds himself, there lie more than two millennia. In addition, the Old Testament writings were themselves written over a period of almost eight centuries. Readers of the Old Testament, therefore, must be thoroughly aware of this chronological gulf. In view of the fact that the Old Testament texts were not all written in the same period, it is necessary to find out the historical context of each text individually. And seeing that the Bible is not a history book but a religious writing that proclaims something, the accounts of so-called historical events must always be interpreted with a great deal of caution.

5. Evolved Scriptures

When one speaks today of the Charter of the United Nations, the Belgian Constitution or the documents of the Second Vatican Council, everyone is aware of the fact that one is talking about documents that came about as the result of an evolutionary process, in which the text was given shape through the work of various writers and/or editors. Well then, similarly, it is highly improbable that a book in the Old Testament was written by a single author. Many writers contributed to each text. For example, traditionally, one could assume that the prophetic book of Isaiah contained the words of the historical prophet Isaiah who, according to the title of the book (Isaiah 1:1), appeared in Judah during the eighth century BC at the time of the Assyrian crisis. However, in Isaiah 44:28 and 45:1, the Persian king, Cyrus, is mentioned, which means that it is difficult to date these texts to a period before 540 BC. Furthermore, the use of the name "Babylon" in Isaiah 43:14; 47:1 and 48:14, 20 indicates that chapters 40–66 are more likely to be connected to the Babylonian crisis of the sixth century BC than to the Assyrian problems of the eighth century. Therefore, it is impossible for the entire book to already have been written in the eighth century BC by the historical prophet Isaiah. The current form of the book, as in all Old Testament books, is rather the result of an extremely complex and protracted process of redaction, rewriting and supplementation.

Moreover, historical certainty about any author of biblical texts is impossible. This problem is further accentuated by the fact that, in antiquity, copyright did not exist. Writers cited each other without referring to their sources. Furthermore, books were published under the pseudonyms of the great names of antiquity, especially with the goal of presenting them as authoritative texts (pseudepigraphy). So, one ascribed the book of Canticles to King Solomon, or the Psalms to his predecessor David.

6. A Multitude of Texts

It is an achievement of biblical scholarship that, today, we have come to realise that biblical literature is the result of cultural and theological ideas from a range of periods that, moreover, have been written down by various authors over a number of centuries in a collection of books that were mostly repeatedly revised and were later passed down in different textual versions. Not a single original autograph (i.e., the actual document produced by the first author) of a biblical book is available. Furthermore, the oldest complete text of the Old Testament, the so-called "Codex Leningradenis," only dates from around the year 1000 AD. However, numerous very old, be they mostly fragmented, manuscripts of Bible texts were discovered in the second half of the twentieth century, of which the finds at the Dead Sea (Qumran, Wadi Muraba'at and Massada) are without doubt the most important. These are Bible texts from the period between the third century BC and the first century AD. Yet, some of these texts contain a scriptural passage that differs markedly from the accepted version, either through intentional reinterpretation or as a result of accidental "mistakes" while copying by hand. In other words, the text of the Bible that we generally use or that we refer to is not *the* text, but rather "a" Bible text. This fact alone prevents us from absolutising this text in a fundamentalistic way.

What is more, the text of the Old Testament was already being translated into Greek from the third century BC. Later, it was also translated into other languages like Latin and Syrian. Often, these translations, as interpretations, present a version that deviates from the standardised text. This all implies that the study of the material text of the Bible must be an important focal point for the exegete. This is so-called textual criticism, in which one, among other things, tries to work out the history of the text as a physical product.

7. Holy Scripture for Jews and Christians

The Bible is more than a "classic" like the works of Homer or Shakespeare. Even though the biblical texts may also belong to the classics of world literature — they are well written, deal with general human themes and are open to all kinds of interpretation —, they still possess an extra dimension. Namely, their function within a faith community. The Bible is a document that, within a group of people, has, in one way or another, gained authority. That is why the Bible is viewed as "Holy Scripture," in which, moreover, one believes that God himself can be heard and the words bear testimony to God's works.

The fact that the Bible has for centuries been regarded as Holy Scripture carries with it the implication that the exegete engages in an equally old tradition of predecessors who have attempted to understand and explain the Bible. In one way, this is of course positive. Many possibilities have already been taken into account and various approaches have already been explored. But in another way, the fact that one is embedded in this process can also be limiting and constricting. Frequently, the reader is inclined to read a scriptural passage in the light of the centuries old tradition, and in so doing, other possible and legitimate interpretations might pass unnoticed. And here, "exegesis" (lead out, interpret) is in danger of becoming "eisegesis" (lead in, preserve). In this case, the text itself no longer speaks. Rather, it is the reader who inserts a meaning into the text that the text does not actually contain. Consequently, one makes the text say things that the text was not intended to say.

The aforementioned factors mean that the Bible in itself, as the basis of the Judeo-Christian tradition, is, for people in the twenty-first century, in effect a "strange" book. On the one hand the Bible is, from a historical perspective, the foundation upon which not only the Judeo-Christian tradition, but indeed the whole of western civilisation is built. On the other hand, however, this biblical tradition, much as it may permeate culture, remains a "strange" and "estranged" foundation. The acknowledgement of this "strangeness" of the Bible can nonetheless be the first step toward adequately interpreting it.

CONCLUSION TO PART I

Against the background described above, one can conclude that the current "crisis" we see in faith and Christianity is a result of two notable factors, namely, on the one hand, the cultural-historical development from pre-modernity, via modernity, to post-modernity, and, on the other, the growing awareness of the "strange" character of biblical writings as one of the results of the modern, more rational approach to the text. Indeed, both factors result in "disenchantment" with religious praxis, as well as with the authority of the Bible as its foundation. The transition from mystery to disenchantment was the spark that ignited a range of possible responses. These various responses to the disenchantment are the subject of the second part of this book.

PART II

RESPONSE TO THE DISENCHANTMENT

INTRODUCTION

The first part focused on the transition from mystery to disenchantment. Against this background, part II will concentrate on the possible reactions that this "disenchantment" with faith and Christianity, and more concretely, with the Bible, evoked.

Obviously, in this regard, the fact that many people have, of course, rejected religion, and Christianity in particular, cannot be overlooked. This reaction, which is the most radical, will not be dealt with any further within the scope of this book. After all, it *de facto* denies the possibility of dealing with the "disenchantment." It leaves no route to reinterpretation open anymore. For this reason, it suffices here to briefly refer to the fact that this attitude manifests itself in a wide variety of ways and, consequently, may not be judged or condemned as a monolithic whole.

First, one can distinguish in this respect "practical atheism," an attitude to life in which God serves absolutely no purpose anymore, and thus is *de facto* absent. Nevertheless, this is not to say necessarily that one also resolutely rejects all forms of religion, defined as coming to know oneself embedded in a transcendent whole. Against the background of the evolution of the place of faith and religion sketched above, it is, after all, apparent that post-modernity brings with it the demand for a religion — albeit usually a god-less religion. Related to this practical atheism is the attitude of "indifference," an attitude in which an (explicit) interest in God, religion, and, more broadly, in finding meaning is as good as nonexistent. In addition to these, one distinguishes the more theoretically asserted and rationally underpinned "atheism." Put simply and generally, this is an attitude and a vision in which one seriously doubts the existence of God or even completely denies it. This atheism can either translate into an agnosticism (one does not know, but makes no effort to work through the problem) or lead to the principled decision that God does not exist or is at least unknowable.

The atheistic option, moreover, has various nuances. Namely, one distinguishes resigned or irenic atheism from aggressive or polemical atheism. In the first, one simply wants to make the best of things, without God — with whom one no longer occupies oneself. In the second, the belief in God is viewed as extremely restrictive, with the consequence that one is convinced that every form of belief in god, and even of religion, must be opposed. Many within this context identify themselves as non-believers. Even though this option may, theoretically speaking, belong to the possibilities, in practice, a life without belief is impossible. Everyone who lives believes. If not in God, then at least in the meaningfulness of life itself. Those who do not believe in the meaningfulness of life, end it. And even this is founded on the impossible to prove conviction, the non-scientifically verifiable belief, that the life that one experiences as meaningless should not actually be allowed to be meaningless.

Alongside the rejection of belief in God and/or of religion, there are, however, also a variety of reactions that do not ignore the "disenchantment," but which nevertheless attempt to "save" God and religion. Lumping these reactions together and trying to systematise them risks not doing justice to all the nuances contained within the plurality of individual and collective answers to the given situation. Nonetheless, in this part we attempt to distinguish between, broadly speaking, two kinds of reaction. On the one hand, we distinguish, generalising somewhat, the "negative" responses that, as a result of the "disenchantment" described, spring forth out of desperation, and that aim at a renewed, demonstrable truth and reality claim as they engage, as it were, in a resistant, restorative search for a recovery of the lost security of certainty. On the other hand, we recognise a "positive" response that, without denying the reality of the disenchantment, attempts to rise above it towards enrichment in a critical relationship with the inherited and recollected articles of faith.

CHAPTER ONE

UPHEAVAL AND RESISTANCE:
THE CONCERN FOR TRUTH AND REALITY

1. Childlike Naivety

When young children come into contact with biblical narratives, they usually give them the same weight as fairy tales. With their childlike naivety, they do not doubt these beautiful stories, in which improbable things happen: talking animals (Genesis 3), a city that collapses when people just blow hard enough on their trumpets (Joshua 6), and Jesus who walks on water (Matthew 14). Children do not, at first, question this. Gradually, however, critical thoughts begin to arise regarding these images: did what is told also actually happen? And so, this critical questioning is of the same substance as the evolution described in the previous part, in which, since the Enlightenment, the centuries-old, self-evident "truths" of the Christian religion were called into question.

Together with the rejection described above, where one discards everything as a fabrication, one can also act as though nothing has happened and simply switch off one's critical thinking. By doing this, one once again nestles into a childlike, pre-critical faith, where one neither asks nor needs to ask oneself any further questions.

2. Historicising Biblical Narratives

a. *Introduction*

With the childlike naivety over, but still holding fast to what is (literally) told in biblical narratives, one finds the so-called historicising tendency. The modern mentality, with its strong orientation toward technology and the scientific investigation of reality, presents everything as doable and explicable. Consequently, if biblical narratives are to "survive" and offer any kind of response, then the events and phenomena that they describe must be rationally interpreted. In this context, the historical character of the biblical account is questioned. Explanations and historical backgrounds are then sought for the sometimes seriously bizarre stories. And although this appears at first sight to be a balancing act between religion and science, it in fact conceals the same conservative attitude as that found in fundamentalistic approaches (see below). Indeed, historicising, taken to its fullest extent, together with the psychologising of biblical narratives that also often accompanies it, is itself a form of biblical fundamentalism. After all, one does not go beyond the disenchantment but instead attempts, in a "modern" way, to make the best of bad situation in order, at all costs, to be able to back the Bible up. This means that it is not always about an objective search for the (cultural-)historical background of the biblical body of thought with a view to correctly understanding the text and what it refers to. It is rather about a reflex to prove that one can still take the Bible story literally, no matter how unbelievable the story may seem at first, because what is described therein is real and historically true. In other words, that which is historically demonstrable is also rationally plausible and therefore continues to be valid. In this regard, consider the numerous pseudo-scientific offerings in books and magazines and the well-known "documentaries" on television that have only one goal in mind: prove that the Bible is right. And even though scholarly exegesis resolutely rejects such approaches, naturalistic and historicising explanations of Bible passages nevertheless succeed in continuously capturing the attention of the media.

    In what follows, this historicising tendency, which has also sometimes strongly influenced and oriented exegetical research, shall be illustrated using approaches to the narrative of the "Plagues in Egypt" in the Old Testament book of Exodus (chapters 7–11). This narrative, in particular, has been questioned to such an extent that there is a real danger of narrow historicism in the answers to the questions, even in scholarly research.

b. *Illustration: The "Plague Narrative" in Exodus 7:14–11:10*

The narrative of the "Plagues in Egypt," which will come up again in this book in the third part when we consider the question regarding the relationship between God, human beings and violence, must be situated at the threshold of the real exodus of the people of Israel from slavery in Egypt. During the course of the negotiating process, in which Moses tries to get the pharaoh to agree to the Israelites' departure from Egypt, the pharaoh's stubborn refusal results in Egypt being struck by a series of ten catastrophes. The Bible narrative attributes these disasters to God, who intended them to be a demonstration of his power in relation to that of Pharaoh. The disasters result in Egypt's deterioration from a flourishing kingdom to a barren, uninhabited and dead land.

In the historicising approach, the events of the "Plague Narrative," so strange at first sight, are related to a range of natural phenomena that occurred in the Egyptian environment. The idea is that the Israelites saw, in the impressive natural events, the work of God. This interpretation is thus supposed to demonstrate how God worked through a series of natural phenomena. Moreover, it is supposed to clarify how Israel interpreted these events in a religious way as God's help. In this regard, one can primarily distinguish two types of explanation.[1]

---

[1] For a more detailed elaboration of this, see: Bénédicte Lemmelijn, "'Zoals het nog nooit geweest was en ook nooit meer zou zijn' (Ex 11,6): De 'plagen van Egypte' volgens Ex 7–11: Historiciteit en theologie," *Tijdschrift voor Theologie* 36 (1996) 115-131 and more recently Bénédicte Lemmelijn, "Not Fact, Yet True: Historicity versus Theology in the 'Plague Narrative' (Ex. 7–11)", *Old Testament*

1. The Egyptian Ecosystem

First, an attempt is made to explain the events in the "Plague Narrative" against the background of various natural phenomena within the Egyptian ecosystem. Moreover, they try to connect the plagues together causally.[2] The one plague must, as it were, immediately follow from the other on the basis of natural causes and effects. Natural phenomena that rapidly follow one another within a period of one year form the basis of this explanation. One encounters in this respect the following explanations. The basis of the whole theory is an unusually heavy rainfall on the East African plateau, the highlands of Ethiopia and the southern parts of the Nile valley. This initial event is then supposed to have resulted in a series of disasters.

The first plague, which tells of how the water turned to blood (Exodus 7:14-25), is explained on the basis of the fact that during the period in which the waters of the Nile rise, around June, they carry with them a large amount of red earth from the mountains of Abyssinia and Ethiopia, and thus all the more so when there is a

Essays 20 (2007) 395-417. References, to scholarly literature that has been consulted and used with regard to the theme described above, can be consulted in the extensive footnotes of the contributions mentioned. Cf. also Bénédicte Lemmelijn, *Het verhaal van de 'Plagen in Egypte' (Exodus 7,14–11,10): Een onderzoek naar het ontstaan en de compositie van een Pentateuchtraditie,* Deel 1: *Status quaestionis van het onderzoek,* unpublished doctoral dissertation, Faculty of Theology, KU Leuven, Promoter Marc Vervenne (Leuven, 1996) 139-152. For an exhaustive text-critical study of the Plague Narrative, cf. also B. Lemmelijn, *A Plague of Texts? A Text-Critical Study of the So-Called 'Plagues Narrative' in Exodus 7,14–11,10,* Oudtestamentische Studiën/Old Testament Studies, 56 (Leiden/ Boston: Brill, 2009).

[2] The purely descriptive, naturalistic explanation as a background to the literary narrative is found in practically all older exegetical commentaries. The causal connection that, as it were, unleashed a chain of catastrophes was primarily stimulated by the contributions of Greta Hort, "The Plagues of Egypt," *Zeitschrift für die Alttestamentliche Wissenschaft* 69 (1957) 84-103; 70 (1958) 48-59 and it also resounds throughout a great many commentaries and contributions.

particularly heavy rainfall. Aside from this, there is a peculiar type of algae and micro-organisms that could have given the water a red colour. The death of fish, which is mentioned as a side effect in the narrative, can supposedly be attributed to the large amount of bacteria that the flood carries with it. The second plague, the appearance of masses of frogs (Exodus 7:26–8:11), is supposed to be due to flooding. Annually, when the Nile bursts its banks, numerous frogs that live in the water are carried onto land. With that, the argument is put forward that the Nile was an excellent habitat for frogs, which, incidentally, regularly became a plague in Egypt. In Palestine, by contrast, there are no frogs. Normally, these frogs would only have appeared in September or October, but due to the abnormal pollution of the Nile by the dead fish from the first plague, the frogs had already overrun the land during the flood period. The countless insects of the third and fourth plagues (Exodus 8:12-28), the larvae of which also develop in the mud of the Nile, eagerly settled on the rotting bodies of dead frogs. These mosquitoes and flies, which have, moreover, been classified as *Stomoxys calcitrans,* are not uncommon in the Egyptian environment, but the unusual situation is supposed to have caused much more severe swarms. The dead frogs were, incidentally, also the cause of the fifth and sixth plagues (Exodus 9:1-7 and 8-12 respectively), in which the spread of bacteria was aided by the buzzing swarms of insects. In this regard, the fifth plague, namely the pestilence that struck only the Egyptian's livestock, is explained as follows: the Egyptian livestock were already grazing on open fields at the time that the water receded and so they were infected by *Bacillus anthracis;* the livestock belonging to the Israelites on the other hand stayed in the Delta region, could not yet move to the open fields and were, consequently, not infected. With regard to the sixth plague – the boils –, lots of skin diseases occurred in Egypt. There was supposedly even a disease called "Egyptian boils" (see Deuteronomy 28:27), which brings to mind skin diseases like smallpox and "Nile pimple." More specifically, it is also proposed that these boils were due to *anthrax* caused by the *Stomoxys calcitrans* of the fourth plague. The seventh plague brought hail and storms (Exodus 9:13-35) that destroyed a large portion of the harvest. This is indeed a strange phenomenon in Egypt. Nonetheless, an explanation for this plague is also put forward. The key lies in Exodus 9:31-32, from which one can infer the point in time at which this plague occurs. In Upper Egypt, according to this explanation, hailstorms are supposed to have occurred occasionally, though not bound by the seasons. In the North, a region with a Mediterranean climate, they only occurred in late spring and early autumn. Between November and March, in Goshen, the region where the biblical account tells us the Israelites lived, there would not, as a result, have been any such storms. In addition, the crops spoken of in verses 31 and 32 were supposedly delayed in their ripening, which could explain why the wheat and spelt were not yet fully grown and so could not be destroyed.

The atmospheric conditions that would have led to a hailstorm could also have caused other plagues. This is how the locusts of the eighth plague (Exodus 10:1-20) supposedly came with the wind. Locusts were a known and feared threat. After their hibernation, the locusts usually moved to Palestine or Egypt in February-March, depending on the direction of the wind. This invasion then attacked plants between March and the beginning of May. For the darkness of the ninth plague (Exodus 10:21-29), the arrival of a hot desert wind was often considered, a wind that darkened everything with enormous dust clouds called the *khamsin*, which would not uncommonly rage for days, leaving chaos in its wake. In that particular year, it was supposedly particularly fierce due to the ever more destructive effects of the plagues following on from one another. That the Israelites were spared is then explained by the fact that they stayed in Goshen, located in a wadi (a river basin) in a region that would be exposed to very little damage by a *khamsin* from the South. For the tenth plague, the death of the first born that is foretold in Exodus 11:1-10,[3] various diseases or deadly polio are sometimes referred to, but it is usually added that in this narrative, every notion of a "natural event" has disappeared. The disaster should be understood as a reprisal for Pharaoh's bid to murder the firstborn Israelites (see also Exodus 4:22-23).

In view of the abovementioned natural explanations, a chronology is also sought in the plagues. Often, it is assumed that the whole drama played itself out between June, the time of the Nile flood, and April of the following year, the time of the Pesach celebrations. The course of events then runs as follows. In June, the Nile bursts its banks. The water becomes very turbid. With the flood, the frogs move onto land in July. During the summer and autumn the afflictions of the mosquitoes, the rashes and other sicknesses make themselves felt. The hailstorm then takes place in January, followed by the locusts in February. March is the month in which the sandstorms rage. The last plague and the exodus, finally, take place around April.

2. A Volcanic Eruption on Santorini (Thera)

Apart from the explanation that relates the plagues to the Egyptian ecosystem itself, still another "natural" explanation of the events mentioned in Exodus 7–11 is proposed.[4] Namely, reference is made

[3] Cf. in this regard, also Bénédicte Lemmelijn, "Setting and Function of Exod 11,1-10 in the Exodus Narrative," *Studies in the Book of Exodus: Redaction – Reception – Interpretation*, ed. Marc Vervenne, Bibliotheca Ephemeridum Theologicarum Lovaniensium, 126 (Leuven: Leuven University Press, 1996) 443-460.

[4] Cf. Eberhard Stechow, "Santorin-Katastrophe und 'Ägyptische Finsternis'," *Forschungen und Fortschritte: Nachrichtenblatt der Deutschen Wissenschaft und Technik* 26 (1950) 174; Joel Block, "The Ten Plagues of Egypt," *Religious*

to a volcanic eruption on the island of Santorini (Thera) in around 1500 BC. This eruption, which has been called the most severe in the last four millennia, caused many unusual natural phenomena in the broad vicinity of the island. The Egyptian Nile Delta, where the plagues of Exodus 7–11 take place, is about a thousand kilometres southeast of Santorini. Therefore, some are of the opinion that the plagues, at least if one dates Moses to the last half of the second millennium BC, can be identified with side effects of this volcanic eruption.

The natural explanation that is proposed on the basis of this fact can be summarised as follows.[5] Between 1500 and 1200 BC, an unusually severe volcanic eruption on Santorini launched an enormous amount of rubble, ash, vapour, bacteria and shockwaves into the atmosphere. The volcanic debris, broken loose by the heat, was blown in a south-easterly direction by the wind and came down again about a thousand kilometers away in Egypt. Moses is then supposed to have interpreted this inexplicable natural phenomenon as the "will of God" and subsequently approached Pharaoh with a request to let the Israelites go. The rose red ash, emanating from the red strata in the rocks of Santorini, landed in the Nile, so that people thought that the water had turned to blood (plague I). The groundwater, which was not affected by the ash, was as a result

Education 71 (1976) 519-526; Günter Kehnscherper, "Philological Hints at Traditional-Historic Relations between the Explosion of the Volcano Santorini (Thera) and the Traditions of the Egyptian Plagues," *Studia Evangelica* 7 (1982) 271-275.

[5] A similar "naturalistic" explanation is offered on the basis of an alternative initial fact. Not the volcanic eruption on Santorini, but a new comet passing close to Earth, in the middle of the second millennium before Christ, could have allegedly caused the Egyptian plagues. This comet, on its way from its perihelion, supposedly came so close to Earth that it touched her with it gaseous tail. This fact then also explains why similar phenomena are also observed and recounted in ancient sources from elsewhere in the world at the time. Cf. Immanuel Velikovsky, *Worlds in Collision* (London: Macmillan, 1950) 60-61, 63, 66, 69-71, 73-76.

still drinkable (see Exodus 7:24). The alkaline ash then polluted the river, whereupon the frogs were forced to leave their natural habitat and seek refuge on land (plague II). Contaminated frogs died and their corpses attracted gnats and flies (plagues III and IV). These insects and the pathogens that go together with the unhygienic conditions described, brought a pestilence upon the animals (plague V) and boils upon the people (plague VI). High levels of water vapour and ash in the atmosphere caused severe storms, rain, and hail (plague VII). The storm winds from the northwest then set the locusts in motion. These supposedly have very highly developed olfactory organs by means of which they, still in their normal habitat on the Red Sea, were able to smell the fresh greenery that was growing better in Egypt thanks to the heavy rains. A massive swarm of locusts then raided Egypt (plague VIII). There are several possible causes of the darkness (plague IX). First, it is proposed that the sun could have been darkened by the enormous amount of ash that was produced by the volcano. Second, it is argued that the winds generated by the eruption, may have caused the previously mentioned phenomenon of the *khamsin* wind. The darkness could also have come about due to the exceptionally large swarm of locusts. Consider the metaphor "it was black with…" Finally, the death of the firstborns (plague X) is traced back to the fact that the masses of ash that were brought by the volcanic storm winds caused the roofs of the Egyptian houses to collapse, resulting in the death of many Egyptians, among them firstborns. The Israelite houses on the other hand were supposedly built of lighter materials so that their collapse was less life threatening.

c. *Conclusion*

On the basis of the above, it can be concluded that this historicising tendency *de facto* tries to find (natural) explanations that make the account rationally acceptable. However, the result is that the Bible narratives are not interpreted as they were meant to be.

In this regard, it is worth noting, incidentally, that older scholarly studies take full account of the natural and historicising explanations, without necessarily agreeing with them per se. However, in more recent research, they are hardly discussed. At most they are mentioned and given some critique. Interest in the strictly historical character of the Plague Narrative does not appear to play a large role in contemporary research, at least as far as it is critically practised. Perhaps this evolution fits within the broader social evolution already presented above. The "modern" society, which was strongly oriented toward science and technology, attached more importance to the explicability, and the historical plausibility that goes with it, than the "post-modern" society does. This once more displays an interest in the literary character of the narrative and for the aesthetic-playful surplus.

Against this background, interest in the biblical passage, in this instance in the Plague Narrative, has gradually moved from the historical to the literary and theological level. The naturalistic and historicising approaches are slowly but surely being nuanced, criticised and radically rejected. Alongside the defenders of the natural explanations there are also researchers who are certainly not proponents of hypotheses concerning a natural and/or historical sequence of events, but who are nevertheless convinced that the description of the plagues is drawn from knowledge of the Egyptian environment. In other words, they rather look at the natural background as a source of inspiration for the literary description.

In addition, it is argued that the stories of the plagues, in their literary form, do not only rely on familiarity with the Egyptian milieu, but also make use of a number of well-known literary motifs. The attempts to explain the plagues in a natural and/or partly rational way do not sufficiently take the genesis and the unique character of the biblical passage into account. Indeed, the narrative should in no way be considered a factual account.

And so one arrives, finally, at a radical rejection of the natural explanations of the plagues. These explanations are not only characterised as unconvincing; they, moreover, fail to appreciate both the literary uniqueness of the narrative and its theological meaning and content. In this regard, emphasis is placed on the argument that the Plague Narratives were not meant to be accurate accounts for future historians. The biblical authors were not reporters who wanted to deliver some sort of eyewitness account. Rather, they wanted to prophetically pass on a religious interpretation of reality. That does not mean that every form of historicity is *a priori* denied. Nevertheless, the question posed by "modern" readers regarding the difference between miraculous occurrences and natural phenomena is inappropriate here. In the mind of the biblical authors, the story is not intended to answer such questions; it endeavours only to be an affirmative proclamation of the fact that God liberated Israel. And in this respect, natural explanations are of little importance. Exodus 7–11 is a literary-theological story, not a historical account.

Against this background, the natural and historicising explanations only demonstrate that the so-called "plagues of Egypt" *could* possibly have happened, but whether that is in fact so is not relevant to the way in which the narrative functions. What is fundamental is the theological message of the story against the background of the intentions and mentality of the biblical authors and redactors. That the literary description of the plagues may indeed refer to a natural background is quite easy to explain. The writers of the Plague Narrative were, of course, real people who stood rooted in the experiences of daily life. They drew the metaphors for the proclamation of the theological message of the series of plagues from this reality.

Consequently, one can conclude that, faced with the "disenchantment," the naturalistic and historicising explanations attempted to hold on to the "truth" of the Bible in a "modern" way. They were, and still are, clung to as if they somehow guaranteed the much desired historical provability and truth of the events recounted. What comes across as "modern" and "scientific," however, is in fact a denial of what the biblical narratives intend.

In the same way, in search of "the absolutely right" of the Bible and doctrine, the fundamentalistic reaction to the "disenchantment" stands out. Therefore, fundamentalism, and biblical fundamentalism in particular, will be elucidated in the next section.

3. Fundamentalism: Between Literal and Symbolic Reading

Within the current discourse, the term "fundamentalism" is often used. Attacks are perpetrated by "fundamentalist Muslim extremists," "fundamentalist" Christians murder doctors who perform abortions, and green "fundamentalists" set fire to hamburger restaurants. These examples clearly illustrate that the concept of "fundamentalism" is an extremely complex and multifaceted one.

In what follows, we shall limit ourselves to religious fundamentalism within the Christian tradition, even though it may appear that a number of its characteristics could also be applied to other forms of fundamentalism.[6] We shall endeavour to define some

---

[6] The description of religious, and particularly Christian, fundamentalism presented here is indebted to Anton Van Harskamp, "Boze droom van het christendom? Verkenningen rond het fundamentalisme als idee en verschijnsel," *Tijdschrift voor Theologie* 33 (1993) 5-26; and particularly Hans Ausloos, "Als de nood het hoogst is, is de redding nabij! Jehovah's Getuigen en het boek Openbaring," *Tijdschrift voor Theologie* 41 (2001) 13-36; Hans Ausloos, "Apocalyptiek en bijbels fundamentalisme," *Het boek Openbaring: Een eindeloos verhaal*, ed. Geert Van Oyen (Leuven: Acco, 2001) 145-178.

parameters that will enable us to identify a particular response to the above mentioned upheaval as "fundamentalism" in the religious sense. First, however, we turn our attention to the term itself.

a. *Fundamentalist Approaches*

It is a perilous undertaking to try to come to a precise, unequivocal definition of fundamentalism. In order to define the notion, one could proceed in various ways. One could attempt to survey all Christian "fundamentalistic" movements in search of a common denominator, and thereby arrive at a definition of "fundamentalism." This method is problematic in various ways. Apart from the fact that surveying all fundamentalistic movements and their bodies of thought would be a colossal task, there appear to be many variations within the movements that usually get labelled as "fundamentalistic." Central to Protestant fundamentalism, for example, is the proposition that the Bible does not so much *contain* the word of God, but rather *is* the word of God. The human authors of the Bible are nothing more than instruments that God used. In manifestations of Catholic fundamentalism, the Bible is, it is true, read in a fundamentalistic way; nevertheless the emphasis is placed on authentic, doctrinal authority. In this respect, one might refer to so-called integralism, in which the individual is totally absorbed into the whole.

In addition to the great variety within Christian fundamentalist groupings, it is especially problematic that, with one exception, no movement calls itself "fundamentalistic." After all, it is anything but honourable to be a "fundamentalist;" on the contrary, the term "fundamentalist" more often functions as a term of abuse that one hurls at others. Just as no religious movement considers itself a sect, but nevertheless still labels others as such, so few consider themselves "fundamentalistic." A fundamentalist is, indeed, the opposite of what one is oneself. By calling others "fundamentalistic," one is saying at the same time, "I am *not* like that; I am a rational being that does not allow his life to be determined by one or another allegedly infallible guru, so-called holy text or its interpretation." This form of negative self-assurance, however, is not at all what was meant by the movement that lies behind the origin of the term "fundamentalism."

The origin of the concept of "fundamentalism" must of course be sought within Christianity and its interpretation of the Bible. Much like the Catholic anti-modernism at the end of the nineteenth century, which largely curtailed scientific research for Catholic theologians – consider the condemnation of "modernistic" theological thought by Pius X's encyclical *Pascendi* (8 September 1907) –, certain currents within Protestantism have vehemently fulminated against the so-called "liberal" (historical-critical) exegesis that primarily flourished in the churches of the Reformation during the nineteenth century.

In 1895, during an American Bible congress of conservatively inclined Protestant, mostly Evangelical, exegetes in Niagara (NY), in reaction to critical Bible studies that appeared to undermine the authority of the Bible, five points were postulated that were considered the "fundamentals" of Christian belief. These concern (1) the literal inerrancy of Scripture, (2) the divinity of Christ, (3) the virgin birth of Christ, (4) the doctrine of the substitutionary atonement of Christ and (5) the bodily resurrection at the second coming of Christ at the end of time. In the years that followed (between 1910 and 1915) a number of tracts appeared with the title *The Fundamentals: A Testimony to Truth*.[7] This self-designation of American Evangelical groups as "fundamentalist" found its way

---

[7] Reuben Archer Torrey, *The Fundamentals: A Testimony to the Truth*, 4 vols. (Grand Rapids, MI: Baker, 1988) (reprint).

into scholarly literature a few years later and so took its place within common parlance.

Nevertheless, even this description of the "fundamentals" of Christian faith cannot be accepted as a clear-cut definition of Christian fundamentalism. Indeed, various elements that appear to be typical of contemporary, Protestantism-inspired fundamentalist movements – one thinks, for example, of a millenarian tendency (see below) –, are given little attention in this description.

Against the background of the problem laid out above concerning a precise definition of fundamentalism, what follows introduces a number of parameters that might be of use in classifying movements as more or less fundamentalistic.

b. *Characteristics of Religious Fundamentalism*

1. Fundamentalist Religion as Ultimate Security

Every form of fundamentalism appears to be, first and foremost, a reaction against the corrosion of the religiously-based identity as outlined in the part I above. The evolution from pre-modernity to post-modernity has meant that the security of certainty that religion offered in pre-modernity have been lost. As such, practically every form of religious fundamentalism takes upon itself the task of defending this lost lifestyle, in which the ethical consequences of religion play a key role. This is apparent from the fact that when Christian fundamentalist movements become active in the political arena, questions regarding life and death and the place of God in society, so-called meaning-giving questions, are almost always their focus. Religious fundamentalist movements within Christianity only become politically active when sexual morals, abortion, euthanasia or homosexuality are on the agenda. In other words, when questions arise that people consider inherent to Christian identity. At the economic level, by contrast, the voice of religious fundamentalist movements is generally seldom audible. In addition, they are convinced that they can once more develop an overarching system of meaning-giving that is able to give an unequivocal answer to all questions, and in which everyone has and knows their proper place.

2. Fundamentalists are a Minority

Characteristic of every form of Christian religious fundamentalism is that they consider themselves a minority, struggling against an uncomprehending majority. Furthermore, in Western pluralistic society, a fundamentalist movement is *de facto* always a minority. Within the group, an austere discipline usually prevails. The movement demands loyalty to the all-encompassing system and its unequivocal doctrine, which is usually presented as being based on divine revelation. Deviations from the rules are not tolerated, which means that critical dialogue and reaching compromises with those who think differently are impossible for fundamentalists.

This minority position of fundamentalist movements can take various forms. On one hand, they can, as a misunderstood minority, choose to withdraw from the majority and lead an isolated existence. On the other hand, they can, in a zealous and separatist manner, openly enter into a confrontation with the outside world.[8] This can manifest itself, among other ways, as an intense fervour for conversion. This idea that a small minority must take a stand against a (hostile) majority is nourished by a strict, dualistic division between good and evil. Good is diametrically opposed to evil.

---

[8] The Zealots were members of a Jewish movement that opposed the Roman occupation of Palestine in the first century AD, because they only recognised God's authority.

There are the good ("us") and the evil ("them"). In Christian forms of fundamentalism, the basis for this dualistic conception of the world and the human being usually lies in the interpretation of biblical narratives.

3. Apocalyptic Thinking

The third barometer for the identification of Christian fundamentalism is an excessive emphasis on apocalyptic modes of thought. For the most part, Christian fundamentalism draws it inspiration in this regard from the biblical apocalyptic literature, which we primarily find in the Old Testament book of Daniel and the New Testament book of Revelation.[9] The latter – the large Christian churches often did not and do not know what to make of it – is, for some communities, the most important book of the biblical tradition, while at the same time, precisely because of its extremely cryptic use of language and imagery, it repels rather than attracts many other Christians.

Apocalypticism is a unique literary genre that takes its name from the last book of the New Testament – the book of Revelation is also known as the book of the Apocalypse or the Revelation of John. The work comprises a number of visions concerning the end of the present world and the coming of a new age. Nonetheless, Revelation cannot simply be dealt with as a prediction of the future. The text, indeed, is not intended to be screenplay that details the contents of a film to be screened in the distant future and the implications of which one can discover when one allows oneself to be lead by imaginative arbitrariness when interpreting the many

---

[9] Besides Daniel, a strong affinity for apocalypticism in Old Testament literature is particularly demonstrable in Isaiah 24–27; Ezekiel 38–39; Joel 3–4; Zachariah 1–6; 12–14.

images in the realm of the Apocalypse. It is true that all sorts of religious crises and traumas that early Christianity had to deal with gave rise to a very militant theology and Christology of Apocalypse, in which Christ is presented as a divine warrior (Revelation 19) or the "Lion of Judah" (Revelation 5:5). In this context, consider the Jewish hostility towards the Christians (Revelation 2:9), the internal conflicts between rich and poor Christians (Revelation 3:17-18) or the traumatic experiences at the hands of the Roman occupiers. Well now, faith in Jesus as Messiah and the belief that God's kingdom culminates in Him take a heavy knock in light of these negative experiences. It was precisely this tension, between, on the one hand, the vision of God's rule, and, on the other hand, the concrete social situation, that brought John to write Revelation as the revelation of the fact that God and Jesus are the true rulers, despite appearances to the contrary. But again, the author of Revelation does not place this revolution somewhere in the distant future. Quite the opposite, he was convinced that it would happen very soon. Therefore, every approach to Revelation that reads like a train timetable, in which the events for the coming millennia can be accurately pinpointed, is of course absurd and reprehensible.

As a school, Apocalypticism developed within Judaism from the third century BC. In this period, Judaism was (once again) confronted with persecution, wars, and occupation by Hellenistic rulers. It became ever more difficult for faithful Jews to continue believing in the goodness of God and in his undertaking to give them possession of the "Promised Land," the central theme of numerous Old Testament texts. In times of adversity, the prophets indeed always held out the prospect of a promising future, but this usually failed to occur. Therefore, they began to put their hope in a salvation at the end of time, when this world would be destroyed in an Armageddon and where a new world, already brought about by God, would descend from the heavens. The apocalyptic literature then also makes a strict distinction between this world, which is corrupt, and the new world in which God, together with a select community of righteous people, will triumph.

The authors of the biblical apocalyptic literature wanted to encourage their contemporaries to persevere. Apocalyptic literature is primarily literature intended to encourage persecuted and marginalised people and groups. In addition to, among other things, pseudonymity, symbolic language, the appearance of angels, a pronounced dualism, and learned interpretations of the numerology in the prophetic literature[10] — one thinks of the complicated views concerning the seventy year-weeks in Daniel 9 —, the marked attention given to the dawning of a period of well-being in another world order, following a period in which calamity and all sorts of crises occur, also belongs to the main characteristics of Apocalypticism. These are the characteristics that distinguish Apocalypticism from classical prophecy.

God had, often long ago, already revealed and unveiled this hidden, future world to a number of insiders. Incidentally, that is precisely what the term Apokalyps (ἀποκάλυψις — un-veiling) means. These insiders recorded their dreams and visions in writing. In addition, it was supposed that these writings were very old, but that they were only made public just before the dawning of the endtime. In reality, however, these texts were written at the time of their alleged discovery. This also implies that various events that have *de facto* already occurred are presented as future events (*vaticinia ex eventu*). The authors of such apocalyptic biblical texts wanted to inspire their original audience not to just let the evil that they were confronted with prevail, but to search for ways to

---

[10] In this regard, the emphasis on the contrast between the few "wise" and the "masses" in Daniel 11:33 is illustrative of the sectarian as an identifying feature of apocalypticism.

combat it. The promise of God's new world, where there is only place for these righteous people, was intended to act as a stimulus in this regard.

In addition to the New Testament book of Revelation, the Old Testament book of Daniel is a typical example of Biblical apocalyptic literature. As "prediction in the rear-view mirror," this book presents itself as a record of the words and experiences of the prophet Daniel in the sixth century BC, while the ideas and predictions indisputably refer to the fortunes of the anti-Jewish Greek ruler Antiochus IV (second century BC). Although Daniel's visions are presented as "predictions" about the distant future, from a scientific viewpoint, it is generally accepted that these texts were only composed in the second century BC at the earliest, and "predict" events the had actually already taken place.

To demonstrate this, we shall consider two passages from the book of Daniel. We shall briefly discuss the second and sixth chapters of the first part of the book (chapters 1–6), which is mostly narrative. Daniel 2 tells of the dream of Nebuchadnezzar, ruler of the Babylonians who had conquered the kingdom of Judah in the sixth century BC, destroying the capital city, Jerusalem, and taking the intellectual stratum of the population into exile. In his dream, Nebuchadnezzar had seen a giant statue. The head was of gold, the chest and arms of silver, the abdomen and thighs of bronze, the legs of iron and the feet, part iron and part clay. Then, without the intervention of a human being, a stone was cut out that pulverized the feet, after which the entire statue fell apart and was blown away by the wind. Nothing remained of the statue. The stone, on the other hand, became a great mountain that filled the whole earth. The question that Nebuchadnezzar puts to his court diviners and magicians is not easy. They must not only explain the dream, but also first tell him the content of the dream. Obviously they do not succeed in this. It is the wise prophet Daniel who, with God's help, manages both tasks. The meaning that Daniel ascribes to the dream is as follows: the head of gold symbolises Nebuchadnezzar himself; the silver chest and arms represent the empire that will follow the Babylonians', namely that of the Medes; the Bronze refers to Persian empire, while the iron legs symbolise the Greek empire under the leadership of Alexander the Great; the feet that are part iron and part clay represent the division that follows the iron Greek world power; finally, the stone refers to a new divine kingdom that will replace all worldly domains.

In the sixth chapter of the book of Daniel, Darius the Mede appears. Who this person is actually meant to be is the subject of a lot of speculation. It is possible that the author has Darius the Persian in mind, who he, nevertheless, mistakenly considers to be a Mede. The content of the chapter is, however, much more important, since it has perhaps, during the course of the tradition, been the chapter that has most captured the imagination. We are told that King Darius, at the instigation of Daniel's opponents, issues a law decreeing that every person who, during a thirty day period, prays to a god or a person other than the king shall be thrown into the lions' den. Daniel, however, continues to pray to YAHWeH, the God of Israel, three times a day, as usual. Daniel's opponents lay charges against him. In accordance with the law, he finds himself in the lions' den. But, saved by his trust in God, Daniel is found the next day without a scratch on him. God had sent his angel to muzzle the lions. Convinced of the power of Daniel's God, Darius sends Daniel's enemies to the lions' den, whereupon they are immediately devoured by the lions.

Daniel 7 begins the second part of the book, which is of a completely different nature to that of the narrative first six chapters. Daniel 7–12 mainly consists of the visions of the prophet Daniel, in which, usually by means of animal symbolism, somewhat analogous to chapter two, reference is made to the successive kingdoms of the Babylonians, Medes, Persians, and Greeks. Furthermore, it is remarkable that the visions only briefly deal with the periods under the Babylonians, Medes and Persians — the period in which the biblical book situates the prophet Daniel —, while all the emphasis is placed on the Greek rule that occurs several centuries later. The persecution of the Jewish religion under the Greek Antiochus IV is particularly prominent.[11] All these empires are tried by the "Ancient One" (Daniel 7:9) — hence the common conception of God as an old man — and stripped of their power. In their place, "one like a human being" (Daniel 7:13) receives eternal dominion and will always stand up for "the people who are loyal to their God" (Daniel 11:32). Furthermore, Daniel turns his attention to the endtime, where an ultimate, eschatological saving of the chosen is envisioned. Perhaps for the first time in the Old Testament literature, Daniel 12:1-3 testifies to a belief in a collective resurrection of at least some of those who have died: "At that time Michael, the great prince, the protector of your people, shall arise. There shall be a time of anguish, such as has never occurred since nations first came into existence. But at that time your people shall be delivered, everyone who is found written in the book. Many of those who sleep in the dust of the earth shall awake, some to everlasting life, and some to shame and everlasting contempt. Those who are wise shall shine like the brightness of the sky, and those who lead many to righteousness, like the stars for ever and ever."

It should be apparent from the above presentation of a few passages from the apocalyptic book of Daniel how the authors of this book, and, for that matter, of apocalyptic literature in general, want to encourage their contemporaries. God's intervention will quickly bring an end to the tyrannising Greek rule, under which second century BC Judaism suffers. The only thing that the Jews have to

---

[11] This also is also true *mutatis mutandis* for Daniel 2.

do is be righteous and trust in God. After all, His kingdom will
soon be established.

The fact that biblical apocalyptic literature is literature aimed
primarily at the encouragement of persecuted, minority groups,
means that these texts are welcomed by all sorts of fundamentalistic minorities who feel persecuted or, at least, misunderstood, and
who live in the midst of a hostile world, the end of which they see
drawing nigh. Moreover, the eschatological component of Apocalypticism, namely the belief that God's endtime intervention will
save the righteous and establish an eternal, divine kingdom for
them, is usually also a central theme in Christian fundamentalist
movements.

4. Millenarianism or Chiliasm

Related to this, it is logical that the twentieth chapter of the New
Testament book of Revelation also assumes an important place in
just about every form of Christian — mainly Protestant — fundamentalism, and it is, therefore, a good means of gauging whether or
not a movement is fundamentalist in character. Revelation 20 talks
about the coming of a thousand year reign. With the coming of this
kingdom, an angel binds the devil for a thousand years, casts him
into the abyss and seals it. During this thousand year reign, all mar-
tyrs, who died for Christ, come back to life and they rule together
with Him. After a thousand years have past, the devil will be freed
again for a short time and then definitively destroyed by God.

In view of the important place that apocalyptic literature assumes
in fundamentalistic movements, it is logical that this pericope about
the thousand year reign also plays a crucial role in most forms of
Christian fundamentalism. In this regard, one uses the terms millenarianism (derived from the Latin *mille*) or chiliasm (derived
from the Greek *chilia*), though this terminology is also used in

recent literature without explicit reference being made to Christian Apocalypticism. A short discussion of this term is important because the concept implies a particular vision of the present reality.

Within millenarianism, one can, roughly speaking, distinguish two strands of thought. Both see a radical break between the present and the coming of the time of salvation. Post-millenarianism considers the thousand year reign as an indication of a period of peace, which, according to some strands, literally lasts one thousand years, and which begins with the second coming of Christ. After (*post*) a period of moral progress, which thanks to the preaching of evangelical ideas is becoming a reality, Christ will come again. Christ's return is the high point of the thousand year reign. Pre-millenarianism, on the other hand, recognises a very radical break between the present world and the thousand year reign. The world in which we live goes from bad to worse. All sorts of disasters and moral decay herald an annihilating event that only a select few will survive. At that moment, Christ will return and establish the thousand year reign. In other words, when things are at their worst, the salvation is near. Therefore, fundamentalist pre-millenarian Christian groups will always point out the negative side of contemporary society: the more wars, the greater the moral decay, and the more destructive the natural disasters, the closer the coming of the thousand year reign. Although there will still be a last stand by the godless, led by Satan, at the end of those thousand years, Satan will nevertheless be definitively defeated, after which a new heaven and a new earth will be established.

In contrast to post- and pre-millenarianism, a-millenarianism — which includes, among others, the vision of the Roman Catholic Church — understands the thousand year reign in Revelation 20 to be a symbolic reference to the time span between Christ's earthly life and the endtime fulfilment of the Kingdom of God. One could also call it "now-millenarianism." Indeed, in accordance with the tradition of the Gospels, they believe that God's kingdom is already being realised *in* history. In the meantime, evil will continue to exist until the moment when the kingdom of God is fully and definitively established.

5. Biblical Fundamentalism

We have shown above that the Bible is important to the emphasis placed on Apocalypticism and millenarianism by Christian fundamentalist movements. The fifth characteristic of the Christian fundamentalist answer to life's questions is its markedly fundamentalistic use of the core Christian document — the Bible. In the first part, we conveyed how the Bible is, in itself, a "strange" foundation. Well, it is precisely this strange document that they read and interpret in a very inflexible way. The members of fundamentalistic communities slavishly follow a ready-made interpretation. At first, it appears that they are being faithful to the Bible, but, in fact, they are avoiding the burden of personal responsibility. They indiscriminately accept what someone else, essentially the Bible, says. And, critical questions are invariably seen as heresy.

(a) Biblical fundamentalism's central point of contention is the literal **"infallibility" of Scripture**, the so-called *"inerrantia."* Biblical fundamentalists are firmly convinced that the Bible, as the word of God, is complete and free of error. One may, therefore, under no circumstances call even the smallest part of it into question. The Bible is always right; and when it is not right, then they ensure that it is *proven* right. This conviction is often justified on the basis of the way in which some biblical passages present themselves as divine revelation. From this it follows that biblical fundamentalism thinks that the Bible can serve as a divine recipe book to solve all manner of current problems, without taking into account the social and literary context in which the biblical traditions took shape. As such, the fundamentalistic reading of the Bible could, of course, be dangerous. It is, at the very least, tempting for people who seek a ready-made answer for all life's problems.

(b) The use of the Bible as a handbook with which one can approach life's current questions, also means that one **reads and interprets the Bible very selectively**, thereby violating and misusing the biblical texts. A simple example will illustrate this. A fundamentalistic use of the Bible condemns male homosexuality on the basis of Old Testament texts like Leviticus 18:22 and 20:13, where it is labelled an "abomination" punishable by death. Making use of these passages to combat homosexuality in the twenty-first century only demonstrates how a fundamentalistic use of the Bible leads to a selective use of the Bible text. Indeed, if one accepts, without question, the law of the book of Leviticus with regard to homosexuality as binding for the twenty-first century, then one must also unquestioningly accept and apply the other laws in Leviticus to today's society. One must shun menstruating women — they are, according to Leviticus 15:19-24, unclean. The eating of mussels is forbidden — "Everything in the waters that does not have fins and scales is detestable to you" (Leviticus 11:12). Foreigners may be used as slaves — "As for the male and female slaves whom you may have, it is from the nations around you that you may acquire male and female slaves" (Leviticus 25:44). In the case of adultery with a married woman, both parties should be put to death (Leviticus 20:10). And the blind, cripples, or people with deformed noses may not become priests (Leviticus 21:18). And so on. These randomly chosen examples from the book of Leviticus clearly show that the use of the Bible as a recipe book in which one thinks one will undoubtedly find the answer to today's questions is altogether wrong.

Nevertheless, this should not imply that the biblical legal texts are wholly worthless. Even if particular laws are usually totally unusable as a result of the massive cultural and historical gulf that lies between us and the period in which they originated, the underlying motives that brought about these and other legal texts can still play a substantial and inspiring role. This will be worked out further in this book by discussing examples from a few Old Testament texts.

(c) Fundamentalist Bible readings often take as their point of departure the mistaken idea that the Old and New Testament Scriptures make **predictions** from the distant past about a future that happens to be the twenty-first century. In addition to the apocalyptic literature, they often appeal to the Old Testament's so-called prophetic literature in this regard. This faulty way of approaching the Old Testament prophet as a diviner of the future is in part due to the use of the word in ancient Greece. The *profètès* at the shrine of Apollo at Delfi translated the incoherent sounds that the priestess (the *Pythia*) made while in a trance. And the fact that they usually expected pronunciations about the future from this *profètès*, meant that the Old Testament prophets were also considered to be predictors of the future. Yet the Greek term προφήτης (*profètès*) originally simply meant "spokesperson" or "messenger." A prophet was, therefore, someone who, on behalf of the deity, conveyed messages to the people. Prophets were men and women who, on God's orders, imparted an intuitively obtained, "revealed" word of God to both kings and (parts of) the population. They did not use astrology, omens or divination. Their messages were not necessarily future orientated. As "divine spokespersons," the prophets had a twofold task: prophets are critics and visionaries.[12] As critics, they reveal how and why Israel has turned away from its devotion and individuality. They confront the present reality with the high ideals of the past and unmask how the present has

---

[12] Erich Zenger, "Entstehung und Afbau des Alten Testaments,"*Lebendige Welt der Bibel: Entdeckungsreise in das Alte Testament*, ed. Erich Zenger (Freiburg/Basel/Vienna: Herder, 1997) 126-140, especially 135.

turned away from these ideals. Prophets are "protestants": they dispute the heresy that everything is good the way it is and should also remain so. As such, they proclaim, as visionaries on behalf of God, a future reality that far surpasses the current one. They announce God's dream to history, thereby relativising the momentary might of the mighty and the passing powerlessness of the powerless. They are God's provocation on all levels of public and religious life. As such, they are, thus, also persecuted, ridiculed and marginalised. Only when the course of history validates their message, spoken in the name of God, are they properly valued. And thanks to this, they have their place in the canon of the Old Testament. When they talk about the future, then it is about the near future, the course of which is apparent from what is going wrong in the present and what went wrong in the past. Only at a later stage did their proclamations, within the framework of a general tendency to apply prophetic promises to the endtime, become a basis for hope in an eschatological liberation of Israel brought about by the Messiah.

(d) Another characteristic of biblical fundamentalism is the so-called **literalism**. They read the Bible literally, regarding the biblical tradition on some points as a trustworthy account of historical events or as accurate information. Everything that is related in the Bible actually happened. Eve was literally made from Adam's rib, Elijah was literally taken up to heaven, and Noah's ark actually existed. With regard to the Old Testament, as proof of the fact that information offered therein must be taken literally and is trustworthy, they avail themselves of the argument from authority: Jesus himself is supposed to have explicitly emphasised the Old Testament's authenticity and authority.[13]

---

[13] With regard to the historicity of Eve, they state, for example, Jesus Christ himself confirmed that Eve actually lived and was not a fictitious person. When the pharisees questioned him about divorce, Jesus drew their attention to the

Nonetheless, this notion of literalism as a characteristic of fundamentalist Bible reading must be nuanced. Indeed, rather than reading *everything* in the Bible literally, they usually shift between literal and symbolic readings at will. This is perhaps one of the most characteristic features of biblical fundamentalism. Still, the fact that certain parts of the Bible contain historical information and others must be read symbolically is beyond question. Indeed, scientific biblical scholarship maintains the same thing. Yet whereas the latter tries, at the end of the research process, to pass a verdict on the literal or otherwise reading of passages and consequently on their historical reliability and the arguments that can be used to support this, it is typical of the fundamentalistic Bible reading that they, without any grounds, take some passages literally and others symbolically. For example, exegesis does not begin from the premise that Balaam's donkey, which is mentioned in Numbers 22–24, could not have been a historical animal that actually spoke. It is only at the end of the research, when it has been shown that the motif of talking animals is a hallmark of myth and folklore, that one decides that Balaam's eloquent donkey is characteristic of a certain kind of literature, the purpose of which is anything but to provide reliable historical information. Biblical fundamentalism, on the other hand, already begins from the premise

Genesis account concerning the creation of the man and the woman (Mt 19:3-6) See Wachttorengenootschap [WTG], *Inzicht in de Schrift*. Deel 1: *A–J* (Brooklyn, 1997) 655. The fact that Jehovah's Witnesses, by taking this position, wholly situate themselves in the camp of biblical fundamentalism is apparent from the following quote from the *magna carta* of Christian fundamentalism: Reuben Archer Torrey, *The Fundamentals: A Testimony to the Truth*, 4 vols. [Grand Rapids, MI: Baker, 1988 (reprint)] 34: "The attitude of Christ to the Old Testament Scriptures must determine ours. He is God. He is truth. He is the final voice. He is the Supreme Judge. There is no appeal from that court. Christ Jesus the Lord believed and affirmed the historic veracity of the whole of the Old Testament writings explicitly (Luke 24:44)."

that the donkey actually spoke. After all, it says so in the Bible, which is the word of God and thus infallible. And if Balaam's donkey did not actually speak, how then can we be sure that what the rest of the Bible says is reliable?

(e) Biblical fundamentalism shows itself to be a master at **taking the Bible out of context**. Depending on the desired outcome, one can, Bible in hand, legitimise or forbid the death penalty. Leviticus 24:21, indeed, states, "one who kills a human being shall be put to death;" but one also reads in Deuteronomy 5:17, "You shall not murder." While Micah 4:3 characterises the time of salvation as a period in which swords will be beaten into ploughshares, Joel 4:10 calls upon people to forge the ploughshares into swords.

Worse still is when one combines biblical quotes, taken out of context, with one another. As an extreme example of such a populist-fundamentalistic handling of the Bible, we shall consider to *The Bible Code*, the work of the American journalist Michael Drosnin.[14] His method is simultaneously simple and laughably simplistic — and therefore fundamentalistic. Drosnin considers the whole Bible to be a chain of letters. As such, he reduces, for example, the first five books of the Old Testament, the so-called Pentateuch, to one line of 304,805 characters. Drosnin then unleashes a computer on this series of letters — one can, of course, no longer speak of a text with meaning. The computer must then combine, from the series of characters, words or names, proposed by Drosnin, with as few letters between them as possible. Hebrew idiom plays no role in this. Indeed, the combinations can just as well be made from right to left as from left to right, from top to bottom as from bottom to top and even diagonally. The whole system can best be likened to the type of puzzle where, in the midst of a whole series of letters, words must be identified. An illustration will make this

[14] Michael Drosnin, *The Bible Code* (New York: Simon & Schuster, 1997).

abstract description clear. In order to see the murder of Prime Minister Rabin of Israel in 1995 already described in the Old Testament, Drosnin — at least by his own account — allows the computer to reconstruct the name "Yitzhak Rabin" using the method described above. The name is found only once. When one splits the 304,805 characters into sixty-three lines of 4,772 characters and a final line of 4,169 letters, then one can read, at a certain place from top to bottom, the name "Yitzhak Rabin." That is to say that there are, between every letter of this name, 4,772 other characters. In other words, the Bible is seen as a giant puzzle, in which one, with the help of the thousands of letters in it, can make combinations to one's heart's content. Not without coincidence, the name of the prime minister of Israel murdered in 1995 is crossed by the formula "assassin that will assassinate," a statement that God did not apparently find necessary to encode (Deuteronomy 4:42), unlike Rabin's name where the required letters are spread out over twenty-three chapters of the book of Deuteronomy (Deuteronomy 2:33–24:16).

The figure below is taken from the sixty-four lines just mentioned. The letters framed in the vertical column form the name Yitzhak Rabin. In the horizontal framed letters, one reads "assassin that will assassinate." The Bible verses from which the letters are taken were found after a little searching. These are given here in the right column.

ת	**י**	ו	ה	צ	ה	י	ה	מ	ה	ל	Dt 2:32
ת	**צ**	**ר**	**י**	**ר**	**ש**	**א**	**ה**	**צ**	**ו**	**ר**	Dt 4:42
י	**ח**	ל	ש	י	ה	ע	ר	צ	ה	ת	Dt 7:20
ת	**ק**	ת	ו	ו	ת	ר	מ	ש	מ	ת	Dt 11:1
י	**ר**	צ	מ	צ	ר	א	מ	כ	א	י	Dt 13:11
א	**ב**	מ	ת	ל	ק	ס	ו	ה	ש	א	Dt 17:2
כ	**י**	ו	ל	י	נ	ב	מ	י	נ	ה	Dt 21:5
י	**נ**	ב	ל	ע	ת	ו	ב	א	ו	ת	Dt 24:16

The "Bible code" is, nevertheless, according to Drosnin, more stringent still. Supposedly, not only the assassination of the Israeli prime minister is announced in the Bible. Drosnin also finds the name of the murderer. For this, he uses Numbers 35:11. In this verse, the author finds the name of Rabin's murderer, Amir, written back to front — but that's exactly why it is a *code*! There is only one problem with this Bible code: without knowing what to look for, you will find nothing.[15]

(f) Not only the Bible is always right. Biblical Fundamentalism is also **always in the right.** In conformity with the univocality with which religious fundamentalistic movements claim to have a monopoly on the truth, the way in which the Bible is read and interpreted is also characterised by univocality. There is one interpretation that is given by a central authority and that, therefore, must be accepted. Biblical fundamentalism permits no "deviant" readings of the Bible. This univocal interpretation obviously demonstrates the need that many people have to get clear and unanimous answers to questions (of meaning) without having to think critically.

In this way, a fundamentalist reading of the Bible distinguishes itself from a critical approach to the text. Just as the whole of scientific theology wants to be a critical reflection on everything that has to do with religion, ethics or society and, therefore, seldom allows itself to make indisputable statements — often giving outsiders the impressions that it never takes a position —, so critical Biblical exegesis also often yields more questions than answers. An accessible presentation of the question of the authorship of the first five books of the Old Testament (the so-called Pentateuch) is, for example, a very tricky undertaking. Within current Pentateuch

---

[15] Michael Drosnin, *De bijbelcode* (Naarden: A. J. G. Strengholt's boeken, 1997) 28: "Zonder te weten waar je naar zoekt, zul je niets vinden."

research, one encounters almost as many answers to the question of the origin of this collection as there are exegetes. For the biblical fundamentalist, the answer to this question is, however, extremely simple: the prophet Moses wrote the Pentateuch. And having been put into writing by someone "whom the Lord knew face to face" (Deuteronomy 34:10), all these books must, without doubt, also be accepted as reliable.

That such a fundamentalistic univocal interpretation of the Bible is wholly in contradiction to the biblical interpretation in the large Christian churches, is apparent from, for example, a document that the Pontifical Biblical Commission — a commission of Catholic Bible scholars — published in 1993, for which Joseph Cardinal Ratzinger, who became Pope Benedict XVI, wrote the preface. In this document, all methods and approaches to the Bible are presented as legitimate, while pointing out their potential shortcomings. Indeed, the document states, "each age must in its own way newly seek to understand the sacred books."[16]

Conscious of the fact that the characterisation of religious and biblical fundamentalism presented above is not only sizeable, but sometimes also perhaps seems complicated, what follows will concretely illustrate the body of thought dealt with by means of a detailed example, namely on the basis of the biblical fundamentalism of the Jehovah's Witnesses.

c. *Illustration: Biblical Fundamentalism among Jehovah's Witnesses*

The Jehovah's Witnesses are undoubtedly a Christian group that just about everyone comes into contact with at some point. In 1884,

---

[16] Commission Biblique Pontificale, "L'interprétation de la Bible dans l'Église," *Biblica* 74 (1993) 451-528 – Cf. also, http://catholic-resources.org/ChurchDocs/PBC_Interp-FullText.htm#Introduction, dd. 07.09.2007.

when the American, Charles Taze Russel (1852-1916), established the *Watch Tower Bible and Tract Society* — since 1931 this society has been primarily known as the "Jehovah's Witnesses" — all the features of a fundamentalist institution were already present. Arising within the evangelical churches of America, during the above-mentioned nineteenth century climate of opposition to liberal Christianity, in which the previously dominant certainties slowly but surely crumbled, the teachings of the Jehovah's Witnesses offered unequivocal and therefore simplistic answers to all manner of questions. Perhaps this, together with the good feeling of being accepted into a group of like-minded people, is one of the reasons for their success. Their moral norms are straightforward. There is no grey, just black and white. In their Bible interpretation, they not only clearly state what the actual and definitive meaning of the text is, the explanation is there for you to take it or leave it. Those who choose to do the latter are doomed.

1. A Righteous Minority versus a Wicked Majority

As a movement that grew out of Protestantism, a fundamentalist approach to the Bible is typical of Jehovah's Witnesses.[17] The fact that they, as a minority, the "good," take a stand against a hostile majority, the "bad," which betrays a dualistic image of the world and human beings, is based on their interpretation of a single verse in the so-called Old Testament "Paradise Narrative" (Genesis 2–3).

After the man and his wife ("Adam and Eve"), at the instigation of the snake, ate of the forbidden fruit six thousand years ago (*sic!*), God, i.e., Jehovah, condemned the snake, in the biblical

---

[17] All the Jehovah's witnesses texts quoted in this book are translated from the Dutch sources (which are explicitly mentioned and referred to in the footnotes), since access to their English equivalents proved to be difficult in Belgium.

narrative, with the following words: "And I shall put enmity between you and the woman and between your seed and her seed."[18] According to Jehovah's Witnesses, this sole verse programmatically indicates the general theme of the Bible, of which they are the only legitimate interpreters. Although this "prophecy" of Genesis 3:15 also applied to the "historical" Eve — an interpretation that testifies to a literal reading of the Bible —, the scope of the prophecy is still much broader. It also articulates the specific position of the Witnesses in today's society. After all, if God's supposed prediction was only applicable to the historical Eve and the historical serpent of six millennia ago, then there would have been an end to the animosity at the moment of Eve's death. The meaning of the "report" of Genesis 2–3 must therefore be more far-reaching. And so both the serpent and the woman also have a symbolic meaning for Jehovah's Witnesses. This meaning, they believe they can track down using their typical and well known method in which biblical quotes are combined with one another at will.

On the basis of two verses from the New Testament, the Witnesses come to the conclusion that the *serpent* in the Old Testament creation narrative is meant to represent "the great dragon [...], the original serpent, the one called Devil and Satan, who is misleading the entire inhabited earth" (Revelation 12:9 – NWT) and "seduced Eve by its cunning" (2 Corinthians 11:3 – NWT).[19] What the *woman* refers to is apparently explained by Revelation

---

[18] This translation is based upon the Jehovah's Witnesses own translation of the Bible: Wachttorengenootschap, *Nieuwe-Wereldvertaling van de Heilige Schrift met studieverwijzingen. Herziene uitgave* (Brooklyn, 1995); orig.: Watch Tower Bible and Tract Society of Pennsylvania (WTS), *New World Translation of the Holy Scriptures – With References* (Brooklyn, 1995), further abbreviated as NWT.

[19] Cf. WTG, *Inzicht in de Schrift. Deel 2: K–Z en Index* (Brooklyn, 1997) 886-887.

12:1-2: "And a great sign was seen in heaven, a woman arrayed with the sun, and the moon was beneath her feet, and on her head was a crown of twelve stars, and she was pregnant. And she cries out in her pains and in her agony to give birth" (NWT). Since women in the Bible, according to Jehovah's Witnesses, often represent organisations that are married to eminent persons — in this respect they refer to, among others, Jeremiah 3:20 in which Israel is depicted as God's unfaithful spouse or to Revelation 21:9-14 where the Christians are called Christ's bride —, the woman in the verses from Revelation represents Jehovah's symbolic spouse.[20] Therefore, the woman who appears on the scene in the Old Testament creation narrative must likewise be a symbolic woman, who represents Jehovah's heavenly organisation comprised of spiritual creatures.[21]

By identifying the snake as Satan and the woman as the symbolic spouse of Jehovah, the Jehovah's Witnesses have biblically attempted to legitimise the foundation of the fundamental dualism between the evil power on the one hand and the good on the other. This dualism is, however, not limited to the supernatural good and the supernatural evil. Genesis 3:15, indeed, is not only about an enmity between a serpent and a woman. God's "prophecy" also applies to the *seed* of the serpent and the *seed* of the woman, that stand diametrically opposed to one another, and that they, moreover, believe they can clearly identify. The "seed of the woman" is supposed to refer primarily to Jesus Christ, who is therefore presented as the son of Eve. Jehovah sent Jesus from heaven in order to restore his dominion over the Earth. In addition, the seed of the

[20] WTG, *De Openbaring: Haar grootste climax is nabij!* (Brooklyn, 1988) 177.
[21] See *ibid.*, 10: "Jehovah's uit geestelijke schepselen bestaande hemelse organisatie."

woman also includes, according to the Jehovah's Witnesses, 144,000 anointed Christians who, together with Christ — the primary part of the seed of the woman — form the secondary part thereof.[22]

For the identification of the "seed of the serpent," the Witnesses base their arguments on Mark's Gospel. According to Mark 3:22, the scribes reproach Jesus saying that he can only drive out demons thanks to Beelzebub, i.e., Satan, who is called the "ruler of the demons." On the basis of this text, Jehovah's Witnesses conclude that the seed of the serpent in Genesis 3 refers, first of all, to Satan's invisible organisation of demons. The seed, however, also refers to Satan's visible organisation on Earth. To support this position, the society now looks to John's Gospel. In John 8:44, Jesus turns on the Jewish religious leaders with the words: "YOU are from YOUR father the Devil, and YOU wish to do the desires of YOUR father" (NWT). Thus, these leaders apparently make up part of Satan's descendants. And, like them, many other people have turned out to be people who do the bidding of Satan.

The nefarious influence of this "human seed" of Satan can, according to Jehovah's witnesses, already be discerned in the early stages of human history. The first person who was born in a normal way, Cain, "who originated with the wicked one and slaughtered his brother" (1 John 3:12 – NWT)), belonged to Satan's seed. Nimrod too, "a mighty hunter in opposition to Jehovah" (Genesis 10:9 – NWT)[23] is allegedly one of the seed of Satan. Indeed, under his leadership, a start was supposedly made to the building of the

[22] The "Great Crowd" is not part of the "seed of the woman." They must serve on Earth, in unity with the heavenly Israel.

[23] The literal translation of Genesis 10:9 reads, "He was a mighty hunter in the sight of the YHWH." Any opposition between YHWH and Nimrod is therefore alien to the Hebrew text.

city of Babylon and its tower (Genesis 11:1-9).[24] It is in Babylon that various elements arise that, as Satan's seed, radically oppose Jehovah. Since Nimrod's founding of Babylon, the influence of Satan's seed has been threefold. (1) Because many people wanted to imitate Nimrod's seizing of power, countless political forces appeared on the scene. (2) Closely associated with the political rulers are the dishonest merchants, of whom Jehovah's witnesses say the following. The merchants of the world have, to this day, selfishly pursued profit, such that in many countries some have become very rich while the majority of the population languishes in poverty. During the industrialised twentieth century, the traders and manufacturers have made huge profits by supplying political powers with diabolical military weapons of mass destruction, including the nuclear arsenals that threaten humanity with extinction. Such selfish business magnates and people like them, together with the military commanders and "strong men," must be counted among Satan's godless seed.[25] (3) In addition to corrupt politics and greedy commerce, the so-called false religion is part of

---

[24] It should be noted that the Bible nowhere names Nimrod as the founder of Babylon. For this claim, Jehovah's witnesses rely on, among others, Flavius Josephus's *Antiquitates*. See WTG, *Inzicht in de Schrift, Deel 2,* 441. For the discussion surrounding the reception of the figure of Nimrod, refer to Claus Westermann, *Genesis 1–11,* Biblischer Kommentar. Altes Testament, 1/1 (Neukirchen/ Vluyn: Neukirchener Verlag, 1974) 686-692.

[25] See WTG, *De Openbaring,* 13: "Tot op de huidige tijd zijn de kooplieden der wereld ermee voortgegaan voor zelfzuchtig gewin te werken, zodat in veel landen enkelen zeer rijk zijn geworden terwijl de meerderheid van de bevolking in armoede verkommert. In dit twintigste-eeuwse industriële tijdperk hebben de handelaars en de fabrikanten grote winsten gemaakt door de politieke machten vol te stoppen met duivelse militaire vernietigingswapens, waartoe ook de kernarsenalen behoren die de mensheid thans met uitroeiing bedreigen. Zulke zelfzuchtige handelsmagnaten en andere personen van hetzelfde slag moeten samen met de 'militaire bevelhebbers' en 'sterke mannen' tot Satans goddeloze zaad gerekend worden."

Satan's seed. According to Jehovah's Witnesses, chapters 17 and 18 of Revelation, which speak of the "the whore of Babylon," deal with this problem. After all, because the original Babylon, founded by Nimrod, signified an open challenge to God, religion also came into play. According to Jehovah's witnesses, ancient Babylon was in fact a cradle of idolatry. When God scattered the builders of the tower, they also spread Babylon's false religion, which is why the scribes and Pharisees at the time of Jesus and the many religions today make up part of the visible seed of the serpent.[26]

The biblical underpinnings of the dualism between the serpent and the woman and their respective "seed," in other words between good and evil, are necessary background in order to be able understand the teachings of Jehovah's Witnesses. They consider Genesis 3:15 to be a declaration of the programme for the whole of history. It isn't any wonder then that this opposition between the seed of the woman and the seed of the serpent concretely translates into a radical opposition between Jehovah's Witnesses, on the one hand, and the rest of world's population, on the other. As the seed of the woman, the 144,000 anointed (the so-called John class) and the "great crowd" (Jehovah's Witnesses) stand on the side of Christ. All the rest are, of course, part of the seed of the serpent and will be annihilated on God's Judgement Day.

2. Between Literal and Symbolic Interpretation

With the theme of the 144,000 chosen anointed, we touch upon another example of fundamentalistic Bible reading by Jehovah's Witnesses, namely, the unfounded hopping between literal and symbolic interpretations. According to the New Testament book of

---

[26] Cf. *ibid.*, 30: "Ja, de geestelijken der christenheid zijn de voornaamste leden van Satans zaad."

Revelation (chapter 7) there will be 144,000 "sealed." On the one hand, Jehovah's Witnesses acknowledge that the number twelve, in both the Old and the New Testament, is a symbolic number. So, they accept that the number twelve in Revelation 7:5-8, when the twelve tribes of Ancient Israel are discussed, is used symbolically. Thus, it is all the more remarkable that they, for no apparent reason, take the number 144,000, albeit a multiple of twelve, literally.[27]

Often, this unfounded alternation between a literal and a symbolic reading takes place in order to make the Bible agree with the results of scientific research that contradict a biblical idea. The concept of the creation of the world in six or seven days offered by the Old Testament creation narrative is, from a scientific point of view, unacceptable. So, despite the fact that Jehovah's Witnesses indeed accept that Adam was the first historical human being — whose creation they can date to the autumn of the year 4026 BC! —, one should nevertheless read the creation in six days symbolically: each of the six days of creation lasted at least a few thousand years. Once again, the Bible is always right.

3. Prediction, Apocalypticism and Millenarianism

Moreover, Jehovah's Witnesses read the Bible as a book full of futuristic predictions. The apocalyptic writings mentioned already play an important role in this regard. They are thought to be writings in which one can read, as if it were a screenplay, about the fortunes that befall the contemporary human being and his society. The theme of the "Thousand Year Reign" is central here. In the teachings of the Jehovah's Witnesses, the year 1914 plays a crucial role. The year is seen as the beginning of the "day of the Lord," on which Christ began his heavenly reign. In 1914, Satan was

---

[27] Cf. WTG, *De Openbaring*, 19.

supposedly cast out of heaven, which also explains the outbreak of World War I.

The starting point for this argument is found, according to Jehovah's Witnesses, in the apocalyptic book of Daniel, which we have already discussed above. As an aside, Jehovah's witnesses believe that the book of Daniel contains an eye-witness account of actual events and, as such, was written by the prophet Daniel between 618 BC and 536 BC. The most important "proof" of the authenticity of the book of Daniel can be found, according to Jehovah's Witnesses, in the fact that Jesus refers to Daniel. Scientific exegesis on the other hand rightly considers Daniel to be a legendary character and dates the book attributed to him to the second century BC.

The fourth chapter of Daniel recounts the Babylonian King Nebuchadnezzar's dream. The ruler sees a giant, beautiful, bountiful tree that reaches to the heavens and that can be seen from all over the world. In its shadow, animals find rest, and its branches are a favourite place for birds. Suddenly, an angel swoops down from heaven and orders the tree to be chopped down. The stump and its roots, however, must be left in the ground in a band of iron and bronze. Heavenly dew will moisten him and he must share the grass of the earth with the animals. The text then says, "Let his mind be changed from that of a human, and let the mind of an animal be given to him. And let seven times pass over him" (Daniel 4:13 – NRSV). For the reader, this makes it immediately clear that the tree is a symbolic representation of a person, namely, the king himself. When the Babylonian sages fail to explain Nebuchadnezzar's dream, the king calls upon Daniel. According to Daniel, the great tree represents Nebuchadnezzar, strong and mighty, whose greatness reaches to the heavens and whose sovereignty reaches to the ends of the earth. That the tree is cut down, and must, as an animal, share the grass of the earth with the

remaining animals for "seven times" means that people will drive
Nebuchadnezzar from human society. Daniel continues, "You shall
be made to eat grass like oxen, you shall be bathed with the dew
of heaven, and seven times shall pass over you, until you have
learned that the Most High has sovereignty over the kingdom of
mortals, and gives it to whom he will. As it was commanded to
leave the stump and roots of the tree, your kingdom shall be re-
established for you from the time that you learn that Heaven is
sovereign" (Daniel 4:25-26).
Jehovah's Witnesses interpret this text from the book of Daniel
in a twofold manner. First, they believe that, twelve months later
(see Daniel 4:29), Nebuchadnezzar's dream literally came true for
the first time. While the king boasted about his empire, that which
he saw in his dream came to pass. The way in which Jehovah's
Witnesses describe this event is worth quoting: "Suddenly, Nebuchadnezzar lost his mind. Driven away from people, he ate plants,
'just like the oxen.' There, outside, among the animals of the field,
it was not some sort of paradise where he sat at ease on the grass,
enjoy the fresh breeze everyday. In what is today Iraq, where Babylon's ruins are situated, the temperatures range from 50 degrees
Celsius in the summer months, to below zero in winter. Without
care and exposed to the elements, Nebuchadnezzar's long, matted
hair looked like the feathers of an eagle and his uncut toe and
finger nails were like bird's claws (Daniel 4:33). What a humiliation for the pride world ruler! (...) Jehovah restored Nebuchadnezzar's mental health after seven times had passed. The king then
acknowledged the Most High. (...) Yes, Nebuchadnezzar came to
realise that the Most High is indeed the Sovereign Ruler of the
kingdom of man."[28]

[28] Translated from WTG, *Daniëls profetie*, 90-92: "Ogenblikkelijk was Nebukadnezar zijn verstand kwijt. Verdreven van onder de mensen at hij plantengroei,
'net als de stieren'. Daar buiten onder de dieren van het veld was het echt niet

Nebuchadnezzar's "mental illness" lasted, according to the book of Daniel, "seven times" (Daniel 4:16, 23, 25, 32). Considering that his hair grew to be as long as the feathers of an eagle and his nails became like bird's claws — which Jehovah's Witnesses, of course, believe literally happened —, the seven times cannot be taken to mean seven days or seven weeks. Relying on certain manuscripts of the Septuagint, i.e., the Greek translation of the Old Testament, and on Flavius Josephus's *Antiquitates,* Jehovah's Witnesses interpret these "seven times" to be "seven years." Moreover, to support this they also point to the other outstanding example of biblical apocalyptic writing, namely, the New Testament book of Revelation. In Revelation 12:6, 14, three and half times/years is equated with 1260 days, which leads the Jehovah's Witnesses to conclude that one year in biblical "prophecies" is 360 days ($1260 \div 3,5 = 360$). Consequently, Nebuchadnezzar's illness lasted, according to Jehovah's Witnesses, literally seven years, i.e. 2520 days.

Nebuchadnezzar's dream in Daniel 4, however, does not only tell us something about what supposedly *de facto* happened to this king sometime in the sixth century BC. At the same time, Jehovah's witnesses transcend this literal reading. The tree should also be seen as a symbol of the universal sovereignty of Jehovah. Before the

een soort paradijs waar hij lekker op zijn gemak in het gras zat, elke dag genietend van een fris briesje. In het huidige Irak, waar Babylons ruïnes gelegen zijn, lopen de temperaturen uiteen van wel 50 graden Celsius in de zomermaanden tot royaal beneden nul in de winter. Zonder verzorging en blootgesteld aan de elementen leek Nebukadnezars lange, samengeklitte haar op de veren van een arend en zijn niet-geknipte vinger- en teennagels werden als de klauwen van vogels (Daniël 4:33). Wat een vernedering voor deze trotse wereldheerser! (…) Jehovah herstelde Nebukadnezars geestelijke gezondheid na verloop van zeven tijden. De koning erkende toen de Allerhoogste. (…) Ja, Nebukadnezar kwam tot het besef dat de Allerhoogste inderdaad de Soevereine Heerser is in het koninkrijk der mensheid."

Jehovah's Witnesses, even go so far, with some reservations, as to consider Nebuchadnezzar's condition to be a case of clinical lycanthropy, a mental illness in which a person believes he or she can turn into an animal. See *ibid.,* 94.

destruction of Jerusalem by Babylon, the kingdom of David and his successors represented Jehovah's sovereignty over the whole world. When Jerusalem was destroyed — this is according to Jehovah's Witnesses what the felling of the great tree of course signifies — divine sovereignty over the world was interrupted for "seven times." They situate the destruction of Jerusalem in 607 BC,[29] while the entire scientific world considers 587-586 to be the period in which Jerusalem fell. The Jehovah's Witnesses then try to work out when these "seven times" will come to an end. For the second fulfilment of this prophecy, the earlier calculation makes little sense. The Jehovah's Witness propose that seeing that the "seven times" constitutes part of a "prophecy," a prophetic rule must also be applied to the 2520 days. This "rule" they find in a "prophecy" by Ezekiel about the Babylonian siege of Jerusalem. Using Ezekiel 4:6 — "one day for each year" — the "seven times" of Daniel 4 must refer to 2520 years. Starting at 607 BC, the Jehovah's Witness thus arrive at 1914.

Thus, we can say that Jehovah's Witnesses, on the basis of an arbitrary combination of Bible texts, conclude that Jesus Christ began his heavenly rule in 1914. That this moment was accompanied by worldwide turmoil, is not only evident from the fact that World War I broke out, but, moreover, according to Jehovah's Witnesses, in the period that followed, various old monarchies, which are part of the seed of the serpent, gradually began to disappear. As an example, they refer to the disappearance of the tsars in 1917. At the same time, they view the instabilities in the political world as precursory "earthquakes" that herald a dramatic upheaval in the area of government. Then, God's kingdom will take control and rule supreme over the earth.[30]

---

[29] See WTG, *Uw koninkrijk kome* (Brooklyn, 1981) 188-189.
[30] See WTG, *De Openbaring*, 106: "Gods koninkrijk (…) het heft in handen nemen en de alleenheerschappij over de aarde voeren."

4. Conclusion

The manner in which Jehovah's Witnesses read the Bible is, without doubt, objectionable, for the sole reason that it is intrinsically flawed. Perhaps, such fierce fulmination leaves a nasty aftertaste for people who afford the Bible a central place in their lives. Still, there is no other option. One must rip *their* bible from their hands — and this holds true for all who read the Bible in a fundamentalistic way — in order to hand them *the* Bible, as it really fits together, as it has really functioned and as it can still potentially make a contribution to our society.[31]

In the introduction to the second part of this book, which described the responses to the disenchantment, it was proposed that one can distinguish two reactions. The first chapter sketched the way in which the "negative" answer, driven by a feeling that one has lost one's religious identity, desperately and stubbornly seeks to retrieve certainty and security. In addition to the pre- or uncritical acceptance of the Bible with childlike naivety, the historicising tendency on the one hand and fundamentalism on the other, particularly the biblical version, are evident. Against this background, the second chapter will delineate the positive reaction to the disenchantment.

---

[31] Cf. Manfred Oeming, *Biblische Hermeneutik: Eine Einführung* (Darmstadt: Wissenschaftliche Buchgesellschaft, 1998) 159.

RISING ABOVE THE DISENCHANTMENT: A CRITICAL APPROACH

In the second chapter, the so-called "positive" response to the disenchantment is described. Without denying the new reality, an attempt can still be made to rise above the disenchantment by seeking a critical yet enriching interaction with the tradition of thought and belief that has been handed down. In this regard, it will first be shown how the Bible and historicity can be critically combined (§1). Then, against this background, the contribution of historical-critical exegesis will be outlined (§2), and, finally, how this evolves towards a plurality of (diachronic and synchronic) approaches that, at the same time, respect both the historical development of the biblical text and its contemporary theological relevance and meaning will be examined (§3).

1. Bible and Historicity

a. *Bible versus Archaeology*

Is the Bible historically accurate or not? What role does archaeology play in this debate? These pertinent questions raise two issues that are not infrequently in the news, although it must immediately be added that the media are often sloppy in their judgement: either the Bible is absolutely right, or it is absolutely wrong. That the Bible is first and foremost a religious book is seldom, if ever, brought up.

That being said, the Bible may be the most translated and even the most sold, perhaps even the most read book in the world, but it is in no way undisputed. Like clockwork, attention is devoted to it in all sorts of media. The Flood and the search for the biblical cities of Sodom and Gomorra are often prominent. Almost always, the common denominator in these reports is the question of the historical reliability of the biblical tradition. The plot is perhaps most recognisable in the conflict between the biblical account of creation, which states that God created heaven and earth out of nothing in six days, and the scientific theories that try to explain the world's existence in terms of the Big Bang and evolution.

Now, this historical reliability of the Bible, which for centuries was never in doubt, has not only taken a knock due to the rise of modernity and the prevalence of the (positive) natural sciences (as discussed above), but other disciplines that were originally intended to safeguard and protect the authority of the Bible have also gradually begun to question the historical calibre of the Bible's content. In this respect, both archaeology and biblical studies played an important role.

When Eusebius of Caesarea, a biblical archaeologist of the third and fourth century, before the term biblical archaeologist even existed, studied the place names that appear in the Bible, he intended to bring the facts of faith and archaeology into accord with one another. By identifying biblical place names with actual sites, Eusebius aimed to demonstrate that the events that the Bible relates were also played out in reality.

Since the Enlightenment and the associated rise of modernity, archaeology has gradually freed itself from its role as the faithful servant of theology. It set out, using its own means and its own methods, to subject the sands of Palestine and the surrounding countries to thorough research. More and more, it became, and becomes, clear that what had until then been accepted as typically biblical attitudes, could in fact not be separated from their ancient-oriental context. Stories of creation and an all-destroying flood are also central for other nations of the Ancient Near East. Furthermore, the Bible appears to be dependant upon these at several points.

On the basis of the vast number of archaeological finds of the last few decades, it would moreover appear that the origin and history of Ancient Israel is much more complex than the Bible would have us believe. For example, what the so-called "Historical books" of the Old Testament (the books from Genesis up to and including Kings) tell us about the patriarchs, slavery in Egypt, mass exodus from that country, years of wondering in the desert, violent occupation of Canaan, the monarchy under David and Solomon and the events in the later northern kingdom of Israel and the southern kingdom of Judah, often appears to contradict the results of archaeological research. So, the biblical account of the occupation of Canaan in the book of Joshua is, from an archaeological perspective, very problematic. Furthermore, regardless of the biblical witness in this regard, there is still no clear archaeological discovery that would even permit the acceptance of something like an Israelite occupation of Canaan.

b. *Biblical History versus History in the Bible*

If we base ourselves on the Old Testament, then the history of Ancient Israel coincides with the fortunes of a single family, the common ancestor of which was a certain Abram of Ur, later called Abraham.[1] During a stay in Egypt, the descendents of Abraham are

---

[1] The scholarly literature on the history of Ancient Israel is inexhaustible. We refer you here to a few, recent, authoritative works: Gösta W. Ahlström, *The History of Ancient Palestine from the Palaeolithic Period to Alexander's Conquest*, Journal for the Study of the Old Testament. Supplement Series, 146 (Sheffield: Sheffield Academic Press, 1993); Rainer Albertz, *Religionsgeschichte*

said to have developed into a nation, a people. This history is largely related in the Pentateuch and the so-called Historical books of the Old Testament, of which the books of Genesis, Exodus, Numbers, Joshua, Judges, Samuel, Kings, Chronicles, Ezra, Nehemiah and Maccabees are especially important. But, here and there in the prophetic literature and in the rest of the Old Testament, we come across notes that appear to refer to the history of Ancient Israel.

In the past, people often tried to use the chronological data supplied in the Old Testament to reconstruct the history of Ancient Israel and to accurately date its highpoints. Yet, because of the lack of a continuous calendar, scholars found it necessary to create a

Israels in alttestamentlicher Zeit (2 vols.), Das Alte Testament Deutsch. Ergänzungsreihe, 8 (Göttingen: Vandenhoeck & Ruprecht, 1992); Siegfried Herrmann, *Geschichte Israels in alttestamentlicher Zeit* (München: Kaiser, 1973); William G. Dever, *Who Were the Early Israelites and Where Did They Come From?* (Grand Rapids, MI: Eerdmans, 2003); Herbert Donner, *Geschichte des Volkes Israel und seiner Nachbarn in Grundzügen* (2 vols.), Das Alte Testament Deutsch. Ergänzungsreihe, 4 (Göttingen: Vandenhoeck & Ruprecht, [2]1996); Baruch Halpern, *The First Historians: The Hebrew Bible and History* (University Park, PA/ San Francisco, CA: Pennsylvania State University Press/Harper and Row, [2]1996); Abraham Malamat, *History of Biblical Israel: Major Problems and Minor Issues*, Culture and History of the Ancient Near East, 7 (Leiden/Boston/Cologne: Brill, 2001); Bruce M. Metzger, *Grundriß der Geschichte Israels* (Neukirchen-Vluyn: Verlag des Erziehungsvereins, [8]1990); James H. Miller and John H. Hayes, *A History of Ancient Israel and Judah* (Philadelphia, PA: Westminster Press, 1986); Nadav Na'aman and Israel Finkelstein (eds.), *From Nomadism to Monarchy: Archaeological and Historical Aspects of Early Israel* (Jerusalem/Washington: Yad Izhak Ben-Zvi, 1994); J. Alberto Soggin, *A History of Israel: From the Beginnings to the Bar Kochba Revolt, AD 135*, trans. from the Italian by J. Bowden (London: SCM, 1984); Thomas L. Thompson, *Early History of the Israelite People: From the Written and Archaeological Sources,* Studies in the History of the Ancient Near East, 4 (Leiden/New York/Cologne: Brill, 1992; [2]1994); Thomas L. Thompson, *The Bible in History: How Writers Create a Past* (London: Brill, 1999). Also, see the yet to be completed series *Biblische Enzyklopädie* (Stuttgart/Berlin/Cologne: Kohlhammer, 1996).

chronology themselves.[2] The starting point for this was Egypt and Mesopotamia. First, using a variety of sources, such as archaeological discoveries, literary texts, inscriptions, and lists of kings,[3] they drew up a general framework in which the events were dated relative to one another: king x ruled for y years before or after king z. Then they tried, within this relative chronology, to determine a few dates with certainty. In this, astronomy played an important role. After all, in both Egypt and Mesopotamia, one comes across texts that connect particular events, which allegedly occurred during the reign of a particular ruler, with solar and lunar eclipses or the positions of the planets. Since one can accurately pinpoint the moment at which, ages ago, astronomical events took place, they succeeded, with apparent precision, in dating the appearance of certain Egyptian and Mesopotamian rulers according to the Gregorian calendar used today. With regard to the first millennium before Christ, this method produced a rather accurate dating of the successive Egyptian and Mesopotamian dynasties. Nevertheless, the further one goes back in time, the larger the degree of uncertainty concerning a precise dating of successive rulers becomes.

It is indisputable that the chronology of events in Egypt and Mesopotamia that they thus derived is important for the reconstruction of the history of Ancient Israel. A number of synchronisms with events in Assyria indeed allow the determination of a few fixed dates within the history of Israel. An example will illustrate

[2] For this, see Mordecai Cogan, "Chronology," *Anchor Bible Dictionary* 1 (1992) 1002-1011; Klaas R. Veenhof, "Geschiedenis van het Oude Nabije Oosten tot de tijd van Alexander de Grote," *Bijbels handboek*. Deel 1: *De wereld van de bijbel*, ed. Adam S. van der Woude (Kampen: Kok, 1981) 286-293.

[3] Besides the fact that such lists are seldom preserved in their entirety and often contain undesirable inaccuracies, one must take into account that ancient oriental lists of kings and inscriptions were seldom written with purely historical motives. An idealistic regard for leaders and deep seated political or military motives certainly played a role here.

this. In 2 Kings 15:19, it says that King Menahem of Israel, after he was conquered by King Pul of Assyria, i.e. Tiglath-Pileser III, gave a thousand silver talents to the latter in the hope that the Assyrian would help the king of Israel hold on to power. Well, in the extra-biblical, so-called tribute list of Tiglat-Pileser, it is likewise mentioned that, among others, "Menahem of Samaria" owed him tribute, a fact that, on the basis of the Assyrian chronology, can be dated to around 738 BC. [4]

Since the Old Testament supplies an abundance of chronological data, such as the durations of the reigns of individual rulers, the life-spans of protagonists, synchronisms between the kings of Israel and Judah, or the indication of the duration of crucial periods, people have tried, starting from the absolute dates that have been determined, to date the events recounted in the Old Testament. Thus, the history of Ancient Israel, as conceived according to the biblical chronology, can be approximately summarised as follows.

Around 2100 BC, Abr(ah)am, the forefather of Israel, left Ur in Babylon and moved to Canaan. Due to famine, Abraham's grandson, Jacob, and his own children went to Egypt in around 1870 BC. The descendents of Jacob, who was also called Israel, stayed in Egypt for about 400 years. If the Old Testament accounts of the patriarchs are merely family chronicles, then from their descendents stay in Egypt onwards, it is the nation of Israel that comes to the fore. In about 1450 BC, the Israelites supposedly left Egypt and began the trek back to the land of their forefathers. After the Israelites had wandered through the desert for more than forty years, they reached the border of Canaan in about 1400 BC. In the centuries that followed, the people of Israel, with their judges, increasingly took control of the country, which, in about 1000 BC

---

[4] James Pritchard, *Ancient Near Eastern Texts Relating to the Old Testament* (Princeton, NJ: Princeton University Press, 1950) 283-284. With regard to the literature of the Ancient Near East, see William W. Hallo (ed.), *The Context of Scripture*, 3 vols. (Leiden/Boston/Cologne: Brill, 1997-2002).

resulted in the establishment of the monarchy under the kings Saul, David and Solomon. After Solomon's death in 931 BC, the kingdom split into two parts — a northern part called Israel and a southern kingdom called Judah — each headed by a king. The northern kingdom fell in 722 BC followed by Judah in 587 BC. On both occasions, a portion of the population was taken into exile. In 538 BC, the exile came to an end and the people could return to settle in their land and worship their god there.[5] With regard to the

---

[5] For this conception of the biblical chronology, which is, according to some experts, a reflection of historical events, see, for example, the conservatively inclined work of Walter C. Kaiser, *A History of Israel: From the Bronze Age through the Jewish Wars* (Nashville, TN: Broadman & Holman Publishers, 1998) 54-55. For the period before the monarchy, they mainly base themselves on the following Old Testament passages. 1 Kings 6:1 mentions that king Solomon began building the temple in Jerusalem in "the four hundred and eightieth year after the Israelites came out of the land of Egypt, in the fourth year of Solomon's reign over Israel, in the month of Ziv, which is the second month..." Since the fourth year of reign is, according to biblical chronology, around 967 BC, the exodus must have taken place in 1447 BC. According to Exodus 12:40, the Israelites lived in Egypt for 430 years, which means that Jacob and his family must have arrived in Egypt in around 1877 BC. According to the counting of the biblical chronological data, the patriarchs must have been in Canaan for 215 years before that. Therefore, Abraham's journey from Haran to Canaan must have happened somewhere around 2092.

Fundamentalistic believers go a step further. Starting from the belief that the biblical figures and events that occurred before Abraham are also meant to be historical, they try to date these on the basis of the chronological data given in Genesis. Thus, they situate the creation at the end of the fifth or the beginning of the fourth century BC. See, for example, for the views of Jehovah's Witnesses, Watch Tower Bible and Tract Society of Pennsylvania, "Chronologie," *Inzicht in de Schrift* 2 (1995) 419-442. The edition of the Nederlandse Evangelische Omroep also goes in this direction. See, for example, *Het ontstaan van Israël: De geschiedenis van het Oude Testament* (Hilversum, 1982). The Jewish calendar is also calculated according to the supposed date of the creation of the World — autumn 3761 BC —, which is arrived at using a combination of biblical chronological data. Thus, the year 2000 AD in the Gregorian calender coincides with the year 5760 in the Jewish calender. For this, see "Calendar," *Encyclopaedia Judaica* 5 (1971) 43-50.

continuation of Israel's history, the Old Testament gives no further chronological information.[6]

The chronology based on the Old Testament says nothing about the historicity of what is recounted. Indeed, it must be clearly stated at the outset that the biblical representation of Israel's history is not a description of a profane history but of a religious one. It is not the relationship to the surrounding nations and countries that is central but the relationship between Israel and its god, who has chosen Israel to be his people. Indeed, it is YaHWeH who chooses Abram and leads him to Canaan. It is YaHWeH who frees his descendents from slavery in Egypt and enters into a covenant with Israel on Mount Sinai. It is YaHWeH who leads the people through the desert and gives them the land, and so on. Moreover, the entire history of Ancient Israel, certainly with regard to the period described in the books of Samuel and Kings, is first and foremost an account of sins against and renunciation of the divinity to whom all thanks are due.

Consequently it must be concluded that the fact that certain representations in the Bible do not correspond to historical reality, does not imply that the Scriptures should be discarded as a fabrication. In fact, the task of archaeology and Bible studies (as well as the associated relevant sub-disciplines) is to identify the underlying reality and the theological wording in the various Bible texts. It is precisely in this regard that historical-critical exegesis produced groundbreaking work.

---

[6] Scholars divide the subsequent centuries into three periods: the Persian (538-331 BC), the Hellenistic (331-63 BC) and the Roman (63-135 BC).

2. The Rise of Historical-Critical Exegesis

a. *From Doubt to Proposition*

Until about the middle of the seventeenth century, people had practically no doubts concerning the historicity of the Old Testament
representations of history. They were taken to be self-evident.
After all, Moses was considered to be the author of the Pentateuch,
Joshua, the author of the book that bears his name, Samuel, the
author of the books of Judges and Samuel, and Jeremiah, the author
of the books of Kings. And such great names — authoritative
prophets who were to a greater or lesser extent all contemporaries
of the events that they recounted — could not and must not be
suspected of having distorted history.

With regard to this attitude, changes gradually start to occur in
the second half of the seventeenth century, when people, due to
inconsistencies in the Bible, begin to call the authorship of Moses,
Joshua, Samuel and Jeremiah into question and the historical-critical approach to the Old Testament begins to win favour. This
approach also meant that people were no longer convinced of the
historical reliability of the Old Testament. Primarily from the
eighteenth century, the question of the historicity of the biblical
tradition, even from within the discipline of biblical studies itself,
took centre stage. Following the research into the origin of the
biblical writings, exegetes have, ever since, devoted their attention
to conflicts and irregularities that occur within the biblical traditions themselves.

The thought of the English bishop, John William Colenso (1814-
1883), a missionary to South Africa,[7] in relation to the so-called
Flood narrative in the book of Genesis is typical of this growing

---

[7] For an introduction to the work of Colenso, see Hans Ausloos, "John William
Colenso (1814-1883) and the Deuteronomist," *Revue Biblique* 113 (2006) 372-
392.

tendency to doubt the historical character of the Bible. How could Noah and his family have fed and cared for all those animals on the ark? If the biblical account says that the whole world was flooded, then would the ark not more likely have been stranded atop Mount Everest instead of the much lower Mount Ararat in modern day Turkey? Moreover, how could the flightless dodo have gotten from Ararat to the island of Mauritius after the flood? And did the kangaroo jump from Turkey to Australia?

Such conclusions, in addition to the purely literary problems that confront one during a thorough reading of the Bible, lie at the base of historical-critical exegesis, which does not consider the Bible to be an objective report of historical facts, but instead a faith-filled reflection upon such facts. At the beginning of the twentieth century, exegetical science conclusively showed that the Old Testament stories could no longer be interpreted as objective, eye-witness accounts of historical facts. The Old Testament texts that paint a picture of how Israel fared are, on the contrary, theological texts that came about via a long and complicated process.[8] The Old Testament is, first and foremost, literature that seeks to proclaim instead of to describe.

---

[8] Cf. in this regard Yairah Amit, *History and Ideology: An Introduction to Historiography in the Hebrew Bible*, The Biblical Seminar, 60 (Sheffield: Sheffield Academic Press, 1999); James Barr, *History and Ideology in the Old Testament: Biblical Studies at the End of a Millennium* (Oxford: Oxford University Press, 2000); Giovanni Garbini, *History and Ideology in Ancient Israel* (New York: SCM, 1988); Klaas A. D. Smelik, "The Use and Misuse of the Hebrew Bible as a Historical Source," *The Rediscovery of the Hebrew Bible*, Amsterdamse Cahiers voor Exegese van de Bijbel en zijn Tradities. Supplement Series, 1, ed. Janet W. Dyk (Maastricht: Shaker, 1999) 121-139; André Wénin, "Le Mythique et l'historique dans le premier testament," *Bible et histoire: Écriture, interprétation et action dans le temps*, ed. Michel Hermans and Pierre Sauvage, Le livre et le rouleau, 10 (Namen: Presses Universitaires de Namur, 2000) 31-56.

b. *Illustration: Proclaimed and Evolved Literature*

As a case in point, we could refer to Genesis 19:30-38 which tells of how the daughters of Lot, Abraham's nephew, got him drunk for two days in a row in order to have sexual intercourse with him so that they could become pregnant by him. The children produced by this incestuous relationship — which according to Leviticus 18:7 is expressly forbidden by God's law — were named Moab and Ammon, the forefathers of the Moabites and the Ammonites. Well now, the author of Genesis 19 is in no way relating a historical event. Rather, the author, by means of an aetiology — i.e. a story that aims to explain the origin of something — wanted to trace the origins of these two peoples, with which Israel had always been at loggerheads, to a scandalous deed, thereby underscoring their inferiority.

A similar conclusion is reached regarding the so-called Historical books. When first read, they appear to describe a "history" spanning from Joshua to the fall of Jerusalem. Although it cannot be denied that the complex of Joshua-Kings is, in its final form, a homogenous whole, exegesis has still demonstrated that it comprises material of various origins, and the different literary genres indicate that the constitutive narratives were originally circulated independently of one another. The tradition of the occupation of Canaan in Joshua 1–12, for example, consists of a number of aetiological legends. They are followed by a long list of the territories of various tribes. Judges 1–12, in which all sorts of stories about sundry heroes are brought together, is followed by a series of stories about one hero, Samson. The story of David is split into a part in which David's ascent is related (1 Samuel 16 – 2 Samuel 6) and a part that primarily focuses on the struggle over who would succeed him (2 Samuel 7 – 1 Kings 2). In the books of Kings, the account of the successive kings of Israel is also interrupted by stories about the prophets like Elijah and Elisha (1 Kings 16 – 2 Kings 9). All these stories were brought together by one or more "Deuteronomic" editors (under the influence of the theological thinking found in the book of Deuteronomy). These editors did not intend to give a purely objective representation of Israel's history. Rather, they wanted to offer a reflection on Israel's past in the light of the prescripts of Deuteronomy — in which the renunciation of idolatry and the requirements of a single, central sanctuary play a crucial role. As a result of the disillusionment and frustration over the loss of Judah and the temple, they wanted to retrospectively explain how Israel could have come to this. And so, they did not write an objective history.

The fact that the Old Testament Wisdom literature (which will be discussed further in the third part of this book) also makes no claim to present historically reliable information is exemplified in the first verse of the book of Job. The expression "There was once a man in the land of Uz" situates the story of Job within the literary genre of the folk tale. Indeed, fairy stories today also often begin with "There once was…" And just as no one knows where Peter Pan's Neverland or the gingerbread house in Hansel and Gretel are, the location of Uz is also unknown. The book of Job is not about history. It is an ahistorical story that plays itself out in an ahistorical world in an ahistorical time.

Finally, the Prophetic literature should also be approached with a healthy dose of scepticism as far as its historical reliability is concerned. Indeed, every prophetic book in the Old Testament has undergone various redactions. For example, it is highly probable that reliably authentic words of the prophet Jeremiah have been handed down in the book of the same name. But there are still many passages in the book of Jeremiah as it stands today that only came about long after the appearance of Jeremiah, although they are often put into his mouth. In other words, we do not encounter

Jeremiah's *ipsissima verba,* but an interpretation and actualisation of his thought by Jeremiah's followers. Regarding the book of Isaiah, it is now also generally accepted that it came about during three different periods, even though the whole book is attributed to one person. The historical Isaiah, whose sayings are passed down in chapters 1–9, probably appeared in the eighth century BC. Isaiah 40–55 was, without doubt, composed at the time of the Babylonian exile (sixth century BC). And the last chapters of the book came about after the exile. All these loose collections of discourses were, over time, added together and redacted, a process during which the words of the historical Isaiah were interpreted and reinterpreted.

c. *Did Not Really Happen and Still True?*

Initially, the doubts concerning the historical reliability of the Scriptures were nipped in the bud by the religious authorities, which often had tragic consequences for the scholars involved. The results that archaeology and biblical studies had recorded since the nineteenth century, indeed, led the traditional understanding of the Bible into a deep crisis. Apart from the easy solution of casting the Bible aside as nothing more than a pile of fabrications, two positions have been possible with regard to the historical character of the Bible since this crisis.

The first possibility, which has already been discussed in detail in the first chapter, consisted of ignoring the achievements of scientific research and in a fundamentalistic way — tending toward religious fanaticism — holding fast to the "inerrancy" of the Bible, attempting to prove this at any cost. Emphasising the fact that the Bible in no way and nowhere goes astray is, after all, the common denominator of every form of biblical fundamentalism. It is for this reason that biblical fundamentalism makes every effort to secure the infallibility of the Bible. To that end, the findings of both archaeology and exegetical research are misused. Accepting that the Bible is the "word of God" is, for biblical fundamentalists, equivalent to saying that every letter of the Bible is infallible. Such an undertaking does intrinsic injustice to the deep and significant meaning that lies hidden in the biblical texts. There is also a second, though perhaps more difficult, way that demands critical insight and nuanced judgement.

The correct manner of approaching Scripture consists of taking the research findings of the various sciences seriously. From the moment that people began to question the historical reliability of the Old Testament tradition, the value of the Old Testament for the reconstruction of the history of Ancient Israel has been judged entirely differently. Indeed, although the Old Testament is above all a religious book with theological insights, it still remains an important source of information for the reconstruction of the history of Ancient Israel, since other sources about the first two millennia before Christ are extremely scarce. Nonetheless, caution is required when one wants to use the Old Testament for the reconstruction of Israel's past. However, in contrast to what some would like to believe on the basis of, among other things, archaeological findings, the acknowledgement that certain parts of the Bible are in conflict with historical reality does not imply that the whole Bible is simply a useless fabrication and fiction. Every biblical text is, indeed, the product of a faith-filled look at the real experiences that Ancient Israel went through. Everyone who wants to sincerely engage the Bible must make a distinction between historical reality and the theological interpretation thereof. In this regard, one should try to track down the underlying message that the biblical authors wanted to bring out of the lived experience of the community. Even if they could prove, beyond a shadow of doubt, that Israel was never enslaved in Egypt, the Exodus narrative would not lose its value. The testimony to the divine liberation from slavery reflects a religious conviction that God turns the history of Israel to the good, a conviction most probably rooted in the historical experience of oppression.

How the Bible can then be understood as religious writings by and for people, is aptly worded by the Leiden exegete, Jan Fokkelman with regard to Old Testament poetry: "The Hebrew poets, for one, are almost always concerned with God, in the second or third person, and this may often be reversed: God keeps poets occupied, in two senses of the word. Poets either express how God touches them, in a positive or negative sense, or tell us how God fascinates them with His presence, or conversely, his distressing absence; this testimony is expressed either in a minor key — in the form of complaints or protests — or in a major key — as hymns of praise or thanks. The narrators and lawgivers, too, stay within the field of religion. Even in those passages where God does not appear as a participant in the action or as a speaking character, the values expressed by the writers are moral, and in the final analysis, religious."[9]

In this way, the resistance and desperation, the longing for a restoration of the premodern certainties, are transcended, not by trying to prove the truth of the Bible by historicisation or fundamentalism, but by critically interpreting the historicity in and through the biblical account in the light of the insight that the Bible is religious literature that has developed over time. This realisation is, however, itself the result of an insight that developed over time, namely, through the growth of biblical studies that gradually focused not on history but on the text itself, and in so doing, introduced different emphases. It is this development that is the subject of the next section.

---

[9] Jan Fokkelman, *Reading Biblical Poetry: An Introductory Guide* (Louisville, KY/London: Westminster John Knox, 2001) 189.

3. From a Diachronic to a Synchronic Approach

The following will describe the way in which historical-critical exegesis evolved after its beginnings. Briefly put, one sees a threefold development, in which the focus gradually and significantly shifts from historical concerns towards literary-theological appreciation.[10]

a. From "Historical-Literary" Concerns to "Literary-Historical" Interests

In the older, classical historical-critical approach to Bible texts, one viewed the text, as it were, as a historical document that was open to investigation. Furthermore, one primarily asked two questions: How did the text come about and what is its historical value? Against the background of this historical interest, people tried, as is apparent from the previous discussion of the "Plague Narrative," to specify a potentially natural background to the events recounted. In this way, they could also continue to postulate the historical character of what was recounted, since they were of the opinion that what could be explained in terms of the (natural) sciences would also be historically plausible. All attention was focused on the historical factuality.

Little by little, however, the interest shifted. More and more, the literary character of the text began to hold sway in exegesis.[11]

---

[10] For a more comprehensive analysis, see Bénédicte Lemmelijn, "Transformations in Biblical Studies: The Story of the History of Research into the 'Plague Narrative' in Exod 7:14–11:10," *Journal of Northwest Semitic Languages* 22 (1996) 117-127; and Bénédicte Lemmelijn, *Het verhaal van de 'Plagen in Egypte' (Exodus 7,14–11,10): Een onderzoek naar het ontstaan en de compositie van een Pentateuchtraditie. I: Status quaestionis van het onderzoek*, unpublished doctoral dissertation, Faculty of Theology, KU Leuven, promoter Marc Vervenne (Leuven, 1996) 164-168.

[11] This development is, incidentally, already clearly noticeable in the discussion of the "Plague Narrative" above due to the fact that the more recent authors

From the end of the nineteenth century onwards, researchers in fact placed ever more emphasis on the literary composition of the biblical text. The historical critique gradually narrowed its focus to diachronic textual studies, in which attention is paid to the origin and development of the text, more specifically in light of a literary question. People wondered how the text had developed over time. They posed questions regarding the literary genre and the "tradition history" (the so-called *Überlieferungsgeschichte*) of the text. The approach became literary-historical. Within this approach, however, yet another evolution occurred.

b. *From "Source Criticism" to "Redaction Criticism"*

In diachronically oriented textual study, the question of development is central. Initially, in order to answer this question, scholars went in search of the various sources that lay behind the texts that we now study. They discovered four main sources, J (Yahwist document), E (Elohist document), D (Deuteronomic document) and P (Priestly document), which were considered to be more or less independent narratives with different features and characteristics. On the basis of these sources, they set about dividing up the text. They tried to make a detailed attribution of every aspect of the narrative, even to the smallest units of a verse, to J, E, D or P respectively. They dissected the literary unity into miniscule parts.

Little by little, the approach changed, however. Research began to apply itself more globally to the narrative's general, broad, underlying redactional layers that are interconnected and that each exert their influence on the final redaction that gives shape to the final literary result. The impact of the (various) redaction(s) on the arrangement of the text is emphasised, but so too is the impact on

do not pay as much attention to the historical aspects of the "Plague Narrative" and the associated natural explanations.

the structural and intrinsic theological aspects of the narrative as a whole. In this approach, the oral tradition is also acknowledged for its important contribution to the creation of the text. In this way, an eye is thus indeed kept on the stratification of the text, but strict source-critical analysis must make way for a broader redactional analysis and evaluation of the text.

As a result of the quest to find the broader influence of redaction on the text as a whole, more attention was thus also given to the theological components in the creation of the literary work. People seemed to grasp that the editor or redactor did not primarily offer a historical report, but rather that he wanted to voice certain important theological affirmations that fundamentally affect the course and tenor of the narrative. This attentiveness to the theological meaning was given even more emphasis in the third developmental phase that we intend to distinguish in the evolution of Old Testament research.

c. *From a "Literary-Historical" Method to a "Literary-Theological" Approach*

So far, it has been made clear that the diachronic textual approaches, in their literary-historical methodology, were interested in the contributions of sources and redactions to the creation of the text. Gradually, the theological aspect also came to the fore.

From about 1970, we notice a new development. Recent research is often not diachronic (in which the origin and development of the text is central) but synchronic (with a focus on the final text).[12] In

---

[12] With regard to the differences and relationship between diachrony and synchrony and the associated development in biblical research, see Jean L. Ska, "Quelques remarques sur Pg et la dernière rédaction du Pentateuque," *La Pentateuque en question: Les origines et la composition des cinq premiers livres de la Bible à la lumière des recherches récentes,* ed. Albert De Pury (Geneva: Labor et Fides, 1989) 95-125, especially 95-97. For an indication of what the recent

this approach, one considers the literary composition as it now stands as a standalone, final version that should be read as such. The question of the way in which the text functions and what its significance is comes to the fore. Synchronic textual studies often propose that the text that we now have is in fact the only text that we can be absolutely certain about.[13] This text is, according to this view, much closer to the original events and the theological interpretation thereof than any speculations or re-orderings on our part could ever achieve.[14] In this respect, it is stressed that the final text is the only source of insight into the oral and written traditions as well as into the historical events behind the narrative. The structure of the final text is of crucial importance here. The text is indeed a standalone literary given. Moreover, literary analysis on the basis of the final text can also often contribute towards an understanding of how sources and traditions are used, that is to say, the interplay between tradition and redaction. The synchronic study of Bible stories, which sees the text as literature with its own integrity, in this way, also explicitly raises the theological message for discussion.

---

evolution in both directions has meant for research into the book of Exodus, we refer you to Helmut Utzschneider, "Die Renaissance der alttestamentlichen Literaturwissenschaft und das Buch Exodus: Überlegungen zu Hermeneutik und Geschichte der Forschung," *Zeitschrift für die alttestamentliche Wissenschaft* 106 (1994) 197-223. For the development of diachronic research, see in particular 202-215; The origin and function of synchronic textual study is discussed between 215-222. Furthermore, in this regard, we refer you to Marc Vervenne, "Current Tendencies and Developments in the Study of the Book of Exodus," *Studies in the Book of Exodus: Redaction – Reception – Interpretation,* ed. Marc Vervenne, Bibliotheca Ephemeridum Theologicarum Lovaniensium, 126 (Leuven: Leuven University Press, 1996) 21-59.

[13] Cf. John I. Durham, *Exodus*, Word Biblical Commentary, 3 (Waco, TX: Word Books, 1987) 126: "Once again, the single absolute certainty is the compilation at hand in the received text."

[14] *Ibid.*, 140: "They are what we have in hand from a time far closer to the events and a living theological interpretation of them than any speculation about them and any rearrangement of them can possibly be."

This all demonstrates the great value of the synchronic approach to Bible texts, as well as the rich contribution it makes.[15] Nonetheless, one should still be careful when applying this approach. There is a risk of one employing this approach polemically or apologetically against historical-critical textual study, such that the different stages in the growth of the literary whole are ignored.[16] The synchronic analysis of the narrative must not lead to too little or even no attention being paid to the multilayered complexity and literary development of the text. The final text is a complex literary composition, but it did not suddenly appear out of nowhere. Moreover, there is also always the risk of overemphasising or isolating formal or structural elements in the final texts such that this too damages the integrity of the final text in all its aspects. Both approaches, diachronic and synchronic, must, therefore, ideally be used to complement one another.

[15] In this regard, we also refer you to the clarifying study made by Jean Louis Ska, which offers an overview of the various aspects within synchronous narrative-linguistic analysis of biblical texts. He discusses, successively, the translation and the delineation of the narrative, the difference between "story" and "discourse," the perspective of time, the plot in its various types, the relationships between teller and reader and their attitude to the text, and the narration standpoint or narrative point of view. See Jean Louis Ska, *"Our Fathers Have Told Us." Introduction to the Analysis of Hebrew Narratives*, Subsidia Biblica, 13 (Rome: Pontificio Istituto Biblico, 1990).

[16] In this regard, see, for example, Cornelis Houtman, *Exodus*, vol. 1: *Exodus 1:1–7:13*, Historical Commentary on the Old Testament, 2: "The work is intended to be a unity and wishes to be understood as a whole. The point of departure for exegesis in this commentary is therefore the text as we have it, the product of its final editing. If the principle of the text as the point of departure for exegesis is taken seriously, the exegete will also continually bear in mind that the results of literary critical studies may not be overlooked, for familiarity with the text confronts the exegete with its undeniable unevenness and tensions which can be explained only in terms of the complex history of its compilation."

CONCLUSION TO PART II

The second part of this book has shown that, with regard to the "crisis" in religion and Christianity that the first part of the book explained in two ways, a twofold response is possible with respect to the "disenchantment" that this crisis brought with it. The first chapter described the seemingly desperate, negative answers. It considered, after a brief look at the attitude of childlike naivety (§1), primarily the historicising tendency (§2) and fundamentalism (§3), which both, in their own way, try, almost frenetically, to demonstrate and protect the (historical) truth of the Bible. The second chapter focused on the "positive" response that tried to transcend the disenchantment by means of critical dialogue. Within the scope of this discussion, we first addressed a nuanced approach to the Bible and historicity (§1). Against this background, the rise of historical-critical exegesis was then outlined (§2), in order to, lastly, describe the evolution from a diachronic to a synchronic approach to the text of the Bible using the threefold development from "historical-literary" via "literary-historical" to "literary-theological."

In what follows, we aim to illustrate how this critical, nuanced handling of biblical texts, without denying or minimising the ancient and "strange" character of the texts, still raises existential questions today and perhaps can also, in a significant way, offer (elements of) an answer to these questions.

PART III

THE BIBLE: A BOOK OF LIFE

INTRODUCTION

In the third and final part of this book, we shall endeavour to critically present the Bible as a text by people and for people about a
God that no human being can ever fully grasp.[1] The biblical tradition contains human beings' reflections on their existential given-
ness, their relations to each other and to reality, and finally to the
One who transcends them. In this sense, it concerns first and foremost musings on being human as such, dealing with good fortune
and setbacks, love and suffering, the hope for fulfilment. In short,
everything that is familiar to people today is also not alien to the
biblical tradition. Biblical narratives — one must never forget this
— are written by people. For that matter, they are not only written
by people, but also revised, suspected, brooded over, rewritten,
translated and ultimately passed on to and through time by people.
They are narratives that try to interpret, to situate, to get a grasp of
and a hold on reality in all its aspects. They are stories by people
who, in the contingent here and now, believed they detected transcendence, experienced transcendence; and who tried to give voice
to their religious convictions in narrative and poetic ways.

In what follows, prior to illustrating this from various points
of view, the first chapter will discuss the relationship between
the two parts of the Christian Bible, namely the Old and the New
Testaments. Then, primarily against the background of the Old

---

[1] See also Bénédicte Lemmelijn, "Bijbelse verhalen: Van mensen voor
mensen, over een God die geen mens ooit vatten kan," *Toekomst voor verhalen
en rituelen? Op het snijpunt van bijbel en geloofscommunicatie*, ed. Paul Kevers
and Joke Maex (Leuven: Acco, 2005) 61-74.

Testament, the existential questions concerning the origin and purpose of human existence (Chapter two), the achievement of peaceful coexistence (Chapter three), and God's involvement in human fortunes (Chapter four) will be successively dealt with.

CHAPTER ONE

THE RELATIONSHIP BETWEEN
THE OLD AND NEW TESTAMENTS

1. Unknown, Unloved

Although it is a definite and indisputable fact that the Christian Bible consists of two parts, namely, the Old and New Testaments, it is remarkable that the first part is, in Christian circles, in reality always considered to be of less importance, less decisive and of less topical value than the New Testament.[1] Despite the fact that the Old Testament far exceeds the New in scope and, moreover, offers many rich opportunities for theology and preaching, the Dutch adage "*Onbekend maakt onbemind*" (unknown is unloved) is clearly applicable to this situation. The literature of the Old Testament has, in recent centuries, almost always been harshly dealt with, if it was dealt with at all.[2]

---

[1] Though familiar with the trend to refer to the Old and New Testaments as the "First" and "Second" Testaments respectively, we have chosen to continue using the more classical terminology for a number of reasons which are laid out in Hans Ausloos and Bénédicte Lemmelijn, "'Oude Testament' versus 'Eerste Testament': What's in a Name?," "*Volk van God en Gemeenschap van de gelovigen" : Pleidooien voor een zorgzame kerkopbouw*, ed. Jacques Haers, Terrence Merrigan and Peter De Mey (Averbode: Altiora, 1999) 46-59.

[2] With regard to the various Christian approaches to the Old Testament in past centuries, see, among others, Erich Zenger, *Das Erste Testament: Die jüdische Bibel und die Christen* (Düsseldorf: Patmos, [3]1987); Erich Zenger, "Heilige Schrift der Juden und der Christen," *Einleitung in das Alte Testament*, ed. Erich Zenger, Heinz-Josef Fabry and Georg Braulik, Kohlhammer Studienbücher Theologie, 1/1 (Stuttgart/Berlin/Cologne: Kohlhammer, [2]1996) 16-17; and Martin

Yet, if one returns to the roots of Christianity, another attitude becomes apparent.[3] For Jesus, who as far as we know never wrote anything himself, most of the books that we now consider to be part of the Old Testament were Sacred Scripture. After all, the New Testament writings did not yet exist for Jesus and his disciples. From both the gospels and the New Testament letters, it seems that the books of the "Old Testament" were normative. The Old Testament is directly quoted 350 times in the New.[4] Furthermore, there are also countless allusions to stories and themes from the Old Testament that were of substantial importance in the composition of the New Testament texts. Moreover, in various places in the New Testament, reference is made to the "Law of the Prophets," "Moses and the Prophets," or "Moses, the Prophets and the Psalms," expressions that probably synthetically refer to what is now called the "Old Testament."[5] One should also not forget the

J. Mulder, "Iets over de relatie tussen Oude en Nieuwe Testament," *Collationes* 21 (1991) 301-314. Also, see the always interesting works of Henning Graf von Reventlow, *Hauptprobleme der Biblischen Theologie im 20. Jahrhundert*, Erträge der Forschung, 203 (Darmstadt: Wissenschaftliche Buchgesellschaft, 1983); and Arnold A. van Ruler, *Die christliche Kirche und das Alte Testament*, Beiträge zur evangelischen Theologie, 23 (Munich: Kaiser, 1955) especially 9-12.

[3] Cf. Alfons Deissler, *Die Grundbotschaft des Alten Testaments: Ein theologischer Durchblick* (Freiburg/Basel/Vienna: Herder, 1995) 13-30. With regard to the place of the Old Testament in the first centuries of Christianity, see Magne Saebø, Christiaan H. W. Brekelmans and Menahem Haran (eds.), *Hebrew Bible/ Old Testament — The History of Its Interpretation*. Vol. 1: *From the Beginnings to the Middle Ages (Until 1300)*. Part 1: *Antiquity* (Göttingen: Vandenhoeck & Ruprecht, 1996); as well as Thomas Söding, *Mehr als ein Buch: Die Bibel begreifen* (Freiburg/ Basel/Vienna: Herder, [2]1996) 11-69.

[4] See the third appendix to the 26th edition of the Greek New Testament by Eberhard Nestlé and Kurt Aland: *Loci citati vel allegati* (739-775).

[5] The formula "Law and Prophets" is not employed in the Old Testament itself, except in the Greek Prologue to Sirach or Ecclesiasticus. This passage also mentions "the other books." For the New Testament use of the expression "Law and Prophets" see, for example, Joseph A. Fitzmyer, *The Gospel According to*

fact that the early Church did not place the Old Testament behind, but in front of the New Testament writings, which gave rise to the two part Christian Bible. Furthermore, it is striking that no changes were made to the Jewish scriptures, not even in passages where the New Testament gives a Christian or Christological reading of the applicable texts. From all these facts, it seems clear that the early Church doubtless saw the Old Testament as the foundation of Christianity.[6] Even the whole polemic between gentile Christians and Jewish Christians, as well as the rift between the "church" and the "synagogue," does not question the fundamental place that belongs to the Old Testament.

From the discussion above, it seems clear that everyone who wants to adequately understand Jesus and his message must also seek to become familiar with the Old Testament and its underlying (Jewish) culture. There can indeed be no New Testament without the Old Testament. However, it is here that we encounter a crucial problem: how are the two Testaments related to one another? How can the Old Testament be understood in a Christian way? Is the

---

Luke 10–24, Anchor Bible (Garden City, NY: Doubleday, 1985) 1116-1117. Cf. in this regard also, Bénédicte Lemmelijn, "Mozes en de profeten," *VBS-Informatie* 30 (1999) 49-52.

[6] In the introduction to *Evangelie en evangelies: Het Nieuwe Testament leren lezen 1*, Nikè-reeks: Didachè (Leuven/Amersfoort: Acco, 1986) 15; Robrecht Michiels refers to Cas Labuschagne, *Gods oude plakboek* (The Hague: Boekencentrum, 1978) 154: "Voor mij staat vast dat we in de kerk het Oude Testament niet kunnen missen, omdat het wegens zijn zelfstandige inbreng aan godskennis van meet af aan in de kerk een plaats heeft gehad naast het Nieuwe Testament. Zonder het Oude Testament zou het Nieuwe niet te begrijpen zijn en min of meer in de lucht komen te hangen. Het is daarom van het grootste belang dat het Oude Testament goed functioneert in het kerkelijk leven." Michiels adds: "Het Nieuwe Testament is geschreven door mensen van het Oude Testament, die een nieuwe en overweldigende ervaring hebben gehad. Het Nieuwe Testament is onder meer samengesteld vanuit het Oude, maar het omgekeerde is niet waar. Wel kunnen christenen het Oude Testament vanuit het Nieuwe lezen" (*Evangelie en evangelies*, 15).

Old Testament instead not pre-Christian or even unchristian? Or is the Old Testament perhaps in fact so Christian that only a Christian can understand it in the correct manner?[7]

2. Diverse Models of Thought

All the questions posed above have been answered in various ways in the past. The quest to define the relationship between the Old and the New Testaments resulted in the development of a number of models of thought, in which, no matter how one looks at it, the Old Testament comes off second best. In addition, it should be noted that the Old Testament, especially since the scholastic theologian Peter Lombard (ca. 1095-1160) and primarily in the context of sundry dogmatic discussions, was less and less respected in its own right. Interest in Old Testament literature was increasingly limited to its usefulness in the corroboration or illustration of ethical or dogmatic-theological propositions. As to the value, meaning and background of the Old Testament texts themselves, however, attention was scarcely paid.

Recently, there has been within the Catholic Church, particularly since Pius XII's encyclical *Divino Afflante Spiritu* (1943), a notable renewal in interest in the unique value of the Old Testament. One only needs to consider certain documents of Vatican II,[8] the attention given to the Old Testament in the liturgy,[9] the document

---

[7] As proposed by Karl Rahner (ed.), *Herders Theologisches Taschenlexikon I* (Freiburg: Herder, 1979) 84: "Als 'vorchristliche' Vergangenheit des neuen und ewigen Bundes, in den hinein das Alte Testament sich aufgehoben hat, ist es nur vom Neuen Bund her adäquat richtig interpretierbar, weil sein wahres Wesen sich erst in der Offenbarung seines *télos* (Röm 10,4) enthüllt."

[8] See for example, the conciliar documents *Dei Verbum* 14-16; *Nostra Aetate* 4; *Lumen Gentium* 5-6.

[9] Cf. André Goossens, "Het Oude Testament in de liturgie," *Collationes* 21 (1991) 397-416; Georg Gafus, "Auswahl mit Schlagseite: Anmerkungen eines

of the Pontifical Biblical Commission on the interpretation of the Bible in the Church,[10] and the many attempts made at clarifying the relationship between the two testaments.

Nonetheless, one must surely see that even these attempts at revaluation could not and cannot change the fact that in Catholicism, and other Christian churches too, the first and most sizeable part of the Christian Bible is not fully appreciated. Furthermore, even though, in the second century, Marcion's attempt to dismiss the Old Testament as a whole was declared heretical, marcionism still seems to raise its head time and again, albeit in more subtle and latent ways.

This is manifest in the negative cleansing of the various approaches developed during the course of history that attempted to demonstrate the relationship between the Old and New Testaments, and where the Old Testament and New Testament are often viewed as being diametrically opposed to one another. Concretely, this concerns three models of thought.

Alttestamentlers zur Leseordnung," *Bibel und Liturgie* 68 (1995) 136-148; Erich Zenger, "Het Oude Testament in de verkondiging vanuit christelijk-joods perspectief," *Sacerdos* 66 (1998) 19-28.

[10] Presented to the pope on the occasion of the 100th anniversary of the encyclical *Providentissimus Deus* (Leo XIII) and the 50th anniversary of the encyclical *Divino afflante Spiritu* (Pius XII) on 24 April 1993. The original text appeared under the title "L'interprétation de la Bible dans l'Église," *Biblica* 74 (1993) 451-528 — the Dutch version can be found in *Kerkelijke Documentatie* 22 (1994) 161-213. For a commentary on this important document see, among others, Jan Lambrecht, "De interpretatie van de bijbel in de kerk," *VBS-Informatie* 25 (1994) 57-67; Jacob Kremer, "Die Interpretation der Bibel in der Kirche: Marginalien zum neuesten Dokument der Päpstlichen Bibelkommission," *Stimmen der Zeit* 212 (1994) 151-166; Pancratius Beentjes, "Pauselijke Bijbelcommissie doet van zich spreken," *Collationes* 24 (1994) 401-409; Georg Fischer, "Kann aus Rom etwas Gutes kommen?," *Bibel und Liturgie* 69 (1996) 171-173.

a. *The Contrast Model*

The contrast model places the Old and the New Testament in direct opposition to one another. This model is largely based on a particular reading of passages from the New Testament's Letter to the Hebrews: Hebrews 8:6 states, "But Jesus has now obtained a more excellent ministry, and to that degree he is the mediator of a better covenant, which has been enacted through better promises;" and Hebrews 8:13 states, "In speaking of 'a new covenant', he has made the first one obsolete. And what is obsolete and growing old will soon disappear." In these verses, the Old Testament is placed in stark contrast to the New Testament. This opposition between the old and new "covenants" primarily manifests itself in two facets. First, the universal nature of the new "covenant" is contrasted with the particularism and nationalism of the old covenant. Second, the antithesis between "law" and "gospel" is emphasised. In other words, through Jesus Christ, the "covenant" between God and Israel has been made "old" and therefore no longer applicable. The classical reference made to support this stance is to the so-called antitheses of the Sermon on the Mount (Matthew 5), where Jesus says, "You have heard that it was said … But I say to you…" The Roman Catholic Church has strongly rejected this dualistic position that bears so close a resemblance to the abovementioned marcionism.

b. *The Fulfilment Model*

The fulfilment model sees the New Testament as the fulfilment of the promises made in the Old Testament. In this model, the Old Testament passage of Jeremiah 31:31-34 assumes a central role:

> The days are surely coming, says the Lord, when I will make a new covenant with the house of Israel and the house of Judah. It will not be like the covenant that I made with their ancestors when I took

them by the hand to bring them out of the land of Egypt — a covenant that they broke, though I was their husband, says the Lord. But this is the covenant that I will make with the house of Israel after those days, says the Lord: I will put my law within them, and I will write it on their hearts; and I will be their God, and they shall be my people. No longer shall they teach one another, or say to each other, 'Know the Lord', for they shall all know me, from the least of them to the greatest, says the Lord; for I will forgive their iniquity, and remember their sin no more.

In a particular Christian interpretation, this text is often regarded to be a sort of Old Testament manifesto for Christianity. The new covenant proclaimed and promised by Jeremiah is well-nigh automatically identified with Christianity.[11]

In reaction to the Christian usurpation of Jeremiah 31:31-34, mediaeval Judaism shifted Jeremiah's promise of the new "covenant" entirely to the messianic time. To be sure, according to the Jewish tradition, Jeremiah did not promise a wholly new Law or Torah for the messianic time. Indeed, the Torah of Moses remains eternally valid. However, the "newness" of the new covenant subsists in the fact that in the messianic time the covenant can no longer be broken, because it will then be inscribed in one's heart and one will, therefore, no longer be able to forget its precepts. Moreover, Judaism points to Matthew 5:17-19, a text that counters

[11] See for example the circa 130 AD Letter of Barnabas (Barn 4:6-8): "*And Moses was in the mountain fasting forty days and forty nights, and he received the covenant from the Lord, even tablets of stone written with the finger of the hand of the Lord.* But they [i.e. the Jews] lost it by turning unto idols. For thus saith the Lord; *Moses, Moses, come down quickly; for thy people whom thou broughtest out of the land of Egypt hath done unlawfully.* And Moses understood, and threw the two tables from his hands; and their covenant was broken in pieces, that the covenant of the beloved Jesus might be sealed unto our hearts in the hope which springeth from faith in Him." Holmes M. Williams (ed.)/Joseph B. Lightfoot and J. R. Harmer (transl.), *The Apostolic Fathers* (Berkeley, CA, 2002) 271-272.

the idea that Jesus intended to renounce the old covenant in favour of the new covenant through Him: "Do not think that I have come to abolish the law or the prophets; I have come not to abolish but to fulfil. For truly I tell you, until heaven and earth pass away, not one letter, not one stroke of a letter, will pass from the law until all is accomplished. Therefore, whoever breaks one of the least of these commandments, and teaches others to do the same, will be called least in the kingdom of heaven; but whoever does them and teaches them will be called great in the kingdom of heaven." Finally, Judaism points out that the characteristic feature of the new covenant according to Jeremiah 31:34, namely that *all* will know God and live according to His commandments, has not yet been fulfilled, not even in Christianity.

In the final analysis, however, both the Christian and the Jewish tradition just outlined, miss the original meaning of Jeremiah 31:31-34. This text was, after all, most likely written in the context of the Babylonian exile (587-539 BC). It forms part of the so-called "Book of Consolation" in Jeremiah, which in no way has the distant future in mind. On the contrary, the Book of Consolation aims to bring a message of hope to those whom it directly addresses, namely the author's contemporaries: "The days are surely coming" (Jeremiah 30:3; 31:27, 31, 38).

A Christian attempt to reconcile the original meaning of Jeremiah 31:31-34 just described — the revelation of which is thanks to historical-critical exegesis — with the idea that the Old Testament anticipates and "predicts" the coming of Jesus Christ, and as such has also been fulfilled, has played an important role in a discussion that has been taking place since 1925 over the *sensus plenior,* a discussion that really got underway following the "permission" granted to engage in critical exegesis in 1943, namely following the encyclical *Divino Afflante Spiritu,* and in which the Leuven professor of exegesis J. Coppens was one of the most important voices.[12] The term *sensus plenior* ("fuller meaning") is usually defined as referring to a deeper meaning that God put into the text, but which the human authors did not make clearly explicit and of which the authors themselves were not aware. Over time, this theory, primarily due to its lack of objectivity, has disappeared from scholarly discourse.

Alongside the fulfilment model, one could also include the related typological reading of the Old Testament. While the fulfilment model primarily bases itself on the Old Testament words that are allegedly fulfilled in the New Testament, typology is more concerned with the events in the Old Testament (*typos*) that seem to have an *anti-typos* in the New Testament. Indeed, for many elements in the New Testament, there is no verbal "prediction" in the Old Testament. One thinks for example of Jesus' crucifixion. Therefore, many Old Testament texts have been regarded as "*typoi*": symbols or signs. Thus, for example, Paul (1 Corinthians 5:7) already considered the slaughter of the Pascal lamb as a *typos* for Jesus' crucifixion.[13]

A similarly related approach can be found in the liturgical use of Old Testament texts. An example will illustrate this. The Gospel reading for the fifth Sunday of Lent (Year A) is that of the raising of Lazarus (John 11:1-45), which is read as a build-up to Easter as the Christian high feast of Jesus' resurrection. The reading from

---

[12] For this, see Henning Graf von Reventlow, *Hauptprobleme*, 39-49; Robert B. Robinson, *Roman Catholic Exegesis since Divino Afflante Spiritu: Hermeneutical Implications*, Society of Biblical Literature. Dissertation Series, 111 (Atlanta, GA: Scholars, 1988) 29-55; Hans W. Seidel and Christoph Dohmen, *Die Erforschung des Alten Testaments in der katholischen Theologie seit der Jahrhundertwende*, Bonner Biblische Beiträge, 86 (Frankfurt am Main: Hain, 1993).

[13] Cf. in this regard, the extremely interesting contribution of Herbert Haag, "Typologische Verständnis des Pentateuch," *Das Buch des Bundes: Aufsätze zur Bibel und zu ihrer Welt*, ed. Herbert Haag (Düsseldorf: Patmos, 1980) 234-249.

the Old Testament comes from the book of Ezekiel (37:12-14), a
part of the vision of the dry bones:

> Therefore prophesy, and say to them, Thus says the Lord God: I am
> going to open your graves, and bring you up from your graves, O
> my people; and I will bring you back to the land of Israel. And you
> shall know that I am the Lord, when I open your graves, and bring
> you up from your graves, O my people. I will put my spirit within
> you, and you shall live, and I will place you on your own soil; then
> you shall know that I, the Lord, have spoken and will act, says the
> Lord.

Unconsciously, the listener is given the impression that the Ezekiel
text, by analogy with the account of the raising of Lazarus, is about
the resurrection of the dead, and that, in other words, the Old Testament foretells what was fulfilled in Jesus Christ. However, when
one takes note of the historical and literary context of Ezekiel 37,
then one is forced to conclude that the vision of the dry bones in
this pericope and its interpretation are indisputably part of the
prophet's own proclamation of redemption to his contemporaries.
The valley full of dry bones is a metaphor for the Israelites and
Judeans who, in the sixth century BC, spend there days in exile, far
removed from their own land, devoid of hope in a better a life, "by
the rivers of Babylon" (Psalm 137:1). Ezekiel must implore these
dry bones to listen to the word of YaHWeH. Only then will Israel
live again — leaving exile for the Promised Land — and know that
YaHWeH is God.

c. *The Evolution Model*

The third and final important model, in which the New Testament
seems to assume precedence over the Old, is the so-called evolution model. This interpretation sees the Old Testament as the preparation for the New. This is often based on the argument that there

is an evolution from the primitive to the developed, from low to elevated, and even from bad to good. In this model, the Old Testament is therefore a sort of prologue to the New Testament; it only prepares the way for the New Testament and cannot be read in and of itself.

Both the fulfilment model and the evolution model implicitly begin from the belief that the Old Testament is only preliminary, unfinished and imperfect. This attitude does not do justice to the Old Testament. As a collection of books, the Old Testament is complete. Therefore, those who would read the Old Testament must try, first and foremost, to allow these texts to tell their stories themselves, independent of the New Testament. Not Christology, but theology, or better, theologies, are central to the Old Testament. In other words, the "talking about God." This of course raises the question of the place of Jesus and the New Testament. Seeing Jesus, professed as the Christ in the New Testament, purely as the "fulfilment" of a vague promise in the Old Testament, does justice neither to the Old Testament nor to the New. As a Christian, one believes and is convinced that Jesus, as the Christ, is the ultimate manifestation of the manner in which God makes himself known in the Old Testament Scriptures. This means that the God of the Old Testament — a God of life — reveals himself in a unique way in Jesus Christ. This then has the consequence that Jesus, during and through his ministry — one thinks, for example, of Jesus' attitudes with regard to the Sabbath (Mark 2:23-28) — and out of his faithfulness, unto death, in the living God, radically challenged the accepted interpretation of the Old Testament laws by the "Scribes and Pharisees" (Matthew 5:20), because in their interpretation the God of life is reduced to a god of letters and laws.

Against the background of this discussion of these models of thought, it is clear that the Old Testament, if it is (still) to mean something to today's Christians, must be read in another way. The Old Testament is indeed of substantial value in and of itself and must be respected as such. The richness that the Old Testament has to offer us is briefly introduced in the following sections and illustrated in the subsequent chapters.

3. The Old Testament: A Book about Living

What can Christians still do with the Old Testament? What does this old book, that is even called "old," still have to offer Christians? Is it not just all a distant, bygone heritage from a time with which we are no longer acquainted? These are familiar questions today. The first two verses of the Letter to the Hebrews already present us with guidance: "Long ago God spoke to our ancestors in many and various ways by the prophets, but in these last days he has spoken to us by a Son..." Every word of the discussion between God and humankind is valuable. Anyone who scraps even one word of a speech or isolates a word from it does not take the speaker seriously. Christianity needs the Old Testament; on that we can agree. Even Jesus could build on the understanding that everyone in his milieu knew who the God of Israel was: the creator, ruler of the world, lawgiver and judge.[14] But as to what the Old Testament could mean for Christians today, we can highlight three elements.

(1) The Old Testament testifies to *a living and life-intervening God*. When Christian theology speaks of a creative and liberating God, then it bases its arguments on the Old Testament. The idea that God is a living God who reveals himself in the lives of those

---

[14] Cf. Herbert Haag, "Das Plus des Alten Testaments," *Das Buch des Bundes: Aufsätze zur Bibel und zu ihrer Welt*, ed. Herbert Haag (Düsseldorf: Patmos, 1980) 304.

who acknowledge him and keep his commandments is the basic axiom of the Old Testament. One can know God as "a God merciful and gracious, slow to anger, and abounding in steadfast love and faithfulness, keeping steadfast love for the thousandth generation, forgiving iniquity and transgression and sin, yet by no means clearing the guilty..." (Exodus 34:6-7). Starting from this relationship, one must tread the path prepared by him. That is the path to which God calls his people and the only possible way of coming to know God. The Münster Old Testament scholar Erich Zenger puts it this way: "He who, ridden with guilt and exhausted, seeks the strength to continue along the way by crying out for YAHWeH's forgiveness, who himself forgives as this God forgives, who himself is kind beyond measure, as is and because it is the way that the biblical God himself walks, he understands and realises who this God is. Neither in contemplating nor caring for an ever so beautiful image of God, nor in the invocation of the ever so proper doctrine is the mystery of this God revealed, but rather only in walking the path to which he calls one."[15] This is also the essence of every prophetic appearance in the Old Testament, that is best summarised by Micah 6:8: "He has told you, O mortal, what is good; and what does the Lord require of you but to do justice, and to love kindness, and to walk humbly with your God?"

(2) The Old Testament keeps Christianity from pursuing salvation (exclusively) in the individual "soul" or in the hereafter.

---

[15] Erich Zenger, *Erste Testament*, 193: "Wer in Schuldverstrickung und Müdigkeit im Schrei um JHWH's Vergebung die Kraft sucht, den Weg weiterzugehen, wer selbst vergibt wie dieser Gott, wer selbst gütig ist über die Maßen, wie und weil dies der Weg ist, auf dem der biblische Gott vorangeht, der begreift und erfaßt, wer dieser Gott ist. Nicht im Betrachten oder in der Pflege eines noch so schönen Bildes dieses Gottes, auch nicht in der Beschwörung eines noch so richtigen Lehrsatzes geht das Geheimnis dieses Gottes auf, sondern nur indem man den Weg geht, auf den er ruft."

Rather, the Old Testament links happiness and liberation with *practical efforts* on the political and social level. In this regard, the prophets are not the only ones who present themselves as critical voices opposed to social injustice; many passages from the books of Exodus, Numbers, Leviticus and Deuteronomy are also illuminating in this context. Redemption and liberation happen to and in Israel *in* history. Moreover, these real experiences of liberation are a call to be liberating too: "Remember that you were a slave in the land of Egypt, and the Lord your God redeemed you" (Deuteronomy 15:15).

(3) The Old Testament offers *guidance and encouragement in everyday life*. Those who have to deal with discouragement, misfortune and despair in their lives, meet, in the Old Testament, people who, in suffering and guilt, in joy and terror, in the thirst for knowledge and in scepticism, in industrious work and in the delights of sexual love, burdened by violence and aggression, still gear their lives to God. The Old Testament is familiar with the highs and lows of human existence. From the very first pages, it speaks about that which has occurred in all times: evil, murder, lies and violence. It does not deny or ignore suffering and death, but seeks to show how life, despite all that, is still worth the effort. It shows that creation and life, people and the world, are intrinsically "*tov*" (good and beautiful) and that the God that we believe in intends good things for humankind and the world. The Old Testament invites one to enjoy life, here and now, and to find joy in it. And also in this regard, it articulates an important supplement to the New Testament. Again, we quote Zenger.[16] "Obviously, the New Testament also talks about joy. But in the New Testament, this joy is often spiritualised. It concerns a joy that often transcends

---

[16] *Ibid.*, 197 (with reference to Haag, "Das Plus des Alten Testaments," 304).

the actual daily reality: joy over the 'reward ... in heaven' (Matthew 5:11-12), joy over Jesus' being present to his disciples (Matthew 9:15; John 15:11), joy through the sending of the Spirit (John 16:20), in short: 'Rejoice in the Lord' (Philippians 4:4). We must ask ourselves, however, whether the human being may only 'Rejoice in the Lord', whether it is not almost inhuman to only find joy 'in the Lord'. In the Old Testament, people find joy in life, in celebrating, at the harvest, in the enjoyment of a meal and particularly the wine, in nature, in love…" In other words, it is a book *by people* — who in all possible human situations or, if you will, in their daily, existential *conatus essendi* tried their hardest to be worthwhile human beings —, *for people* — who, in a completely different context, nonetheless also try today to give meaning to their humanity —, *about a God* who is more than all the attempts to "grasp" Him, but who, at the same time, surpasses both them and us in love.

CHAPTER TWO

ORIGIN AND GOAL OF HUMAN EXISTENCE
THE CREATION POEM IN GENESIS 1:1–2:4

"I believe in God the Father Almighty, Creator of Heaven and earth…" These words begin the so-called catholic "Apostle's Creed," so named because they are seen to be the faithful summary of the beliefs of Jesus' disciples. With these words, Christianity has traditionally hailed God as "Creator." In so doing, the Christian tradition follows the Old Testament traditions concerning the creating God.[1]

During the history of scholarly research, it has often been alleged that the theme of God as Creator is secondary, even in the Old Testament. In this regard, it has usually been argued that the biblical Israel first encountered traces of God in the events surrounding its liberation from Egypt and only later called this liberating God

---

[1] With regard to the creation poem in Genesis 1:1–2:4, the literature is nearly inexhaustible. We refer here to a few accessible studies: Othmar Keel and Silvia Schroer, *Schöpfung: Biblische Theologien im Kontext altorientalischer Religionen* (Göttingen/Freiburg: Universitätsverlag, 2002); Ellen van Wolde, *Verhalen over het begin: Genesis 1–11 en andere scheppingsverhalen* (Baarn: Ten Have, 1995); Marc Vervenne, "Mens, kosmos en aarde: een exegetische reflectie over Genesis 1–3,"*De mens: verrader of hoeder van de schepping?*, ed. Johan De Tavernier and Marc Vervenne, Nikè-reeks, 26 (Leuven: Acco, 1991) 27-62; and Marc Vervenne, "The Compositional Texture of the Priestly Overture to the Pentateuch," *Studies in the Book of Genesis: Literature, Redaction and History*, ed. André Wénin, Bibliotheca Ephemeridum Theologicarum Lovaniensium, 155 (Leuven: Peeters/University Press, 2001) 35-79; Walter Vogels, "The Biblical Creation Myth of Gen 1:1–2:4a," *Kerygma* 21 (1987) 3-20.

"creator." Nevertheless, one cannot escape the fact that the biblical
authors put the creation narrative, or better, the creation narratives,
at the beginning of the Bible. From a theological point of view, this
is an important observation. The first chapters of the Bible, after
all, do not focus on the relationship between YAHWEH and the
People of Israel but rather on the relationship between God and
humankind *tout court*. From the perspective of a believer who
believes in God as a person, one wants to be able to say something
about the human person, his environment and his relationship to
God. The image of God sketched here is, moreover, not that of a
God who is primarily concerned with a single nation, namely
Israel. God is the God who created the entire world, including all
its people. Before one is a Jew or a Christian, one is part of God's
"salvation history," his journey with humankind; one is part of
"salvation history" because one is a human being as such. This
implies, at the same time, that the reproach often made with regard
to the Old Testament — namely that the Old Testament presents a
particularistic image of God, in contrast to the universalistic image
of God that the New Testament supposedly presents —, at least as
far as the first chapters of the Bible are concerned, is invalid.

The question concerning how human beings came to exist, which
at the same time implies the question concerning the purpose of
human existence, is an eternal question. It is one of the universal
questions that have been considered by all people of all cultures.
The question of our origin and our purpose is an existential question, even today.

Against this background, the following will focus on the "creation poem" of Genesis 1:1–2:4. In the first section, the text will be
situated and defined within its literary context. The second section
presents a succinct analysis and discussion of the text. The third
and final section will highlight the theological significance and
function of the text.

1. In the Beginning... Two Creation Narratives

a. *Two Creation Narratives*

When one reads the first three chapters of the book of Genesis, it is immediately clear that they are constituted by two different creation narratives. After a passage in which one reads that everything was created over a period of six or seven days, the biblical account suddenly says again that there is nothing: "In the day that the Lord God made the earth and the heavens, when no plant of the field was yet in the earth and no herb of the field had yet sprung up — for the Lord God had not caused it to rain upon the earth, and there was no one to till the ground; but a stream would rise from the earth, and water the whole face of the ground — then the Lord God formed man..." (Genesis 2:4-7). God, as the biblical authors see it, begins creation all over again. Moreover, the vocabulary of Genesis 1:1–2:4 also differs from that of the subsequent chapters. So, Genesis 1 continually speaks of *Elohim* ("God"), while Genesis 2–3 speaks of *уанwен Elohim* ("уанwен God"). The style of the two narratives also differs. Genesis 1 is not really a "narrative" in the strict sense of the word. It is more of a poem that, in a solemn, monotonous, liturgical and stereotypical way, sums up the various elements of creation. Genesis 2–3, by contrast, is a dramatic tale in which we are told how the man and his woman ("Adam" and "Eve") find themselves in the paradisiacal Garden of Eden, only to be driven out of it.

Based on these observations, among others, biblical scholars have, for centuries, accepted that two different traditions have been brought together in Genesis 1–3. The fact alone that the biblical authors passed on both texts together also makes it clear that they did not want these to be seen as historical accounts of the past. Both texts were written with the intention of explaining the current reality and proclaiming, above all, how creation should be viewed

in light of this reality. The creation narratives are not a description
of the past, but rather an attempt to interpret the present through
the lens of a faith-filled reflection. In what follows, this will be
made clear using the example of the first creation narrative.

b. *The Delineation of the Text*

In most recent Bible translations, Genesis 2:4a is indicated as the
end of the first creation narrative. The New Revised Standard
Version also makes a division after the first part of Genesis 2:4:
"These are the generations of the heavens and the earth when they
were created."

   The second part of Genesis 2:4 ("In the day that the Lord God
made the earth and the heavens...") is thus considered to be the
beginning of the so-called Paradise Narrative, which is generally
said to end at Genesis 3:24.

   This splitting of Genesis 2:4 into two parts (the end of the first
and the beginning of the second narrative) is based on the traditional source-critical analysis of the book of Genesis, which reached
its peak during the course of the twentieth century. On the basis of
the abovementioned differences, among others, between Genesis 1
on the one hand and Genesis 2–3 on the other, the first creation
narrative was seen as "Priestly" (P), while the second was ascribed
to the "Yahwist" source (J). Genesis 2:4b was also usually attributed to this author. This division was based, for example, on the
use of the divine name. Genesis 2:4b uses the so-called tetragrammaton, YaHWeH, comprising four characters, (in Hebrew, only
consonants are written), whereas verse 4a refers to God using the
word "*Elohim*" ("God"). Moreover, the vocabulary used in each
of the two parts of the verse differs: Genesis 2:4a uses the Hebrew
term ברא (*bara'* – "to create"), as opposed to עשׂה (*'asah* – "to
make") in verse 4b. Consequently, it was decided that Genesis

2:4b must be the original beginning of the so-called Paradise Narrative.

A few critical comments, however, must be made with regard to this rigorous splitting of verse 4. Firstly, let it be said that the "paradise narrative" does not use the tetragrammaton *tout court*, but indeed a combination of the two divine designations (YaHWeH Elohim). In the first creation narrative on the other hand, only *Elohim* appears. The divine name can thus only be used with difficulty as the basis for the division of the text into two separate "sources."

Secondly, it appears that the alternating use of creation terminology [ברא (*bara'* — "to create"), as opposed to עשׂה (*'asah* — "to make")] is typical of the vocabulary of the first creation narrative (see for example *bara'* in Genesis 1:2, 21, 27; 2:3 versus *'asah* in Genesis 1:7, 16, 25, 26, 31; 2:2, 3). This therefore seems to suggest instead that the whole of Genesis 2:4 should be seen as the conclusion to the first narrative.

Finally, in the book of Genesis, the *toledot*-formula already mentioned (usually translated as "this is the history of...") mostly functions as an element that binds two wholes. By using this formula, the author/editor does not so much want to end one part and begin a new part as make a link between the two parts. Although, as we shall see later, Genesis 2:4 clearly appears to serve a function in the first creation narrative, at the same time, it seems to be composed as a transition into the second creation narrative. Therefore, we can best ascribe Genesis 2:4 to the editor who not only refashioned the creation narrative that lay before him, which we now encounter in Genesis 1, but who, simultaneously, linked it to the likewise already extant "Paradise Narrative."

In what follows we shall study the first creation narrative as a literary work of art. We shall investigate what this passage is trying to say and how it is trying to say it on the basis of an analysis of the text. Genesis 1 is a poem. And, as in every form of Old Testament poetry, the author of this passage was concerned about the fusion of form and content. Therefore, we shall begin the analysis, after the presentation of the text itself, with an overview of the structure of Genesis 1:1–2:4.

2. Genesis 1:1–2:4: A Vision of a Perfect World

a. *The Text*

[Chapter 1] In the beginning when God created the heavens and the earth, ²the earth was a formless void and darkness covered the face of the deep, while a wind from God swept over the face of the waters. ³Then God said, 'Let there be light'; and there was light. ⁴And God saw that the light was good; and God separated the light from the darkness. ⁵God called the light Day, and the darkness he called Night. And there was evening and there was morning, the first day.

⁶And God said, 'Let there be a dome in the midst of the waters, and let it separate the waters from the waters.' ⁷So God made the dome and separated the waters that were under the dome from the waters that were above the dome. And it was so. ⁸God called the dome Sky. And there was evening and there was morning, the second day.

⁹And God said, 'Let the waters under the sky be gathered together into one place, and let the dry land appear.' And it was so. ¹⁰God called the dry land Earth, and the waters that were gathered together he called Seas. And God saw that it was good. ¹¹Then God said, 'Let the earth put forth vegetation: plants yielding seed, and fruit trees of every kind on earth that bear fruit with the seed in it.' And it was so. ¹²The earth brought forth vegetation: plants yielding seed of every kind, and trees of every kind bearing fruit with the seed in it. And God saw that it was good. ¹³And there was evening and there was morning, the third day.

¹⁴And God said, 'Let there be lights in the dome of the sky to separate the day from the night; and let them be for signs and for seasons and for days and years, ¹⁵and let them be lights in the dome of the sky to give light upon the earth.' And it was so. ¹⁶God made the two great lights — the

greater light to rule the day and the lesser light to rule the night — and the stars. [17]God set them in the dome of the sky to give light upon the earth, [18]to rule over the day and over the night, and to separate the light from the darkness. And God saw that it was good. [19]And there was evening and there was morning, the fourth day.

[20]And God said, 'Let the waters bring forth swarms of living creatures, and let birds fly above the earth across the dome of the sky.' [21]So God created the great sea monsters and every living creature that moves, of every kind, with which the waters swarm, and every winged bird of every kind. And God saw that it was good. [22]God blessed them, saying, 'Be fruitful and multiply and fill the waters in the seas, and let birds multiply on the earth.' [23]And there was evening and there was morning, the fifth day.

[24]And God said, 'Let the earth bring forth living creatures of every kind: cattle and creeping things and wild animals of the earth of every kind.' And it was so. [25]God made the wild animals of the earth of every kind, and the cattle of every kind, and everything that creeps upon the ground of every kind. And God saw that it was good.

[26]Then God said, 'Let us make humankind in our image, according to our likeness; and let them have dominion over the fish of the sea, and over the birds of the air, and over the cattle, and over all the wild animals of the earth, and over every creeping thing that creeps upon the earth.'

[27]So God created humankind in his image,

in the image of God he created them;

male and female he created them. [28]God blessed them, and God said to them, 'Be fruitful and multiply, and fill the earth and subdue it; and have dominion over the fish of the sea and over the birds of the air and over every living thing that moves upon the earth.' [29]God said, 'See, I have given you every plant yielding seed that is upon the face of all the earth, and every tree with seed in its fruit; you shall have them for food. [30]And to every beast of the earth, and to every bird of the air, and to everything that creeps on the earth, everything that has the breath of life, I have given every green plant for food.' And it was so. [31]God saw everything that he had made, and indeed, it was very good. And there was evening and there was morning, the sixth day.

[Chapter 2] Thus the heavens and the earth were finished, and all their multitude. ²And on the seventh day God finished the work that he had done, and he rested on the seventh day from all the work that he had done. ³So God blessed the seventh day and hallowed it, because on it God rested from all the work that he had done in creation. ⁴These are the generations of the heavens and the earth when they were created.

Genesis 1 imbeds God's work of creation within the schema of seven days or one week. The structure of the week is one of completion. No day is added; no day is left out. By framing the work of creation within the schema of a week, the author wants to clearly show that creation is complete and completed. Obviously, one can raise the objection that the world is far from flawless and that reality is far from perfect. But in so doing, one touches upon the essence of what Genesis 1 is trying to say. The poem is not saying anything about how it once was; it instead wants to emphasise how creation ought to be — perfect! And the author of Genesis 1 also strives to attain this perfection.

b. *The Structure of Genesis 1:1–2:4*

In the text as it now stands, inclusive of Genesis 2:4, the following structure can be discerned. Genesis 1:1 is the title verse, which forms an inclusion with Genesis 2:4, the closing verse (and at the same time, the hinge verse between the first and the second narratives). This is apparent from, among other things, the fact that the expression "the heavens and the earth" and the verb "created" (*bara'*) appear in both the title and the closing verses.

The actual activity of creating begins in verse 3 ("God said"). Indeed, all of the subsequent paragraphs begin with the same expression (1:6, 9, 11, 14, 20, 24, 26). Consequently, one can, based on the structure of the text, infer that verse 2 does not yet form part of the actual creation poem. It is, instead, an overture in which the disorder and turmoil that precedes God's intervention is evoked. This verse has Genesis 2:1-3 as its counterpart. The seventh day is characterised by complete and perfect order and peace: "Thus the heavens and the earth were finished, and all their multitude. And on the seventh day God finished the work that he had done, and he rested on the seventh day from all the work that he had done. So God blessed the seventh day and hallowed it, because on it God rested from all the work that he had done in creation."

In contrast to this order and peace, Genesis 1:2 emphasises the chaos and turmoil. This is evident from the construction of the verse, where, in three parts, the chaotic and disordered state of the primal situation is brought out: "… the earth was a formless void / and darkness covered the face of the deep, / while a mighty wind swept over the face of the waters." This translation is perhaps more correct than the widely accepted spiritual rendering "the spirit of God hovered over the waters." The Hebrew word *ruach* (רוח) literally means "wind." And in Hebrew, the word "God" (*elohim* — אלהים) can also be used to indicate a superlative. The sound of the Hebrew expression *tohu wavohu* (והו ובהו) also evokes the chaos of the primal situation, which is characterised by threatening darkness. What is important is that it is not the attractive darkness of approaching evening that is being described here. Rather, this threatening darkness is best related to the ominous darkness of an approaching thunderstorm.

The body of the text (verses 3-31) deals with the six workdays of the week. Here, two parts can clearly be distinguished. The first three days describe the creation of the basic structure (verses 3-13): time and space — take note that plants and trees that are created on the third day are also seen to be part of this basic structure. The subsequent three days describe the fittings that will fill this basic structure (verses 14-31). Moreover, as is apparent from the schema laid out below, the two large parts of the six day creation week correspond to one another (days 1-3 on the one hand and days 4-6 on the other). The fittings of the fourth day (the sun and the moon) correspond to the basic structure of the first day (day and night). Birds and fish populate, on the fifth day, the dry land and the sea, which were made on the second day. The land animals (vv. 24-25) are the "decoration" of the dry land (vv. 9-10). And there is also a connection between the human beings and the plants (vv. 11-13), since the plants are meant to serve as food for the human beings.

Consequently, it seems as if the body of the creation narrative is very rigidly structured. Nonetheless, a closer reading of the text reveals something peculiar. After the first work of creation, the text concludes in verse 5, "And there was evening and there was morning, the first day." Likewise, after the second work of creation, we read in verse 8: "And there was evening and there was morning, the second day." However, after the third act of creation (verses 9 and 10) one would expect to find a similar formula as a conclusion of the third day ("And there was evening and there was morning, the third day"). This is missing, however. In its place, verses 11 and 12 just tell us how God proceeds with a new act of creation. Only after this, in verse 13, do we find the expected stereotypical formula. As a result, there are, on the third day, two works of creation. So, in this respect too, verses 3-13, in which an account of the creation of the basic structure is given, form a diptych with the three subsequent days of creation (vv. 14-31). Here too, four activities take place over three days: one on the fourth day (the heavenly bodies), one of the fifth day (fish and birds are named together), and two on the sixth day (the land animals and human beings).

In summary, the structure of Genesis 1 can be represented as follows:

A	**Title Verse**		God created the heavens and the earth	(1:1)
	B	**Overture**	disorder and turmoil	(1:2)
		C **Body**	creation in six days	(1:3-31)
		day 1 work 1	day and night	(1:3-5)
		day 2 work 2	sky and sea	(1:6-8)
		day 3 work 3	dry land	(1:9-10)
		work 4	plants	(1:11-13)
		day 4 work 5	sun and moon	(1:14-19)
		day 5 work 6	birds and fish	(1:20-23)
		day 6 work 7	animals on the land	(1:24-25)
		work 8	the human being	(1:26-31)
	B'	**Conclusion**	order and peace	(2:1-3)
A'	**Hinge verse**		YaHWeH God made/created the heavens and the earth	(2:4)

c. *Structure within the Individual Creative Acts*

Having considered the structure of Genesis 1:1–2:4 as a whole, the individual works of creation also deserve closer inspection. Even a superficial reading of the text reveals a relatively stereotypical construction. Each creative act begins with an introductory formula ("And God said" – verses 3, 6, 9, 11, 14-15, 20, 24 and 26). This is followed by the divine command ("Let there be" – verses 3, 6, 9, 11, 14-15, 20, 24 and 26). Then, except for the fifth day, there follows the effect ("And it was so" – verses 3, 7, 9, 11, 15, 24 and 30). Moreover, with the exception of the second day, each creative act is evaluated ("And God saw that it was good" – verses 4, 10, 12, 18, 21, 25 and 31). Finally, at the end of every day, there is a concluding formula ("And there was evening and there was morning" – verses 5, 8, 13, 19, 23 and 31).

Nevertheless, this almost perfect schema is repeatedly broken. At the production of the fifth work of creation (verses 14-15) we read, for example, "And God said, 'Let there be lights (…).' And it was so." Thus, one concludes that at the end of verse 15 the lights are in actual fact also there. Yet the text in verse 16 goes on: "God made the two great lights." If the lights already appeared at God's command, why then, according to verse 16, does God still have to make them?

In order to solve this problem, it makes sense to distinguish the stereotypical elements that the creative acts have in common from the variations. These variations primarily concern the use of verbs. Within the stereotypical schema of "And God said" followed by "And it was so," God's creative actions are indicated by means of different verbs: God "separated" (verses 4 and 7), God "called" (verses 5, 8 and 10), God "made" (verses 7, 16 and 25), God "set" (verse 17), God "created" (verses 21 and 27) and God "blessed" (verses 22 and 28).

The different kinds of verbs that are used in, on the one hand, the common parts and, on the other, the variations reveal two differing concepts of creation. In the stereotypical parts, God creates by means of his will to create. God speaks and things appear. In the variations, God must himself act: God separates, names, makes, creates, places and blesses. Consequently, it appears that in Genesis 1:1–2:4 an editor may have reworked two visions of creation into a single poem: a text in which God's creation by his "word" was central and a text in which God actively had to roll up his sleeves.

The author/editor of the text we have before us deliberately chose to preserve both ideas. On the one hand, he wanted to let God create purely by speaking a word. From this point of view, God does not have to do anything to bring things into existence. For God, it is sufficient to speak and things happen according to his word. Perhaps it was also this author or editor who bundled the eight works of creation together over six days of creation, and did so with theological interests in mind, i.e., he wanted to legitimise the Sabbath as the seventh day of the week and a day of absolute rest. That is why, on the other hand, the author wanted to safeguard the notion of the creative acts of God. God, of course, would not need much rest if he had only spoken. After six days of labour, there is the seventh day of absolute rest for God. And just as God rested on the seventh day, so too should human beings, made in God's image and likeness, keep the seventh day as a day of rest.

In this regard, it is worth noting that the ancient Greek translation of the Old Testament, the Septuagint, reads, in Genesis 2:2, instead of "the seventh day," "the sixth day." Indeed, in the Hebrew text it seems as if God did not rest completely on the seventh day; he "finished" his work. Within Judaism — the Septuagint translation of the Torah appeared in the third century BC — that was unacceptable: the Sabbath is absolutely sacred, also for God!

3. Theological Function and Meaning

a. *A Historically Reliable Account?*

The chapter on fundamentalism demonstrated how a fundamentalistic reading of the Bible concerns itself with trying to bring the creation narrative into agreement with a scientific explanation of the origin of the world. Furthermore, there is a strong revival, particularly in the United States, in creationism, in which the biblical representation of the origin is put forward as a reliable source of information about the past.

Those, however, who would take the text seriously, must immediately see that the creation poem in Genesis 1:1–2:4 has anything but a historically reliable account of the origin of the world in mind. The text does not pretend to be scientifically reliable and should not be read that way. Some examples will make this immediately clear. For a few centuries now, it has been firmly established as a scientific fact that light comes from the sun. Experience, however, teaches us something completely different. There are days on which there is indeed light, but the sun cannot be seen at all. Therefore, it would seem that, if one bases one's argument on this experience, the light and the sun are two different things. It is no wonder then that, according to the biblical vision of creation, the creation of the light (day 1) and the creation of the sun (day 4) are attributed to two distinct creative acts. Moreover, everyday experience seems to suggest that the moon and the stars are also light emitting heavenly bodies, even though we now know scientifically that the moon has the sun to thank for its "light." Indeed, we still speak of sunrise and sunset, even though science showed centuries ago that it is not the sun that revolves around the world but the other way around. Such expressions — like the word "moonlight" — are remnants of a pre-scientific worldview that was nevertheless based on sensory perception.

When one bases oneself on sensory perception, then one must also conclude that the world is a flat disc, covered by a firmament, the ends of which meet at the horizon (see diagram). There is water above the earth (rain) that is held back by a dome, the vault of heaven, but which sometimes falls to earth as it flows through the floodgates of heaven. And because there is also water that bubbles up out of the earth at springs, the conclusion that there is also water under the disc of earth is not quite so surprising.

Such images, based on an Old Testament worldview, lead to the conclusion that every attempt to bring the biblical creation myth into agreement with the results of research conducted in the positive sciences is altogether mistaken and must necessarily end in a hopeless biblical fundamentalism. The Bible is, of course, first and

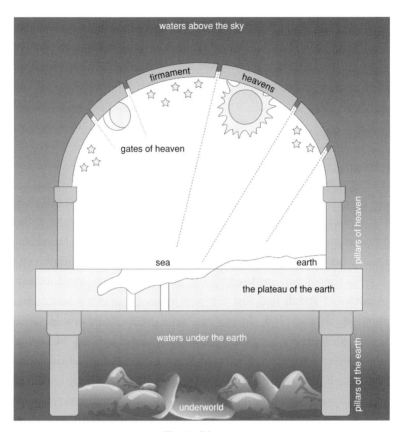

Fig. 1. Diagram

foremost, a testimony of faith that was not intended to be a scientific account. Science and the Bible each speak their own language.

Therefore, one could then, of course, also call the biblical creation poem a "myth." The use of this term, however, in no way implies a fake, a fiction or an illusion. The term refers, indeed, to an attempt, by means of a symbolic story, to articulate the transcendent that is intuitively sensed — in the case of the biblical creation narrative, that God stands at the origin of everything. As such, the biblical creation narrative is also "true," yet this in no

way implies that it "actually happened." Indeed, the first words of
the creation poem already reveal its mythical nature. The expression "In (the) beginning" — note that in the Hebrew no article is
used — refers to a time when there was still no time.

b. What the Creation Poem Wants to Make Clear

1. God as Mighty Creator

The author or editor responsible for the text of Genesis 1:1–2:4 as
it now stands composed his creation narrative in the context of the
Babylonian exile (587-537 BC). The northern kingdom of Israel had
already been absorbed into the Assyrian empire in the eighth century BC after it was invaded by the Assyrians. Now, the southern
kingdom of Judah had lost the war against Assyria's successor,
Babylon. The capital, Jerusalem, and the central temple were
destroyed, bringing a definitive end to the royal dynasty of David.
In addition, the Judean elite were taken into captivity in Babylon.
This disastrous turn of events for Judah gave the (exiled) Israelites
the impression that Marduk, the Babylonian supreme deity, was
more powerful than YaHWeH, Israel's God. Indeed, not only had
Israel lost the battle, but YaHWeH, as Israel's God, came out of the
conflict as the big loser.

Against this background of disillusionment and doubt — there
probably more than a little uncertainty with regard to YaHWeH —
the creation poem in the first chapter of the book of Genesis proclaims God as a mighty creator. Moreover, Israel's God is not only
professed to be the creator of Israel, but of the entire universe:
everything owes its existence to God. This also implies that YaH-
WeH is more powerful than any other deity, including Marduk, who
is subordinate to YaHWeH. This polemical tone regarding Babylon's
supreme god is also apparent in the fact that the Genesis narrative

clearly states that the sun and the moon, which were gods in the various cultures that surrounded Israel, are nothing more than God's creations. Moreover, it is striking that the "sun" and the "moon" are not even called by name; the author downgrades them to "two great lights" (1:16).

2. A Trustworthy God

The way in which the author/editor of the creation narrative has organised his material shows that he also wanted to use his text to testify to a trustworthy God. God speaks *and* acts according to his word. God practices what he preaches. Or, as one might say of an honourable person: he means what he says, says what he means and also does what he says. The author wants to underscore the trustworthiness of Israel's God with this story. And this was more than necessary for the Israelites in exile. In other words, for the author/editor of Genesis 1:1–2:4, creation is an essential witness to God's faithfulness.

3. The Seventh Day: A Day of Rest

The whole poem culminates in the seventh day, the day of God's rest. For the Jews, this is the Sabbath. And although Genesis 2:1-3 does not refer to the Sabbath by name, this still clearly resounds through the Hebrew text: "And on the seventh (*hasjevii*) day God finished the work that he had done, and he rested (*wajisbot*) on the seventh (*hasjevii*) day from all the work that he had done. So God blessed the seventh (*hasjevii*) day and hallowed it, because on it God rested (*jisbot*) from all the work that he had done in creation."

For the Israelite exiles, the Sabbath was something new to hold on to. The destruction of Jerusalem in 587 BC meant that the exiles needed to find an alternative for the demolished temple. Furthermore, while in a strange and faraway land, they wanted to save and protect the Israelite religion. Therefore, the creation narrative's emphasis on the Sabbath is designed to both legitimise and explain. It seeks to legitimise why people should observe the seventh day of the week as a day of rest, namely because God also took a rest on the seventh day from the work that he had been doing. And at the same time, it seeks to give an explanation for the establishment of the Sabbath as a religious institution. Indeed, in all likelihood, the origin of the Sabbath can be found in an ancient agricultural practice that sought to ensure that people and animals could rest at the end of a working week. This profane custom, a remnant of which one still encounters in a legal text in the book of Exodus ("For six days you shall do your work, but on the seventh day you shall rest, so that your ox and your donkey may have relief, and your home-born slave and the resident alien may be refreshed." — Exodus 23:12), was perhaps later fleshed out in a religious way to become a day of rest to the glory of God. As an aetiology — a story that seeks to explain the origin of something — the creation narrative traces the origin of the Sabbath back to God himself.

4. From Chaos to Order

According to the first creation narrative, the act of creation was no *creatio ex nihilo*. It was a transformation of chaos and disorder into order and cosmos. Herein too lies a hidden message for the exiled Israelites. They lived in Babylonian chaos. The narrator, however, points out that God, even in the worst chaos, can bring order. And the order that God brings about is qualified: it is good (*tov*). When God creates light, it is said that it is "good" (Genesis 1:4). This, however, is not said of darkness, which constitutes part of the chaos (1:2). God does give both light and dark a purpose though:

the light God calls "day;" the darkness God calls "night." The sombre and threatening darkness of the primal chaos is thereby given a place in the ordered cosmos. In this case too, the author seems to base his argument on his everyday experience of the world: on the one hand, darkness can be extremely threatening, but on the other, the darkness of night is at the service of human beings as they try to sleep.

In other words, as a didactical poem, Genesis 1:1–2:4 proclaims the order of the world. Everything is planned and has its place. This planning and regulation is emphasised in the structure of the text, as was demonstrated earlier. Indeed, the idea that order and regulation were a central focal point in ancient Israelite society is apparent from the countless legal texts in which transgression of the order — and therefore the concomitant descent into disorder — is radically condemned.

5. Human Beings Are Special

From the structure of Genesis 1:1–2:4, we can see that the human being occupies a special place in creation. After all, the creation of the human being comes at the end of the poem. The whole universe is ordered and the scene seems to be set for the human being to make his appearance. On the one hand, there can be no human being without nature. Nature, in a broad sense, was always the context, essential to life, that the Israelites found themselves in. Without rain, livestock and fish, they could not live. On the other hand, nature is subordinate to the human being. This is clearly apparent from the place given to sea monsters; they are created by God and are thus reduced to being creatures (Genesis 1:21) — nature is demythologised.

The author of Genesis 1 makes it clear, in various ways, that the human being is the highpoint of creation. As such, the poet's vision is without doubt anthropocentric. The way in which the creation of the human being is depicted is different in many respects from the rest of God's creative acts.

First, the paragraph in which the creation of the human being is recounted is much more expansive than the account of the other works of creation. Moreover, with regard to the creation of the human being, the divine command so characteristic of all the other paragraphs, "Let there be," is missing. The creation of the human being begins in another way: "Let us make humankind...." In this verse, which in the past has been erroneously thought to be a reference to the Trinity due to the use of the plural form, God consults himself as it were. Sometimes, it is also argued, by making reference to Job 1:6, that God is consulting his heavenly court or that this plural form should be seen as a "royal we."

Second, with respect to the creation of the human being, it is striking that the creation of the plants and land animals evidently issues from the land itself: "The earth brought forth vegetation" (Genesis 1:12); "Let the earth bring forth living creatures of every kind" (Genesis 1:24). Humankind, by contrast, comes directly from God.

Third, the poet says, in contrast to the other works of creation, that God made the human being "in our image" and "according to our likeness" (Genesis 1:26). This is not a statement about the outward physical appearance of God, as if the human being could form an image of God. Indeed, with regard to depictions of God, Ancient Israel was very strict: "You shall not make for yourself an idol" (Exodus 20:4). What "being an image of God" really means is made clear in the rest of the verse: the human being must "have dominion over the fish of the sea, and over the birds of the air, and over the cattle, and over all the wild animals of the earth, and over every creeping thing that creeps upon the earth." And in verse 28, God addresses the human beings directly: "Be fruitful and multiply, and fill the earth and subdue it; and have dominion over the fish of the sea and over the birds of the air and over every living thing that moves upon the earth." Just as God rules over Creation, so too, human beings are commissioned to rule over Creation. Against the background of the increasing realisation of the fragility of Nature, these verses have, especially since 1970, been deemed responsible for the ecological deterioration of Creation.[2] After all, the creation narrative allegedly preaches an extreme anthropocentricism in which the human being has, by order of God, been given absolute sovereignty over Creation and in which the biblical creation narrative allegedly gives humankind a licence to exploit Creation.

It is correct to say that Genesis 1 awards the human person a central place. Indeed, we have just seen how the author of Genesis 1 demonstrates his conviction that the human being is the highpoint of Creation. After all, as the "image of God," the human being is considered to be of immense value throughout the biblical tradition. This is already apparent from the many Old Testament prescriptions that all have the wellbeing of the human being in mind and that wish the human being a long and happy life. At the same time, however, this emphasis on the human being conceals a polemic against other visions of creation known to the author of the creation narrative. In the Babylonian creation narrative — the *Enuma Elish* —, with which the author was undoubtedly familiar, the human being is created from the blood of a rebellious god and made to serve the gods. In complete contrast to the Ancient Babylonian idea in which the human person is little more than a slave

<hr>

[2] See, in this regard, Lynn White, "Die historischen Ursachen unserer ökologischen Krise," *Gefährdete Zukunft: Prognosen anglo-amerikanischer Wissenschaftler*, ed. Michael Lohmann, Hanser Umweltforschung, 5 (Munich: Hanser, 1970) 20-29; and Carl Amery, *Das Ende der Vorsehung: Die gnadenlosen Folgen des Christentums* (Reinbek: Rowohlt, 1972; [2]1974).

to the gods, the biblical author sees the human being as the crown of Creation.

In the biblical creation narrative, the human being is oriented to the world. The earth is the domain in which the human being must prove himself. The human being must "rule" over the world. Sadly, it may be true that, with this verse in hand, the exploitation of the earth has been legitimated. Nevertheless, the verse actually has a completely different implication. "Having dominion" does not mean the same thing as misuse. Dominion, here, has to do with "authority." Real authority, in the true sense of the word, is put at the service of the other and contributes to the development of the world. Moreover, the lordship of the human being is related to God's blessing (Genesis 1:28). And, in biblical thought, "blessing" is the exact opposite of "cursing." Those who lose God's blessing are cursed. If the biblical blessing is synonymous with "solidarity" — God is in solidarity with humankind and stands at its side —, then the "curse" is the same as breaking this solidarity. Furthermore, is appears that, although Genesis 1 accentuates the importance of the human being, the human being is and remains still (only) a creature. In Genesis 1:27 the author repeats three times that God "created" human beings. For this, the Hebrew verb *bara'* is used, a word that always and only has God as its subject. For the other verbs that the author uses in connection with God's creative acts ("to make," "to separate," "to call"), the human being can also be the subject. This is not, however, the case for the word *bara'*.

The fourth and final point is that while the creation of plants and animals talks about various kinds, this is not mentioned with regard to the human being. Indeed, it is said that humankind *tout court* is made "in our image, according to our likeness" (Genesis 1:26). In saying this, the author undoubtedly wants to emphasise the equality within humanity. The fact that this equality is more of an ideal than a reality makes the central argument of Genesis 1 clear: the creation narrative describes an ideal world. Not "how it was," but "how it should be" is the focus. Moreover, this seems all the more evident from the diet that humans and animals are prescribed. Indeed, it is remarkable that both human beings and animals are, according to Genesis 1, vegetarians. That this was the author's intention, is made apparent by a comparison with the flood narrative in Genesis 6–9, which is a return to a state of chaos (cf. the deep). After the Flood, God approved a new "diet" for the human beings of the new creation. Human beings may now eat meat (Genesis 9:1-4). The difference between eating plants and eating animals has to do with the difference between "animate" and "inanimate" life (see above where it is shown how the creation of plants in Genesis 1 on the third day means that plants thus form part of the basic structure of creation.)

In conclusion, one could say that the creation poem of Genesis 1:1–2:4 deals, as do most myths, with an ideal state of affairs, a situation of peace and harmony, a world without violence and death. This is not the world as it has ever been. The creation narrative paints a picture of the world as it ought to be: a world without bloodshed. As such, the creation poem is an appeal to humankind, as the image of God, to strive for a world of peace and harmony.

CHAPTER THREE

ACHIEVING HUMAN COEXISTENCE

When the biblical, and particularly the Old Testament, tradition refers to human existence, and more concretely to human society or coexistence, it is clear that it is not giving a utopian, unrealistic account that does not tally with human experience. On the contrary, it very realistically — even though it may be from the perspective of a hopeful ideal — tells the story of everyday life with its crises and high points, defined and also influenced by the full and colourful spectrum of possible positive and negative emotions and desires. In this context, it is evident that society also needs to be regulated.

This chapter addresses this aspect from two angles. The first section, against the background of the so-called "Ten Commandments" or the "Decalogue," reveals the boundaries that must be taken into account in order to prevent human society — both in the human-human sense and the human-divine sense — from sliding into chaos. Here, in light of the prohibition of murder, we shall pay particular attention to the way in which the intrinsic value of life is emphasised. The second section discusses the biblical concern for social justice, as illustrated by the Old Testament law concerning the so-called "Jubilee Year."

1. From Human to Human, from Human to God: The Decalogue in Exodus 20:1-17

The importance and the impact of the Decalogue, or the so-called "Ten Commandments," on the development of Judeo-Christian thinking can not be overestimated. The directives that were written down in Exodus 20:1-17 (parallel in Deuteronomy 5:6-21), have influenced, in no small way, not only Christian thought, but also (Western) culture as such.[1] For generations, these "ten words" formed the ethical manual for human thought and action. And for generations, Bible scholars have tried to explain and interpret this pericope. A proper understanding of the (original) text is a *conditio sine qua non* for its legitimate, contemporary application.

This section comprises two parts. First, the actual pericope as a whole, namely Exodus 20:1-17, will be briefly introduced.[2] Then,

---

[1] An exhaustive comparison of Exodus 20 and Deuteronomy 5, which would focus on the redaction history, is not carried out here. We limit ourselves in the scope of this book to a more content oriented theological overview of the version presented in Exodus 20, which is usually considered to be the older of the two.

[2] See several recent contributions to exegetical research on the Decalogue: Jan Holman, "De tien geboden in het Oude Testament," *Een lichte last? De tien geboden in de Katechismus van de katholieke Kerk: Uitleg en commentaar*, ed. Karl-Wilhelm Merks and Frans J. H. Vosman (Baarn: Gooi en Sticht, 1998) 11-44; Axel Graupner, "Die zehn Gebote im Rahmen alttestamentlicher Ethik: Anmerkungen zum gegenwärtigen Stand der Forschung," *Weisheit, Ethos und Gebot: Weisheits- und Dekalogtraditionen in der Bibel und im frühen Judentum*, ed. Henning Graf Reventlow, Biblisch-Theologische Studien, 43 (Neukirchen: Neukirchener Verlag, 2001) 61-95. In this regard we also refer the book on which the author in the article mentioned also worked as a co-author, namely Werner H. Schmidt, Holger Delkurt and Axel Graupner, *Die zehn Gebote im Rahmen alttestamentlicher Ethik*, Erträge der Forschung, 281 (Darmstadt: Wissenschaftliche Buchgesellschaft, 1993). Those who seek more literature will also find an expanded bibliography in this book. Another overview that seeks to make the ten commandments relevant for today, with a meditative reflection, can be found in André Chouraqui, *Les dix commandements aujourd'hui: Dix paroles pour réconcilier l'homme avec l'humain* (Paris: Laffont, 2000). See also Joëlle Ferry, "Le décalogue, une loi pour l'homme?," *Revue de l'Institut Catholique de Paris* 80 (2001) 155-170; and Marc-Alain Ouaknin, *Les dix commandements* (Paris: Seuil, 1999). With regard to the Jewish point of view, see, for example, Mose Weinfeld, "The Decalogue: Its Significance, Uniqueness, and Place in Israel's Tradition," *Religion and Law: Biblical-Judaic and Islamic Perspectives*, ed. Edwin Firmage,

we shall look more closely at a concrete directive from this text, namely the prohibition of murder, both against the background of the text itself and in the light of the history of its subsequent reception and implementation.[3]

a. The Decalogue in Exodus 20:1-17

1. The Text

[1]Then God spoke all these words: [2]I am the Lord your God, who brought you out of the land of Egypt, out of the house of slavery; [3]you shall have no other gods before me.

Bernard Weiss and John Welch (Winona Lake, IN: Eisenbrauns, 1990) 3-47; Mose Weinfeld, "The Uniqueness of the Decalogue and Its Place in Jewish Tradition," *The Ten Commandments in History and Tradition*, Publications of the Perry Foundation for Biblical Research, ed. Ben-Zion Segal and Gershon Levi (Jerusalem: Perry Foundation for Biblical Research, 1990) 1-44; and in the same book, also the more general Moshe Greenberg, *The Decalogue Tradition Critically Examined*, 83-119.

[3] The present section is a (partial) reworking of Bénédicte Lemmelijn, "'Als je mijn volgeling wil zijn, pleeg je geen moord': De betekenis van Exodus 20,13 in de context van de decaloog," *De verruwing voorbij: Over de kwetsbaarheid van alle leven*, Cahier voor vredestheologie, 20 / Pax Christi-Pocket, ed. Roger Burggraeve, Johan De Tavernier, Didier Pollefeyt and Jo Hanssens (Leuven: Davidsfonds, 2004) 151-177. The footnotes in the contribution just mentioned furthermore refer to particular studies that were especially inspiring for this section too, namely, among others, Jan Holman, *De tien geboden in het Oude Testament*, 11-44; Axel Graupner, *Die zehn Gebote*, 61-95; and especially Cornelis Houtman, *Exodus: Vertaald en verklaard*. Vol. 2: *Exodus 7:14–19:25*, Commentaar op het Oude Testament (Kampen: Kok, 1989); and Cornelis Houtman, *Exodus: Vertaald en verklaard*. Vol. 3: *Exodus 20–40*, Commentaar op het Oude Testament (Kampen: Kok, 1996). These commentaries have been translated, respectively in Cornelis Houtman, *Exodus*. Vol. 2: *Exodus 7:14–19:25*, Historical Commentary on the Old Testament (Leuven: Peeters, 1996); and Cornelis Houtman, *Exodus*. Vol. 3: *Exodus 20–40*, Historical Commentary on the Old Testament (Leuven: Peeters, 2000).

⁴You shall not make for yourself an idol, whether in the form of anything that is in heaven above, or that is on the earth beneath, or that is in the water under the earth. ⁵You shall not bow down to them or worship them; for I the Lord your God am a jealous God, punishing children for the iniquity of parents, to the third and the fourth generation of those who reject me, ⁶but showing steadfast love to the thousandth generation of those who love me and keep my commandments. ⁷You shall not make wrongful use of the name of the Lord your God, for the Lord will not acquit anyone who misuses his name. ⁸Remember the sabbath day, and keep it holy. ⁹For six days you shall labour and do all your work. ¹⁰But the seventh day is a sabbath to the Lord your God; you shall not do any work – you, your son or your daughter, your male or female slave, your livestock, or the alien resident in your towns. ¹¹For in six days the Lord made heaven and earth, the sea, and all that is in them, but rested the seventh day; therefore the Lord blessed the sabbath day and consecrated it. ¹²Honour your father and your mother, so that your days may be long in the land that the Lord your God is giving you. ¹³You shall not murder. ¹⁴You shall not commit adultery. ¹⁵You shall not steal. ¹⁶ You shall not bear false witness against your neighbour. ¹⁷ You shall not covet your neighbour's house; you shall not covet your neighbour's wife, or male or female slave, or ox, or donkey, or anything that belongs to your neighbour.

2. The Literary Context

If one wishes to read, comprehend, analyse and discuss a biblical pericope, then it is essential that one first situates the text in its literary context. Indeed, no biblical text stands isolated on its own. Every text is part of a broader framework to which it gives meaning and from which it likewise receives meaning. When one takes a biblical text out of its context, then, as we have seen in part II in the discussion of fundamentalistic approaches to the Bible, it can lead to interpretations that were never originally intended and that make the (isolated) text arbitrarily say whatever one wants. Therefore, the text of the Decalogue in Exodus 20:1-17, if it is to be understood correctly, must first be defined and situated in both its immediate and its broader literary contexts.

The "ten words" in Exodus 20:1-17 is like a gift wrapped in many layers of packaging, like the prize in the children's party game, "pass the parcel." The gift is packed in a box, then stuffed into a larger box and finally wrapped in colourful paper. The Decalogue, like all biblical texts, is not an isolated unit. It is carefully wrapped in its broader literary context and then again in its immediate context. Moreover, the text itself functions in an introductory manner by presenting the guiding principles for the interpretation of what follows it.

In its broader context, this text is firstly part of the larger whole that is Exodus 19–40. This part of the book of Exodus tells of how Israel and God, after the exodus from Egypt and the long trek through the desert during which their relationship was clarified and purified, finally conclude a "covenant" that states the conditions and lays down the foundations for life in the Promised Land. In its immediate context, the Decalogue is introduced by Exodus 19:1-25. This is a pericope that sets the scene for the actual meeting with God, creating the atmosphere, and that should in fact be read together with the "ten words." Exodus 20:1-17, the Decalogue itself, is followed by a short description of Israel's reaction to God's appearance (vv. 18-21), finally transitioning into the beginning of the so-called "Book of the Covenant" (Exodus 20:22–23:33), a *crux interpretum*,[4] in which a whole series of more

---

[4] In this regard see, Hans Ausloos, *Deuteronomi(sti)sche elementen in Genesis–Numeri: Een onderzoek naar criteria voor identificatie op basis van een literaire analyse van de epiloog van het 'Verbondsboek' (Exodus 23,20-33)*, 3 delen, Unpublished doctoral dissertation, Promoter Marc Vervenne (Leuven, 1996); Hans Ausloos, "The 'Angel of yhwh' in Exod. xxiii 20-33 and Judg. ii 1-5: A Clue to the 'Deuteronom(ist)ic' Puzzle?," *Vetus Testamentum* 58 (2008) 1-12;

detailed and very specific laws are formulated. As such, the Decalogue in Exodus 20:1-17 forms the core of "God's Rulebook." It
is, as it were, the concise formulation upon which the other regulations depend.

3. A Historically Situated and Evolved Text

While the second chapter of the second part of this book makes the
general assertion that biblical texts are proclaimed and developed
literature, this is particularly true in the case of the text of the
Decalogue. More than likely, most readers came to know of the
Decalogue as a simple list of "ten commandments" during cate-
chism classes or Sunday school. Alas, the biblical text itself is a
lot less unequivocal. In fact, the number, subdivision, and order of
the prescripts handed down are hotly debated.[5]

Hans Ausloos, "The Risks of Rash Textual Criticism Illustrated on the Basis of
the Numeruswechsel in Exod 23:20-33," *Biblische Notizen* 97 (1999) 5-12; Hans
Ausloos, "Exod 23,20-33 and the 'War of yhwh'," *Biblica* 80 (1999) 555-563;
Hans Ausloos, "Deuteronomi(sti)c Elements in Exod 23,20-33? Some Methodo-
logical Remarks," *Studies in the Book of Exodus: Redaction – Reception – Inter-
pretation*, ed. Marc Vervenne, Bibliotheca Ephemeridum Theologicarum Lovanien-
sium, 126 (Leuven: Peeters/University Press, 1996) 481-500; Hans Ausloos, "The
Septuagint Version of Exod 23:20-33: A 'Deuteronomist' at Work?," *Journal of
Northwest Semitic Languages* 22/2 (1996) 89-106. Cf. also Eckart Otto, *Wandel
der Rechtsbegründungen in der Gesellschaftsgeschichte des antiken Israel: Eine
Redaktionsgeschichte des 'Bundesbuches' Ex XX 22–XXIII 13*, Studia Biblica, 3
(Leiden: Brill, 1988); and Ludger Schwienhorst-Schönberger, *Das Bundesbuch
(Ex 20,22–23,33)*, Beihefte zur Zeitschrift für die alttestamentliche Wissenschaft,
188 (Berlin/New York: de Gruyter, 1990). *Infra,* in the second section of this
chapter, the "book of the Covenant" also comes repeatedly to the fore.
   [5] See Cornelis Houtman, *Exodus, vertaald en verklaard.* Vol. 3, 15-17. Concerning the number, see also for example Paul L. Maier, "Enumerating the
Decalogue: Do We Number the Ten Commandments Correctly?," *Concordia
Journal* 16 (1990) 18-26; Ronald Youngblood, "Counting the Ten Commandments," *Bible Review* 10 (1994) 30-35, 50-52.

As far as the *number* and with it the related issue of the subdivision are concerned, there is a difference between the Jewish view, the Roman Catholic vision based on the Church fathers Clement of Alexandria and Augustine, and the option taken by the Eastern Churches that appeal to Philo of Alexandria and Josephus. Protestant opinions are divided. At the centre of the debate are the questions of whether the introduction in Exodus 20:2 also functions as a commandment, whether Exodus 20:3-6 should be split into two independent prescripts and whether the same should also be done with Exodus 20:17.

Alongside the number, the *order* also differs in the various traditions of the text. The Masoretic (the accepted Hebrew *textus receptus*) and the Septuagint (the oldest Greek translation) versions of both Exodus 20 and Deuteronomy 5, the versions passed down by both Philo of Alexandria and Pseudo-Philo, and finally the versions found in the Nash Papyrus (a papyrus that originated in Egypt between the second century BC and the first century AD) all differ in their respective ordering. It primarily concerns the sequence of verses 13, 14 and 15. Furthermore, elsewhere in the Bible, when the commandments of the Decalogue are mentioned together, they are not always quoted in the order found in Exodus 20. This is the case for example in the Old Testament texts of Jeremiah 7:9 or Hosea 4:2 and in the Gospels according to Matthew 19:18-19, Mark 10:19 and Luke 18:20.

In *which moment* should the appearance of the present version of Exodus 20 be situated?[6] The ancient belief that Moses was the author of the Decalogue can be retained in so far as it concerns a number of fundamental, and indeed possibly very old, prescripts. However, they were probably only redacted into their current form during or after the Babylonian exile (587-537 BC). Moreover, it is

---

[6] See Cornelis Houtman, *Exodus, vertaald en verklaard*. Vol. 3, 20.

clear that the "ten words," which function as the summary of and guide to God's directives, cannot have come about at the beginning of the development, but rather, by virtue of their very nature, can only have come about as a synthetic reflection that aims, as it were, to present a "credo" of the relationship of Israel to its God.[7]

In addition, there is the fact that, as already pointed out in the second chapter of the first part of this book, the contemporary reader is always a "third party" when reading the Decalogue today. The "ten words" are not addressed to people of the twenty-first century. The *original addressees* of the Decalogue in Exodus 20:1-17 seem, first of all, to be the people of Israel, or more specifically, the individual, adult, male Israelite. Based on the content of Exodus 20:1-17, it addresses someone who is the head of a family and who has a say over his family members and subordinates, someone who takes part in the cult and who has considerable possessions at his disposal.[8] Someone who, to put in Greek terms, has time to devote himself to the "*politeia*" of religion, culture and politics, because others support him in sorting out the more practical aspects

---

[7] See also Jan Holman, *De tien geboden*, 18. See also Axel Graupner, *Die zehn Gebote*, 62: "Der Dekalog steht nicht am Anfang der Geschichte von Recht und Ethos in Israel, sondern eher an ihrem Ende." In the same way, the central commandment of Leviticus 19:18 concerning love of neighbour is not the origin of all the other concrete prescripts that surround it but rather a concise summary that developed to capture what the rest was really all about. In this regard see Werner H. Schmidt, Holger Delkurt and Axel Graupner, *Die zehn Gebote*, 147-148.

[8] See also David Clines, "The Ten Commandments: Reading from Left to Right," *Words Remembered, Texts Renewed*, ed. Jon Davies, Journal for the Study of the Old Testament. Supplement Series, 195 (Sheffield: Sheffield Academic Press, 1995) 102-103: "It is, in short, one might say a balding Israelite urban male with a mid-life crisis and a weight problem, in danger of losing his faith" and 110: "a member of the Volvo driving, property-owning class." See also John Barton, *Ethics and the Old Testament* (Harrisburg, PA: Trinity Press International, 1998) 5: "(...) broadly speaking the kind of person who had the vote in most Western democracies a century ago."

of life. Or, to put it yet another way, someone who belongs to the *"deinde philosophari,"* because others take care of his *"primum vivere."* Concretely, this means that women, children and slaves are not, or at least not directly, taken into consideration at all.

This fact, however, cannot and may not be used as a pretext to simply dismiss the content of the Decalogue's prescripts or to dismiss the text, from a feminist perspective, as outmoded and irrelevant. It is true that not everyone is a man, but it is also true that not every man who reads the Decalogue today is an Israelite. Not only the Decalogue, but every Bible text is, in its style, formulation and content, culturally and historically specific. Nevertheless, this limitation can be easily transcended by a broader, contemporary interpretation of the intrinsically rich meaning of the pericope's content. After all, as a result of a well-defined historical-cultural context, the Decalogue may indeed primarily be addressed to the male Israelite, but this in no way implies that its prescripts were also only meant to apply to one group. One must, in this instance, distinguish between the addressees and the validity of the prescripts.[9] The commandments indeed seem to protect not only the male Israelite but are valid for all Israelites, whatever there social status or gender may be. This social concern, incidentally, is clearly expressed in the explication of the Sabbath law (Exodus 20:8-11) that applies not only to the man but also to his wife, his children, his male and female slaves, his guests (the alien) and even to his animals.

In conclusion, one can say that the Decalogue, ultimately passed down as the "ten words," is in any case the result of a complex evolutionary process. Various building blocks (consider the classical

---

[9] See for example Athalya Brenner, "An Afterword: The Decalogue — Am I an Adressee?," *Feminist Companion to Exodus and Deuteronomy*, ed. Athalya Brenner, The Feminist Companion to the Bible, 6 (Sheffield: Sheffield Academic Press, 1994) 255-258.

diachronic exegetical research that primarily found Priestly and
Deuteronomistic elements in the Decalogue) have together given
form to the whole. Perhaps this was done on the basis of a sort of
"primal Decalogue." Nevertheless, on that point there is still disa-
greement between scholars. What is, however, very likely and
almost certain is the fact that a number of editors worked on it.[10]
With this we reach the core of what was described at the end of part
II, namely the awareness of the fact that the biblical texts present
themselves as literature that grew and developed over time (cf. diachronic textual studies). The final result (which is the focus of synchronic study) nonetheless appears to be intended as a self-contained
whole comprising ten prescripts. In this regard, the biblical number
ten possibly symbolised the all-encompassing nature of God's laws
while at the same time functioned as a mnemonic tool.

4. Theological Meaning and Function

The end product of Exodus 20:1-17 is a carefully composed theological whole in two respects. Both form and content testify to a
profound reflection on the core of the relationship between people
themselves and between people and God.

In terms of *form*, the common name given to the Decalogue —
the "Ten Commandments" — is in fact an inadequate title. An
attentive reading of Exodus 20:1-17 immediately reveals that most
of the provisions are not actually formulated as commands, but
rather as prohibitions. This is clearly apparent in the original

[10] A lot has been written about this. See, by way of example, Frank Lothar
Hossfeld, *Der Dekalog: Seine späten Fassungen, die originale Komposition und
seine Vorstufen*, Orbis Biblicus et Orientalis, 45 (Freiburg/Göttingen: Herder,
1982); André Lemaire, "Le décalogue: Essai d'histoire de la rédaction," *De la
Torah au Messie,* ed. Maurice Carrez (Paris: Desclée, 1981) 159-195; Bernard
Lang, "Neues über den Dekalog," *Theologische Quartalschrift* 164 (1984)
58-65.

Hebrew text; the repetition of the negative particle לֹא (*lo*) immediately catches one's eye. The prescripts rendered in Exodus 20:1-17 are formulated as apodictic law. Apodictic law is characterised by the formulation of unequivocal prescripts. The mention of sanctions in the event that the laws are transgressed is usually omitted. In casuistic law on the other hand — which is formulated conditionally (if…, then…) — the penalty is indeed mentioned. As an apodictic collection, the Decalogue also makes no mention of sanctions with regard to those who do not follow the law.

The formulation of the Decalogue as a series of prohibitions may at first provoke resistance in today's readers, people who live in the post-modern society of the twenty-first century, which deludes them with the vision of their absolute, seemingly unassailable autonomy. Against the background of this contemporary sensitivity, attempts are often made to formulate the prohibitions of the Decalogue in a positive way, thereby respecting this notion of freedom. Well now, this positive formulation in the form of a commandment is in fact precisely what limits freedom. Indeed, upon closer inspection, the fact that the Decalogue predominantly consists of prohibitions creates a large degree of freedom. Or, as Jan Holman puts it: "The predominantly negative formulation appears to be an ingenious way of guaranteeing the future validity of the Decalogue. […] After all, a positive wording would always require re-adjustment in accordance with the altered circumstances. Moreover, a Decalogue that was already concretely fleshed out would not appeal as strongly to our own moral responsibility and creativity."[11] In the final analysis, a command states in absolute terms what must be

---

[11] Jan Holman, *De tien geboden*, 20: "De overwegend negatieve formulering blijkt een geniale vondst om de geldigheid van de decaloog voor de toekomst te garanderen. […] Een positieve verwoording zou immers telkens weer om bijstelling vragen, overeenkomstig de veranderende omstandigheden. Bovendien zou een reeds concreet ingevulde decaloog niet zo sterk appelleren aan onze eigen morele verantwoordelijkheid en creativiteit."

done; a prohibition provides a boundary that may not be crossed, but otherwise leaves open a whole range of positive possibilities. In this sense, the Decalogue aims to provide boundaries that — quoting Houtman —must "be observed, so that the relationship of YHWH with Israel will not be disturbed. [...] As outlining the parameters, the requirements mean to avert chaos and preserve harmony and order in society."[12] The Decalogue is, in this sense, primarily understood as an appeal to our own responsibility.

In terms of *content*, one can distinguish two kinds of prescript in Exodus 20:1-17.[13] Very generally, one can make a distinction between verses 3-11 on the one hand and verses 12-17 on the other. The first part, Exodus 20:3-11, defines the relationship between Israel and YaHWeH. The second part, Exodus 20:12-17, is mainly concerned with laying down rules of a social nature, namely with respect to one's parents and one's neighbours. Yet even these social ordinances are inspired by the authority of YaHWeH such that they likewise become religious prescripts. The whole of Exodus 20:3-17 should, for that matter, be read against the background of the introduction in Exodus 20:1-2, in which YaHWeH bases his legitimacy as Israel's God on the fact that he liberated them from Egypt. Incidentally, these introductory verses capture three of the fundamental characteristics of Old Testament spirituality, namely its historical ground, the prohibition of idols and YaHWeH's claim to exclusivity.[14] With regard to the latter, it should however be noted that this exclusivity in the context of the Decalogue expresses more of a henotheistic than a monotheistic tone. Henotheism professes one god who, in comparison with other gods, is held to be superior. I.e., there is no *a priori* denial of the potential existence of other gods.

---

[12] Cornelis Houtman, *Exodus*. Vol. 3: *Exodus 20–40*, 12.
[13] *Ibid.*
[14] See Jan Holman, *De tien geboden*, 19.

Mature monotheism, on the other hand, acknowledges the existence of only one god and therefore also only worships this one god. In actual fact, the Decalogue in Exodus 20 is far from being the only collection of prescripts on the Old Testament. The "ten commandments" as such herald the so-called "Book of the Covenant" (Exodus 20:22–23:33), which records an extensive collection of many more specific ordinances. Then there is also, for example, the so-called "Holiness Code" in Leviticus 17–26. Finally, there are obviously the numerous laws and prescripts in the book of Deuteronomy. Nevertheless, in both this context and in the later reception history, the Decalogue has earned a special, perhaps even unique, place.[15] Three features underscore the power of its prescripts.[16] First, the use of the number "ten" underlines the importance of the Decalogue. Second, the grammatical use of direct speech, namely the fact that YaHWeH himself promulgates and proclaims the prescripts, has also in no small way contributed to the importance attached to Exodus 20.[17] Indeed, although only verses 3-6 are, strictly speaking, written as direct speech, the whole of the Decalogue is, of course, interpreted as YaHWeH's own law.[18] This means that the Decalogue is given weighty, if not indeed the weightiest, authority.[19] Finally, and with this we perhaps touch upon the core of the matter, the Decalogue appears to function as a sort of framework of interpretation[20] that is applicable to religion in general and to Israel's religion in particular. It primarily concerns

---

[15] See, in this regard, also Patrick Miller, "The Place of the Decalogue in the Old Testament and its Law," *Interpretation* 43 (1989) 229-242.

[16] See Cornelis Houtman, *Exodus, vertaald en verklaard.* Vol. 3, 19.

[17] See, for example, Ernest W. Nicholson, "The Decalogue and the Direct Address of God," *Vetus Testamentum* 27 (1977) 422-433.

[18] See, Cornelis Houtman, *Exodus, vertaald en verklaard.* Vol. 3, 19.

[19] See Jan Holman, *De tien geboden,* 15.

[20] See Cornelis Houtman, *Exodus, vertaald en verklaard.* Vol. 3, 21.

the relationship between God and humanity. This has meant that
the Decalogue has, over the course of history, also exercised a
relativising function with regard to the countless other, more specifically cultic and ritual, prescripts that have been handed down.
In the Decalogue, one finds, as is often stated today by those following in the footsteps of Norbert Lohfink, the expression of
unchangeable ethical values (the foundational principles), while
other rules and prescripts relate more to changeable ideas and time-
specific issues (the concrete application).[21] In this way, the Decalogue developed into, in Cornelis Houtman's words, a "constitution for YHWH's pact with Israel."[22] More concretely we could say:
"All in all, anyone who acknowledges YHWH as his Lord finds in
the Decalogue a number of clear rules which are not to be transgressed under any circumstance."[23]

[21] See Norbert Lohfink, "Kennt das Alte Testament einen Unterschied von
'Gebot' und 'Gesetz'? Zur bibeltheologischen Einstufung des Dekalogs," *Studien
zur biblische Theologie*, ed. Norbert Lohfink, Stuttgarter Biblische Aufsätzbande.
Altes Testament, 16 (Stuttgart: Katholisches Bibelwerk, 1993) 206-238. Cf. also
Norbert Lohfink, *Bibelauslegung im Wandel* (Frankfurt am Main: Knecht, 1967).
See also Axel Graupner, *Die zehn Gebote*, 93.
[22] Cornelis Houtman, *Exodus*. Vol. 3: *Exodus 20–40*, 7 "The number of cultic
and moral rules in the Pentateuch is large. All express the will of God, but their
multiplicity and diversity obscures the foundations of the relationship between
YHWH and Israel, the essentials of how the relationship is to be sustained. The
decalogue provides the needed clarity. With a variant on Matt. 22:40 one could
say: on these ten commandments hang all the law and the prophets." In this
regard, see also, Frank Lothar Hossfeld, "Der Dekalog als Grundgesetz: Eine
Problemanzeige," *Liebe und Gebot: Studien zum Deuteronomium*, ed. Reinhard
G. Kratz and Hermann Spieckermann, Forschungen zur Religion und Literatur
des Alten und Neuen Testaments, 190 (Göttingen: Vandenhoeck & Ruprecht,
2000) 46-59. Cf. also Werner H. Schmidt, Holger Delkurt and Axel Graupner,
Die zehn Gebote, 148: "Allerdings möchte wohl schon der Dekalog selbst als
Zusammenfassung der Grenzziehungen und Anstöße zur Lebensführung, als eine
Art Grundsatzprogramm, verstanden werden."
[23] Cornelis Houtman *Exodus*. Vol. 3: *Exodus 20–40*, 7.

Against the background described above, what follows will, by way of example and on the basis of the discussion of a particular concrete prohibition, namely the prohibition of murder, demonstrate how this foundational norm has been broadened during the course of its interpretation history.

b. The Prohibition of Murder in Exodus 20:13

1. The Text and Its Original Meaning

The original Hebrew text of Exodus 20:13 only consists of two words: לא תרצח, a negative particle (*lo*) and a verb form (*tirzach*). Analysed grammatically, it concerns a *qal yiqtol* second person singular of the root רצח (*ratzach*), which in this respect is called a *prohibitivus* and which facilitates the expression of a prohibition in legal texts.[24] Literally translated it reads: "You may not murder." Incidentally, it should be noted that the New Revised Standard Version translation quoted above — "You shall not murder" — more closely and adequately renders the Hebrew text than the widespread "Thou shalt not kill" found in, among others, the King James Version and the New American Bible.

In actual fact, the meaning of this text is relatively limited in its original context. The verb used, רצח (*ratzach*), which means "to kill," is actually an appropriate term chosen from others that have a similar meaning, namely מות (*mut:* to die), הרג (*harag:* to murder, to slaughter) and קטל (*qatal:* to kill). This term very specifically means the killing *of* a person *by* a person, in other words, the act of killing where a person is both the subject (in this case an

---

[24] Bruce K. Waltke and Michael P. O'Connor, *An Introduction to Biblical Hebrew Syntax* (Winona Lake, IN: Eisenbrauns, 1990) 510: "A *non-perfective of prohibition* expresses negative instruction in legal literature. The use of לא with the non-perfective is common in legislative contexts."

Israelite) and the (implicitly) suffering object of the action.[25] Taken
on its own, this term refers to killing, with or without malice afore-
thought. However, in the specific context of the Decalogue, the
term more than likely refers to premeditated murder. After all,
unintentional manslaughter could not reasonably be the object of
an apodictic prohibition. Someone who is deeply convinced that the
killing of another person is principally and absolutely impermis-
sible can still of course, as a result of (extreme) circumstances, lose
control and kill someone. In addition to the literal meaning of
murder, the prohibition can also be interpreted figuratively as "indi-
rect killing," such as that which may result from malicious plots,
degrading exploitation, and humiliation through base scandal and
lies. An example of such a use of the term can be found in Ecclesiasticus 34:26-27: "To take away a neighbour's living is to commit murder; to deprive an employee of wages is to shed blood."

When one reads Exodus 20:13 — "You may not murder" — in
its literary context, then, it would appear that this apodictic prohibition is really about a social norm. Incidentally, remember that
Exodus 20:13, as has already been explained above, is part of the
"social" section of the Decalogue (20:12-17). The prohibition of
murder should, first and foremost, prevent the undermining of
coexistence in society. Said in very concrete terms, this means that,
in the context of the Decalogue as described above, it is addressed
to the Israelite with regard to his fellow citizen. This implies that
Exodus 20:13, at least in its original context and meaning, is not
applicable to the (legally applied) death penalty or the killing of
one's fellow human beings in a war situation (pacifism), nor to
abortion or euthanasia, nor to the killing of animals (vegetarianism)
or suicide.[26] If one were to propose this, then the biblical narratives,

<hr />

[25] See Cornelis Houtman, *Exodus, vertaald en verklaard*. Vol. 3, 68.
[26] See Cornelis Houtman, *Exodus, vertaald en verklaard*. Vol. 3, 69-70; see
also Werner H. Schmidt, Holger Delkurt and Axel Graupner, *Die zehn Gebote*,
107-108, especially 111: "Allerdings bleibt das sechste Gebot thematisch, vom

which aim to provide the reader with exemplary guidance, would themselves be in constant transgression of this law. Exodus 20:13 is, in the literary and theological context of the Decalogue, primarily meant to be a prescript that addresses the problem of murder as a factor in the breakdown of society. It articulates a prohibition of the killing of one's fellow human being as "undermining society."[27]

2. The Prohibition of Murder and Its Biblical Elaboration

The fact that Exodus 20:13, when its context as a social prescript is strictly observed, is only applicable to the premeditated killing of a fellow human being has not prevented a much broader interpretation of this verse during the course of the Bible's reception history. In practice, it is in fact used as an argument against the death penalty, and against waging war as a solution to conflicts, and as an argument in support of respect for life. This broader interpretation is based on the elaboration in both the New Testament and the broader theological horizon of the Old Testament itself.

Jesus' preaching in the New Testament extends the figurative meaning that "murder" had already been given in the Old Testament (see above), albeit not *ex nihilo*, in a remarkable fashion (see, for example, Matthew 5:21-22 and 1 John 3:15).[28] Not only is a person that literally murders someone else found guilty of murder, but so too are those who exploit, hate, belittle and are otherwise

Sachbereich her, eingeschränkt; es umfaßt nicht das durch die Gemeinschaft bzw. deren Institution beschlossene oder vollzogene Töten, den Krieg, die gerichtliche Todesstrafe, erst recht nicht die Tiertötung."

[27] Cornelis Houtman, *Exodus*. Vol. 3: *Exodus 20–40*, 60; see also Werner H. Schmidt, Holger Delkurt and Axel Graupner, *Die zehn Gebote*, 109: "Das Gebot sucht das Leben des Nächsten zu schützen, so den inneren Frieden der Gemeinschaft — vor tieferen Störungen — zu bewahren."

[28] For a more detailed discussion of the relationship between Exodus 20:13 and Matthew 5:21-22, see Piet Van Boxel, "You Have Heard that It Was Said," *Bijdragen, tijdschrift voor filosofie en theologie* 49 (1988) 362-377.

cruel. This radicalisation of Exodus 20:13 ultimately results in the transformation of the prohibition of murder into a commandment to love one's fellow human being.[29] Nevertheless, even in this context, it must be added that this very same commandment — that is in fact literally quoted — also comes from the Old Testament.[30] In any case, the boundary that the prohibition in Exodus 20:13 lays down (and which obviously also defines that which is desirable) appears to have been transformed, in the New Testament, into an ideal.

In the *Old Testament*, the prohibition of murder in Exodus 20:13, which, as shown above, was in its immediate literary and cultural-historical context in fact limited to a crucial (social) rule that sought to preserve the functioning of society and was thereby addressed primarily to male, well-to-do Israelites, is opened up in a twofold manner. First, it is expanded in the light of a deeply rooted, fundamental respect for life, over which YaHWeH alone has control and decides. Second, it is remarkably enriched by the hope in an (end-time) messianic peace, which, by its very nature, is averse to every form of violence, and thus *a fortiori* to death.

In the Old Testament, the prohibition of murder is, theologically, first grafted onto the fundamental respect for life in general. With this, reference is made to the fact that the human being is created in God's image and likeness, meaning that the human being is thus under a higher protection. God is the one who created life, created everything, and assigned human beings their place in it. As such,

[29] See, as part of the double commandment, for example Matthew 22:37-39; Luke 10:27; Romans 13:9; Galatians 5:14. See Cornelis Houtman, *Exodus, vertaald en verklaard*. Vol. 3, 70.

[30] Cf. Deuteronomy 6:4-9; 11:13-21; Numbers 15:37-41 regarding what concerns the love of God and Leviticus 19:18, 34 with regard to the relationship to one's neighbour. See also in this regard Werner H. Schmidt, Holger Delkurt and Axel Graupner, *Die zehn Gebote*, 149.

YAHWEH is the Lord of creation and Master of life and death.[31] Life belongs to him alone. A noteworthy example of this theological train of thought, which refers to Genesis 1:26-28, can be found in Genesis 9:6: "Whoever sheds the blood of a human, by a human shall that person's blood be shed; for in his own image God made humankind." In this verse, the prohibition of murder is legitimised on the basis of the belief that the human being is made in the image of God.[32]

In addition, the Old Testament is permeated by the prophetically inspired anticipation of the dawning of the messianic age. The associated hope in a blessed future captures both the idea of peace among people (and peoples) and the idea of peace among animals as the definitive and final triumph over death.[33] Peace between peoples implies the absence of war, of weapons and thus also of death. What is striking here is that the peoples consciously place themselves under God's rule. He is the one who administers justice and offers wisdom. In other words, this ultimate peace is not a

---

[31] See also the theology of the so-called "Plague narrative" in Exodus 7–11. The story alls aims to demonstrate that YAHWEH is Lord over life and death. Cf., in this respect, also Bénédicte Lemmelijn, "Not Fact, Yet True: Historicity versus Theology in the 'Plague Narrative' (Ex. 7–11)," *Old Testament Essays* 20 (2007) 395-417.

[32] This reflective, theological background as the basis for the prohibition of murder is not discussed in Exodus 20:13 itself. See Cornelis Houtman, *Exodus, vertaald en verklaard.* Vol. 3, 69. Cf. Johan Lust, "'For Man Shall His Blood Be Shed': Gen 9,6 in Hebrew and in Greek," *Tradition of the Text: Studies Offered to Dominique Barthélemy in Celebration of his 70th Birthday*, ed. Gerhard J. Norton and Stephen Pisano, Orbis Biblicus et Orientalis, 109 (Freiburg/Göttingen: Universitätsverlag/Vandenhoeck & Ruprecht, 1991) 91-102.

[33] See Werner H. Schmidt, Holger Delkurt and Axel Graupner, *Die zehn Gebote*, 111-113; See also Jan Holman, *De tien geboden*, 33. Cf. in this regard also Heinrich Gross, *Die Idee des ewigen und allgemeinen Weltfriedens im Alten Orient und im Alten Testament*, Trierer Theologische Studien, 7 (Trier: Paulinus, 1956; ²1967).

purely human achievement. Texts about the kingdom of peace can be found in, for example, Isaiah 11 or Zachariah 9:10. This idea is put very succinctly in Isaiah 2:2-4 (parallel in Micah 4:1-3):

> In days to come the mountain of the Lord's house shall be established as the highest of the mountains, and shall be raised above the hills; all the nations shall stream to it. Many peoples shall come and say, 'Come, let us go up to the mountain of the Lord, to the house of the God of Jacob; that he may teach us his ways and that we may walk in his paths.' For out of Zion shall go forth instruction, and the word of the Lord from Jerusalem. He shall judge between the nations, and shall arbitrate for many peoples; they shall beat their swords into ploughshares, and their spears into pruning-hooks; nation shall not lift up sword against nation, neither shall they learn war any more.

More all-encompassing than just peace between people, there is also a striving towards a more global harmony between human beings and nature: peace between people and animals on the one hand and peace among animals themselves on the other. With regard to the peace between people and animals, one sees incidentally two differing visions in the Old Testament.

The first, more realistic idea describes the peace as the exclusion of those wild animals that form a threat to humanity. Examples of texts that advocate this vision can be found in, among others, Leviticus 26:6 and Isaiah 35:9. Ezekiel 34:25 puts it thus:

> I will make with them a covenant of peace and banish wild animals from the land, so that they may live in the wild and sleep in the woods securely.

The other idea, perhaps somewhat more idealistically, included wild animals in its vision of peace. In this respect too, there is again a theological reference to the restoration of the original harmonious situation at the creation. Texts that articulate this view can be found, for example, in Genesis 1:29; 2:16, 19-20 and very clearly in Hosea 2:18:

I will make for you a covenant on that day with the wild animals,
the birds of the air, and the creeping things of the ground; and I will
abolish the bow, the sword, and war from the land; and I will make
you lie down in safety.

When it comes to peace among animals themselves, then we can
refer to the familiar words of Isaiah:

The wolf shall live with the lamb,
the leopard shall lie down with the kid,
the calf and the lion and the fatling together,
and a little child shall lead them.
The cow and the bear shall graze,
their young shall lie down together;
and the lion shall eat straw like the ox.
The nursing child shall play over the hole of the asp,
and the weaned child shall put its hand on the adder's den
(Isaiah 11:6-8).

The wolf and the lamb shall feed together,
the lion shall eat straw like the ox;
but the serpent – its food shall be dust!
They shall not hurt or destroy
on all my holy mountain, says the Lord (Isaiah 65:25).

This clearly expresses the idea that not only murder, i.e. violent
death, but death itself will also ultimately disappear under YaHWeH's
reign. In later Old Testament texts, this idea develops into the hope
of resurrection and life after death. An example of this can be
found in Isaiah 26:19; Psalm 22:30; 73:26 and Daniel 12:2.

In conclusion, one can say that although Exodus 20:13 cannot
and may not be expansively interpreted in its immediate context,
other Old Testament pericopes have opened up the meaning of the
prohibition of murder to a remarkable extent. As such, the task
falls to contemporary readers to think beyond the strict meaning of
the verse and to give shape to the echo of the deeper intention of
this biblical prescript. Nevertheless, this actualisation must occur

without letting go of the original text. In this regard, we quote
Werner H. Schmidt: "Die Frage nach der Gegenwartsbedeutung
der Zehn Gebote vermag der Exeget, solange er Exeget bleibt, nicht
unmittelbar zu beantworten, sondern nur soweit aufzunehmen, als
er sie an den Text zurückbinden kann und dort Anhalt findet."[34]

c. *The Decalogue and the Relevance of Biblical Ethics*

After the perhaps somewhat disenchanting reading and interpretation of the "ten words" in Exodus 20:1-17 supplied above, one can,
with both feet planted firmly in the twenty-first century, ultimately
ask the question as to what actually remains of it. The Decalogue
as a whole, and the prohibition of murder in particular, came into
existence long ago in a world that is absolutely nothing like ours.
The broader messianic perspective of peace that the other Old Testament pericopes depict and that, for Christians, was heralded by
Jesus, but that still (largely) entails an eschatological expectation,
has thus not yet come about. Many dreams, little reality...

This observation introduces a fundamental question. How can
biblical ethics in general and the Decalogue in particular still really
be relevant nearly three thousand years later? This question cannot be exhaustively dealt with within the scope of this section. It
should really form the basis of an entire study in its own right.[35]
Nevertheless, we shall attempt, primarily following in the footsteps

---

[34] See Werner H. Schmidt, Holger Delkurt and Axel Graupner, *Die zehn
Gebote*, VIII.

[35] For a thorough discussion of this issue, see John Barton, *Ethics and the Old
Testament* (Harrisburg, PA: Trinity Press International, 1998); John Barton,
"Understanding Old Testament Ethics," *Journal for the Study of the Old Testa-
ment* 9 (1978) 44-64; John Barton, "The Basis of Ethics in the Hebrew Bible,"
Semeia 66 (1995) 11-22; Walter Kaiser, *Towards Old Testament Ethics* (Grand
Rapids, MI: Eerdmans, 1983); Eckart Otto, "Forschungsgeschichte der Entwürfe

of John Barton, to tentatively formulate a few elements of an answer.[36]

It goes without saying that it is not easy to "useably" apply the ancient, culturally and historically determined material of the Old Testament to ethical reflection today. Two attitudes must be avoided in this regard. Neither the fundamentalistic acceptance of the literal text as law, simply because of the fact that it supposedly concerns *Sacred Scripture*, nor the equally fundamentalistic smoothing out of the difficulties in the text by so-called non-literal, more spiritual and symbolic interpretations can bridge the enormous gap of both time and culture in a critical, rational and responsible manner. Even a text like the Decalogue, which nevertheless widely served as a source of inspiration for Western ethical thought, is further from us than we might think, precisely because of a constant actualisation. Does that mean that we can do nothing more with this text? No. One should, however, be properly aware of the difficulties that must be taken into account when the Old Testament as a whole and the Decalogue in particular are to be brought to bear in contemporary ethical reflection. They offer no cut-and-dried answers to today's ethical problems. It is not a key that fits every lock. In this regard, it suffices to refer to the problems described in the second chapter of part I of this book.

With Barton, we can emphasise three fundamental issues in this regard.[37] First, the texts themselves are, as a result of their often strange and even violent character, sometimes shocking or at least bizarre. Immediately related to the text itself is the fact that what

einer Ethik im Alten Testament," *Verkündigung und Forschung* 36 (1991) 3-37; Eckart Otto, *Theologische Ethik des Alten Testament,* Theologische Wissenschaft, 3/2 (Stuttgart/Berlin/Cologne: Kohlhammer, 1994); Werner H. Schmidt, "Ansätze und Absichten alttestamentlicher Ethik," *Bibel und Kirche* 40 (1985) 94-100.

[36] See John Barton, *Ethics and the Old Testament*, 1-18.

[37] See *ibid.*, 5-7.

Barton calls its "underlying assumptions"[38] result in a similarly large culture shock. A second difficulty concerns the fact that, though there are very many Old Testament texts that have ethical implications, they go about things in very different and sometimes even contradictory ways, simply because they came about over a period of perhaps as much as a thousand years. Finally, the Old Testament texts reason and argue using moral categories that are often no longer ours. In this regard, consider for example the important concept of purity and impurity. All these problems make the application of Old Testament moral reflections to today's ethical context anything but simple.[39]

Does this mean that the Old Testament texts are simply "dead wood," [40] or do they, even if we deal critically with this tradition, still indeed have something to say? The answer is decidedly positive.[41] There are of course texts that are wholly out of date and that are effectively nothing more than a pile of musty, yellow paper. There are, however, also texts that touch upon the core of the human being and humanity in such a way that the message that they expound, albeit a historically coloured version, remains universally and limitlessly relevant. Such texts do not necessarily have to be religiously tinted, but the biblical tradition, which is of course religiously tinted, can at least in this way still offer rich insights, even in our contemporary culture.

When one studies the Decalogue in Exodus 20:1-17 more closely, against the abovementioned background, one must undeniably

---

[38] *Ibid.*, 5.

[39] See *ibid.*, 7: "So the initial difficulty of the proverbially bloodthirsty nature of Old Testament morality turns out to be almost the least of our troubles. Much more troublesome are the Old Testament's rootedness in a culture which is not ours, its internal contradictions, and its use of categories of thought which are alien to modern thinking about morality."

[40] *Ibid.*, 7.

[41] *Ibid.*, 7-8.

admit that this text is also clearly imbued with a social and cultural-historical context, that, at least in some respects, is (thankfully) no longer our own.[42] At the beginning of this section, for example, we already referred to the "patriarchal" context in which the Decalogue is formulated. Moreover, it seems that the prescripts concerning the relationship to God as well as the second series, which relates to the relationship with one's fellow human beings, are perceived as religious prescripts. They are, in other words, rooted in a theocratic system, in which religion was certainly not a private matter. Nevertheless, the second series of prescripts, and more specifically the very generally formulated verses concerning murder, adultery, and theft (even if adultery is here considered to be a subdivision of theft: the woman being considered the man's possession),[43] leads one to suspect that this concerns a society that shared a clear and explicit consensus regarding respect for life and for others' property. This is even more strongly apparent from the last verse which even forbids the "coveting" of another's possessions. The intention here is a state of mind that is at once generous and not jealous. So, positively speaking, in the Decalogue, even if strictly speaking it only addresses the free man, one can identify a social order that at least limits one's autonomy in the sense that it expects exclusivity with regard to the relationship with YaHWeH and demands mutual respect in relations with one's fellow human beings. It is precisely these values that are valid for all time.

Barton concludes that the Old Testament ethical considerations, understood in this way, are in fact more subtle, better thought-out

[42] *Ibid.*, 8-12.

[43] In this regard, see also Hans Ausloos and Bénédicte Lemmelijn, "Man en vrouw schiep Hij hen (Gn 1,27): Het bijbelse concept van het huwelijk en zijn receptie in de conciliaire documenten van Vaticanum II," *Levensrituelen: Het Huwelijk*, ed. Roger Burggraeve, Michel Cloet, Karel Dobbelaere and Lambert Leijssen, Kadoc-studies, 24 (Leuven: Universitaire pers Leuven, 2000) 164-178, especially 168.

and more relevant than they perhaps at first appear.[44] They contain truths and values that are so deeply human that they can offer clarification and insight to all generations. Nevertheless, a paradox again arises in this affirmation. Indeed, no matter how generally human and universal the ethical core of the Old Testament may be, the expounding of these is all the more concrete and manifold.[45] After all, the Decalogue, which is relatively general in its formulation, is, within the biblical tradition, the exception to the rule. The majority of ethical directives and implications are touched upon in the context of very concrete narratives about very contingent people and events. For this reason, the ethical thought of the Old Testament sometimes seems "maddeningly unsystematic" to modern eyes.[46] This fact stands in stark contrast to the way in which ethical reflection is nowadays done, i.e., from the principle to the application and not vice versa. According to Barton, in this regard we can find a connection in the philosophy of Martha Nussbaum, who received an honorary doctorate from the Catholic University of Leuven in 1997. Nussbaum gave new impulse to moral philosophy precisely by using particularity as a starting point in order to, accordingly, even if the formulation of general principles results, also return again to the particular and individual as the real substrate for moral judgement.[47] It is not the intention of this book to comment on this philosophy, let alone judge it. However, if Nussbaum is articulating a valid intuition

[44] See John Barton, *Ethics and the Old Testament*, 14.

[45] See *ibid.*

[46] See *ibid.*, 15.

[47] See *ibid.*, 15-16. Barton refers to Martha Craven Nussbaum, *The Fragility of Goodness: Luck and Ethics in Greek Tragedy and Philosophy* (Cambridge: Cambridge University Press, 1986); and Martha Craven Nussbaum, *Love's Knowledge: Essays on Philosophy and Literature* (New York: Oxford University Press, 1990).

with her proposition, then the Old Testament tradition, in all its determinedness and with all its concrete and historically and culturally specific formulations, may be such that it can also inspire us today in the quest for deeper, ethical insights upon which we can base our own behaviour. Perhaps, it can do so all the more in the contemporary post-modern cultural context. No matter how far removed it may be from the original *Sitz im Leben* of the Old Testament texts, post-modernity, averse as it is to great systematic discourse and coloured by a renewed sensitivity to narrativity, may ironically be more open to learning from the particularity of the Old Testament.

d. *Conclusion*

"Die Zehn Gebote suchen zwar eine Vielfalt des Lebens zu umfassen, sind jedoch mit Absicht nicht auf bestimmte Einzelsituationen bezogen, sondern reden eher grundsätzlich-allgemein und sind darum stets neu zu konkretisieren."[48] This quote summarises the preceding discussion of the Decalogue and its application to ethical reflection today. The Decalogue, through its general formulation, is intended, indeed, to be a direction giving guide,[49] the expression of a fundamental conviction that, though it may be limited by its cultural-historical context in Exodus 20:1-17, can also function as a source of moral inspiration today, and that consequently must be continuously concretely filled in. As a result, it is does not concern a number of absolute laws that YAHWEH, as a sovereign and capricious despot, imposed upon the Israelites. No obedience to

---

[48] Werner H. Schmidt, Holger Delkurt and Axel Graupner, *Die zehn Gebote*, 145.

[49] See also Axel Graupner, *Die zehn Gebote*, 94: "Die Stärke des Dekalogs liegt gerade darin, daß er nicht alles und jedes umfaßt, sondern sich auf Wesentliches konzentriert, dabei in den Formulierungen Allgemeingülltigkeit anstrebt."

alien legislation is demanded. Rather, they are the expression of YAHWEH's concern. They are founded upon the consciousness that He led Israel out of Egypt, or in other words, that He saves them and stands by them. Therefore, the Decalogue ultimately functions as an ethical call to responsibility in freedom. The human being should live in such a way that he protects the lives of others, and moreover, helps them to flourish. And that he does this in imitation of the manner of his God. Or, in the words of Werner H. Schmidt: "Die Zehn Gebote werden getragen durch die voranstehende Zusage 'dein Gott'. Dab Verbote und Gebote nicht das Allerletzte und Endgültige sind oder zu sein brauchen, deutet das Alte Testament selbst an."[50]

We conclude this section with the words of Jan Holman, who very aptly and comprehensively expresses what we have tried to say: "The great initial fact of salvation, the exodus from slavery in Egypt to the freedom of the Promised Land, casts its glow over the ten commandments. It seems to be an important element in the basic structure of the Bible. The salvation-historical indicative (God's merciful blessings) always precedes the ethical imperative (moral instructions). The indicative and imperative moods may not function separately. Alas, we lost sight of this connection. The Ten Commandments, detached from God's liberating deeds, went off and led their own life in the service of an endless, drab slavery to obligation. The new vision of the Decalogue resulted in an ethos of the grateful answer. Now, the ten words again demarcate a living space for us in which we are called to freedom, and upon which God's blessing rests."[51]

---

[50] Werner H. Schmidt, Holger Delkurt and Axel Graupner, *Die zehn Gebote*, 149.

[51] The quotation above has been translated from Dutch into English. For the original wordings, see Jan Holman, *De tien geboden*, 20: "Het grote voorafgaande heilsfeit, de uittocht uit het slavenhuis van Egypte naar de vrijheid van het

No matter how concrete and culturally and historically determined it may be, the Decalogue testifies to such a deeply human
concern that even today, albeit in completely different circumstances, it makes an appeal to our humanity. A comparable example
that pertinently raised the question of the realisation of our peaceful coexistence can be found in the Old Testament social legislation dealing with the so-called "Jubilee Year" (Leviticus 25).[52]
Historically and culturally determined as it is, this legislation can
of course not immediately be applied in our society. However, in
this too, the underlying concern, namely the maintenance of the
precarious balance between self-interest on the one hand and the
common good on the other, is so fundamental that it remains a
priority on the social agenda to this day.

2. Social Justice: The Jubilee Year in the Judeo-Christian Tradition

On 10 June 2005, the finance ministers of the G8 — the seven
richest countries and Russia — agreed to cancel the debts owed by

beloofde land, werpt zijn glans over de tien woorden. Het blijkt een belangrijk
element van de grondstructuur van de Bijbel te zijn. De heilshistorische indicatief
(Gods weldaden) gaat steeds vooraf aan de ethische imperatief (morele richtlijnen).
Die aantonende en gebiedende wijs mogen niet los van elkaar functioneren.
Helaas hadden wij hun samenhang uit het oog verloren. De tien geboden waren,
los van Gods bevrijdend handelen, een eigen leven gaan leiden in het diensthuis
van eindeloze, grauwe plichtenslavernij. De nieuwe visie op de decaloog resul-
teerde in een ethos van het dankbare antwoord. De tien woorden bakenen voor
ons nu weer een levensruimte af waarbinnen wij tot vrijheid geroepen zijn, en
waarop Gods zegen rust."

[52] In this regard, see also Hans Ausloos, "Sabbatjaar, jubeljaar, heilig jaar: De
actualiteit van een oudtestamentische traditie," *VBS-Informatie* 30 (1999) 81-96;
and particularly Hans Ausloos, "Invrijheidstelling en kwijtschelding van schuld:
Werkelijkheid of utopie? Het jubeljaar in de joods-christelijke traditie," *Krachten
voor de toekomst. Lessen voor de xxiste eeuw*, ed. Bart Raymaekers and André
van de Putte (Leuven: Leuven University Press, 2000) 118-142.

eighteen of the world's poorest countries to, among others, the International Monetary Fund. This is thanks to the efforts of countless people over the years — from the singer Bono, of the Irish rock group U2, to Pope John Paul II — to bring an end to the unbearable burden of debt borne by many so-called Third World countries.[53] After all, when nations sometimes have to annually spend more than a third of their available resources settling national debt — whatever its origins may be — and in so doing barely retain enough resources for healthcare or education, one can certainly speak of an unbearable burden. Indeed, in such countries, the repayment of national debt paves the way for a downward spiral into poverty for the entire population.

It is no coincidence that it is often these countries that are regularly discussed with regard to all sorts of slavery that affect large parts of the population. Indeed, poverty and slavery still seem to be inextricably linked to one another, even at the beginning of the twenty-first century. Despite the fact that the Slavery Convention was signed in 1926 and the fact that the Universal Declaration of Human Rights prohibits slavery and human trafficking, according to the organisation *Anti-Slavery International*, approximately twenty million people still live in a state of debt-slavery or bonded labour.[54] Although slavery has been forbidden in the African country of Niger since 1960, a law came into force in 2004 that made it possible for the owners of slaves to be sentenced to serve long prison terms, which demonstrates that slavery still *de facto* exists.

The plea for the cancellation or at least the thorough review of the burden of international debts borne by such countries aims to cast off the burdens of the past so that, with regained freedom,

---

[53] For more information about campaigns that appeal for the cancellation of debts, see, among others *http://www.jubilee2000uk.org/* en *www://erlassjahr.de*

[54] In this regard, see http://www.antislavery.org.

however precarious that may be, a vision of a new life can be stimulated. An attempt is being made to bring about a time in which the weak and marginalised can set their lives on another course. A time that should be the beginning of the end for world-wide slavery.

This all encompassing idea of "cancellation of debt" is in no way new. It stretches back to and finds its source of inspiration in the Old Testament book of Leviticus. The twenty-fifth chapter of this book tells us that God, via Moses, orders the Israelites to declare every fiftieth year a "jubilee year." This year should be a year of "freedom": belongings lost to debt should be released and those in bondage should be given their freedom. However, these very radical precepts did not come about in a vacuum. On the contrary, they have a long and complicated prehistory. Highlights of this will be presented here.[55]

---

[55] Some outstanding studies regarding the jubilee year legislation: Rainer Albertz, "Die 'Antrittspredigt' Jesu im Lukasevangelium auf ihrem alttestament-lichen Hintergrund," *Zeitschrift für die Neutestamentliche Wissenschaft* 74 (1983) 182-206; Rainer Albertz, "Die Tora Gottes gegen die wirtschaftlichen Sach-zwänge: Die Sabbat- und Jobeljahrgesetzgebung Lev 25 in ihrer Geschichte," *Ökumenische Rundschau* 44 (1995) 290-310; Jeffrey Fager, *Land Tenure and Biblical Jubilee*, Journal for the Study of the Old Testament. Supplement Series, 155 (Sheffield: Sheffield Academic Press, 1993); Jean-François Lefèbvre, *Le jubilé biblique: Lv 25 – exégèse et théologie*, Orbis Biblicus et Orientalis, 194 (Fribourg/Göttingen: Academic Press/Vandenhoeck & Ruprecht, 2003); Arndt Meinhold, "Zur Beziehung Gott, Volk, Land im Jobel-Zusammenhang," *Bibli-sche Zeitschrift* 29 (1985) 245-261; Eckart Otto, *Theologische Ethik des Alten Testaments*, Theologische Wissenschaft, 3/2 (Stuttgart/Berlin/Cologne: Kohlham-mer, 1994) 249-256; Eckart Otto, "Wirtschaftsethik im Alten Testament," *Infor-mationes Theologiae Europae. Internationales ökumenisches Jahrbuch für Theo-logie*, ed. Ulrich Nembach, Heinrich Rusterholz and Paul Michael Zulehner (Frankfurt am Main: Lang, 1994) 279-289; Eckart Otto, *Gottes Recht als Men-schenrecht: Rechts- und literaturhistorische Studien zum Deuteronomium*, Bei-hefte zur Zeitschrift für Altorientalische und Biblische Rechtsgeschichte, 2 (Wies-baden: Harrassowitz, 2002) especially 219-239; Gnana Robinson, "Das

a. *Ancient Israel in Crisis*

1. From Inheritance to Landlordism

We can say little with certainty about the origin of the people of Israel. We can only make a general assertion from a historical point of view that Ancient Israel probably began to develop during the end of the second millennium before Christ. Nevertheless, from the material findings, we can still gain some insight into the organisation of ancient Israelite society. It probably consisted mainly of small-scale farmers and herders. Possibly in order to safeguard each family's chance of survival and to offer protection against landlordism, the principle that land could not be sold was central. After all, if one denies farmers and herders their land, then they lose their livelihood and they fall directly into a state of poverty. This rule was, moreover, also religiously motivated: the people of Israel received their land from God as an inheritance.

As it turns out, however, as time passed this principle of inheritance seems to have been observed less and less. Or was it doomed to failure from the start as a utopian vision rather than plausible reality? During the time of the monarchy (from the tenth century BC onwards), the rulers sought to expand their estates at the expense of the peasantry. The story of Naboth's vineyard in 1 Kings 21:1-29

Jobel-Jahr: Die Lösung einer sozial-ökonomischen Krise des Volkes Gottes," *Ernten, was man sät*. FS. Klaus Koch, ed. D. R. Daniels (Neukirchen-Vluyn: Neukirchener Verlag, 1991) 471-491; John van Seters, "The Law of the Hebrew Slave," *Zeitschrift für die alttestamentliche Wissenschaft* 108 (1996) 534-546; Mose Weinfeld, "Sabbatical Year and Jubilee in the Pentateuchal Laws and the Ancient Near Eastern Background," *The Law in the Bible and Its Environment*, ed. Timo Veijola (Helsinki/Göttingen: Vandenhoeck & Ruprecht, 1990) 39-62; Raymond Westbrook, *Property and the Family in Biblical Law*, Journal for the Study of the Old Testament. Supplement Series, 113 (Sheffield: Sheffield Academic Press, 1991) 36-57; Christopher J. H. Wright, "Jubilee, Year of," *Anchor Bible Dictionary* 3 (1992) 1025-1030.

testifies to such behaviour and the opposition to it. Indeed, this story is part of what is called the "Deuteronomic history," i.e. the Old Testament books of Joshua, Judges, Samuel and Kings. In general, the authors of the Deuteronomic history wanted to explain the disastrous fortunes of Ancient Israel by pointing out how it had abandoned God's commandments. And so the story of Naboth's vineyard seeks to demonstrate the wickedness of the ruling monarch, which is attributed to idolatry. According to the story, King Ahab wanted to expand the royal estates by incorporating Naboth's vineyard, which bordered on the king's palace. Ahab would have given him an even better vineyard in return or paid him for it. Naboth, however, responds as follows: "The Lord forbid that I should give you my ancestral inheritance" (1 Kings 21:3). At the instigation of the queen — the non-Israelite Jezebel — Naboth is murdered and his property is incorporated into the royal palace. The sentence that YAHWEH sends to Ahab via the prophet Elijah is clear: "In the place where dogs licked up the blood of Naboth, dogs will also lick up your blood" (1 Kings 21:19).

The loss of inherited property — one of the foundations of ancient Israelite society — and the associated social injustice is strongly opposed by the prophets from the beginning of the eighth century BC onwards. In the prophetic book of Micah, the author declares: "Alas for those who devise wickedness and evil deeds on their beds! When the morning dawns, they perform it, because it is in their power. They covet fields, and seize them; houses, and take them away; they oppress householder and house, people and their inheritance" (2:1-2). In the same period, the prophet Isaiah makes similar accusations: "Ah, you who join house to house, who add field to field, until there is room for no one but you, and you are left to live alone in the midst of the land!" (5:8); "The Lord enters into judgement with the elders and princes of his people: It is you who have devoured the vineyard [a metaphor for the people of Israel]; the spoil of the poor is in your houses. What do you mean by crushing my people, by grinding the face of the poor?" (3:14-15).

The tendency for the rich to get richer by appropriating the property and goods of others is possibly connected to the inability of many people to pay the imposed taxes, which was almost certainly the case when crops failed or there was a livestock plague. After all, the king's expeditions against neighbouring countries, the maintenance of the army and the construction of immense buildings were only possible thanks to the imposition of high taxes. Against this background, crop failure or livestock disease could have disastrous consequences in a society of farmers and pastoralists in which people were wholly at the mercy of nature. In order to be able to pay the taxes imposed, they had to borrow from more wealthy citizens who invoked stringent credit laws. Indeed, it appears that one could legitimately charge sky-high interest rates. If a debtor was not in a position to pay this interest, then the creditor was free to attach the debtor's possessions. If this did not suffice, then the creditor could take the debtor, his wife and his children into service as slaves — so-called debt slavery — or he could sell them.

2. In Search of a Way out of a Disturbed Social Order

It goes without say that such practices can entirely disrupt a community, and even destroy it. Apparently, people were already all too aware of this three thousand years ago; consider the prophetic critique of the prevailing establishment. This prophetic criticism was, furthermore, contagious. In the wake of this criticism, a number of attempts at reform were made, the results of which we find in the three most important collections of laws in the Old Testament. These are, in the order in which they were written, the so-called "Book of the Covenant" (Exodus 20:22–23:33), the "Deuteronomic Law" (Deuteronomy 12–26) and the Priestly "Law of Holiness" (Leviticus 17–26). These legal texts were not created at the same time. Rather, each collection is itself a testimony to a phase in the developmental process of the social and religious thought of Ancient Israel. Moreover, in this regard we must emphasise that these laws were not juridically enforceable. Non-compliance brought no penalty or prison term with it. Nevertheless, people were convinced that non-observance of the regulations, which of course carried the weight of God's law, profoundly disrupted the relationship with God, which defined the course of the history of Israel as a people. This religious framework of Ancient Israel implies, incidentally, that practically all Old Testament prescripts that deal with socio-economic life have a theological legitimisation.

This takes nothing away from the fact that the motive behind these prescripts — and this must apply to all laws — is the desire for a well-grounded balance between self-interest and the common good.[56] It is widely known and accepted that the pursuit of self-interest and the associated competition are important drivers of the economy.[57] The realisation of this principle implies a diversification of society into successful and less successful people, into rich and poor. However, an entrenched division between the various strata within a society is an extremely dangerous catalyst for social conflicts that can very easily escalate. Therefore, if an economic order is not to become self-destructive and is to bring the functioning of the whole of society into play, then it needs a number of

---

[56] See Eckart Otto, *Wirtschaftsethik*, 279-289.

[57] See, for example, the insights of the Scottish philosopher Adam Smith (1723-1790) in his work *Inquiry into the Nature and the Causes of the Wealth of Nations* (1776).

social mechanisms that prevent whole segments of the population from slipping into extreme poverty.

It has already been stated above that "setting free" is the central concern of the Old Testament "jubilee year." In Leviticus 25:8-10, this is concisely summarised:

> You shall count off seven weeks of years, seven times seven years, so that the period of seven weeks of years gives forty-nine years. Then you shall have the trumpet sounded loud; on the tenth day of the seventh month — on the day of atonement — you shall have the trumpet sounded throughout all your land. [10]And you shall hallow the fiftieth year and you shall proclaim liberty throughout the land to all its inhabitants. It shall be a jubilee for you: you shall return, every one of you, to your property and every one of you to your family.

This also explains the origin of the term "jubilee year." The Hebrew literally says: "it will be a *jobel*-year." It is possible that this is connected to the fact that the proclamation of the jubilee year would be sounded on the (rams)horn. The English term "jubilee year" goes back to the Vulgate. In the fourth century AD Latin translation of the Bible, the Hebrew word *jobel* is rendered into Latin using a word play — *annus jubilaeus*. With it, the Church Father gave a transcription of the Hebrew term and referred to the prevalent Latin word for *jubilum* ("shepherd's song") by which the joyful character of the jubilee is emphasised.

In the rest of Leviticus 25, this general rule of "setting free" — the Hebrew original uses the technical term דרור (*deror*) — is made more specific. Nevertheless, according to verses 11-12, the "jubilee year" must, first of foremost, be understood thus: "That fiftieth year shall be a jubilee for you: you shall not sow, or reap the aftergrowth, or harvest the unpruned vines ... you shall eat only what the field itself produces." In other words, human coexistence is central to this prescript, in which rest for people, animals and land is underscored. For this reason, we shall next consider the institution of the "sabbatical year."

b. The "Sabbatical Year" (Leviticus 25:1-7 and 18-22)

The institution of the "sabbatical year," which verses 1-7 and 18-22 deal with, is peculiar to the book of Leviticus. According to these verses, YaHWeH, via Moses, commands the Israelites to allow the land to lie fallow every seventh year once they arrive in the Promised Land:

> [1]The Lord spoke to Moses on Mount Sinai, saying: [2]Speak to the people of Israel and say to them: When you enter the land that I am giving you, the land shall observe a sabbath for the Lord. [3]For six years you shall sow your field, and for six years you shall prune your vineyard, and gather in their yield; [4]but in the seventh year there shall be a sabbath of complete rest for the land, a sabbath for the Lord: you shall not sow your field or prune your vineyard. [5]You shall not reap the aftergrowth of your harvest or gather the grapes of your unpruned vine: it shall be a year of complete rest for the land. [6]You may eat what the land yields during its sabbath — you, your male and female slaves, your hired and your bound labourers who live with you; [7]for your livestock also, and for the wild animals in your land all its yield shall be for food. (…)
>
> [18]You shall observe my statutes and faithfully keep my ordinances, so that you may live on the land securely. [19]The land will yield its fruit, and you will eat your fill and live on it securely. [20]Should you ask, 'What shall we eat in the seventh year, if we may not sow or gather in our crop?' [21]I will order my blessing for you in the sixth year, so that it will yield a crop for three years. [22]When you sow in the eighth year, you will be eating from the old crop; until the ninth year, when its produce comes in, you shall eat the old.

What the land itself yields will be sufficient to survive during the seventh and eighth years. This law is underpinned by religious arguments. Firstly, if people observe these regulations, YAHWEH will bless the land such that people will not run short. Secondly, it is said that the land must observe the Sabbath *in honour of YAHWEH*. After all, it is he who, according to Old Testament conviction, gave the land to the Israelites.

1. The "Sabbatical Year" and Its Textual Prehistory

The prescript about the "sabbatical year" had a long prehistory and is rooted in the concern for an enduring society. It may go back to an ancient farming practice that, unlike what we encounter in Leviticus, was not originally legitimised on religious grounds. We find possible evidence of this practice in the Book of the Covenant. Exodus 23:10-11 prescribes the following:

> For six years you shall sow your land and gather in its yield; but the seventh year you shall let it rest and lie fallow, so that the poor of your people may eat; and what they leave the wild animals may eat. You shall do the same with your vineyard, and with your olive orchard.

The original meaning of this prescript — which is here not yet referred to as a "sabbatical year" — possibly lies in a concern that the soil should not be completely and utterly depleted. The land too must, at the proper time, be given a chance to recuperate (the so-called *restitutio in integrum*). In addition, the "sabbatical year" has a charitable function. What the land itself brings forth is intended for the poor and the destitute. And in order to be sure that the poor would have enough food, the work in olive orchards and vineyards must also stop during the seventh year. After all, olive trees and grapevines still produce ample fruit without human intervention.

Furthermore, it should be noted that this septennial rest may not have been applied to the entire territory of Israel at the same time.

The practice may instead have been applied to sections. This is apparent from, among others, Exodus 21:2-3, where it is said that slaves should also serve for six years. This means that the "seventh year," i.e., the year of "liberation," would not be the same for all slaves. The same can be said with regard to sections of agricultural land. This arrangement implies not only that the owners never have to allow all their properties to lie fallow at the same time, which means that they are always assured of food and income, but it also ensured that it was possible to permanently alleviate the needs of the poor. They could always go to lands that were in their seventh year.

2. The Deuteronomic Elaboration of the "Sabbatical Year"

A few centuries later, the Deuteronomic reformers applied this agricultural practice to the issue of debt:

> [1]Every seventh year you shall grant a remission of debts. [2]And this is the manner of the remission: every creditor shall remit the claim that is held against a neighbour, not exacting it from a neighbour who is a member of the community, because the Lord's remission has been proclaimed. [3]From a foreigner you may exact it, but you must remit your claim on whatever any member of your community owes you. [4]There will, however, be no one in need among you, because the Lord is sure to bless you in the land that the Lord your God is giving you as a possession to occupy, [5]if only you will obey the Lord your God by diligently observing this entire commandment that I command you today. [6]When the Lord your God has blessed you, as he promised you, you will lend to many nations, but you will not borrow; you will rule over many nations, but they will not rule over you. [7] If there is among you anyone in need, a member of your community in any of your towns within the land that the Lord your God is giving you, do not be hard-hearted or tight-fisted towards your needy neighbour. [8]You should rather open your hand, willingly lending enough to meet the need, whatever it may be. [9]Be careful

that you do not entertain a mean thought, thinking, 'The seventh
year, the year of remission, is near', and therefore view your needy
neighbour with hostility and give nothing; your neighbour might cry
to the Lord against you, and you would incur guilt. [10]Give liberally
and be ungrudging when you do so, for on this account the Lord your
God will bless you in all your work and in all that you undertake.
[11]Since there will never cease to be some in need on the earth, I
therefore command you, "Open your hand to the poor and needy
neighbour in your land."

This passage (Deuteronomy 15:1-11) makes use of the motif of the
seventh year. It says that one should remit or forgive all debts
every seven years. Verse 9, perhaps unlike the Book of the Covenant, seems to suggest that this is a regulation that should be
applied throughout the country at one and the same time, an exception being made with regard to foreigners. Moreover, the Deuteronomic law is much more radical than the prescript regarding the
sabbatical year in the Book of the Covenant. The poor, weighed
down under the burden of their debts, are no longer left to depend
on what they can scrape together in the fields, although Deuteronomy continues to provide for this possibility (see Deuteronomy
24:19-22). People have apparently abandoned the rule that they
should leave the land to lie fallow every six years. According to
the Deuteronomic law, after at most six years have past, all debts
must be forgiven. The destitute are then able to start again with a
clean slate.

Such complete remission of debts is not unique to the Old Testament. One also comes across it in other cultures of the ancient Near
East. However, unlike in Deuteronomy, where it concerned a recur-
rent septennial affair, the forgiveness of debts in ancient eastern
society was an exceptional act of clemency by a ruler, for example,
on the occasion of his accession.

That the regulation concerns a cyclical remission of debts of
course has enormous material and financial consequences for the

moneyed classes. It is also not surprising, then, that these people, as the seventh year approached, would often refuse to lend to their poor compatriots. On this point, however, the Deuteronomic law shows itself to be quite ingenious. The observance of the regulation is defined as an act of divine worship and religiously legitimised: it is forgiveness *in honour of* ΥΑΗΨΕΗ. Furthermore, it emphasises that meeting the needs of poor compatriots will be rewarded by God's blessing (verses 10-11).

3. The Finalisation of the "Sabbatical Year" in Leviticus 25

Against the background of what had become, during the Babylonian exile (587-538 BC), the generally accepted religious practice of the Sabbath, which obliged one to respect the seventh day as a day of absolute rest — since God himself rested after He brought about Creation in six days — the Priestly authors of Leviticus 25 react against the all too anthropological Deuteronomic interpretation of the ancient practice of allowing the land to rest after six years. By reintroducing the "sabbatical year," they want to reinstate this custom. Nevertheless, they still consider the Deuteronomic concern that debts should be forgiven to be extremely valuable. That is why, alongside the introduction of the "sabbatical year," in which Creation's recuperation is central, most of Leviticus 25 concerns itself with the problem of debt, the aim of which is to ensure the well-being of the human person and society.

In addition to the emphasis on the sabbatical year, two series of prescripts can be distinguished in Leviticus. Verses 13-34 concern the return of forfeit property. Verses 39-55 focus on the release of people. Both complexes are connected to one another by the interest prohibition. The central position of the latter reflects the main concern of Leviticus 25. What follows discusses these three collections.

c. *The Interest Prohibition (Leviticus 25:35-38)*

1. The Text and its Underlying Concerns

In the context of Leviticus 25, the interest prohibition assumes a central position (verses 35-38). This suggests that combating extreme poverty in the population was a top priority for the author of Leviticus 25:

> [35]If any of your kin fall into difficulty and become dependent on you, you shall support them; they shall live with you as though resident aliens. [36]Do not take interest in advance or otherwise make a profit from them, but fear your God; let them live with you. [37]You shall not lend them your money at interest taken in advance, or provide them food at a profit. [38]I am the Lord your God, who brought you out of the land of Egypt, to give you the land of Canaan, to be your God.

It is no coincidence that the author of Leviticus 25 places this pre-script in the centre between regulations around the release of forfeit possessions and the setting free of people. If an Israelite falls into poverty, one may not leave him in the lurch, but must render assistance, unconditionally. If one takes this central prescript seriously, then even the remaining prescripts regarding the jubilee year — release of forfeited properties and regaining personal freedom — would in fact be unnecessary. No one would forfeit his possessions or would find themselves in such poverty that their freedom had to be put at risk. Once more, the Old Testament text testifies to a utopian ideal that at the same time however represents a call and an invitation to real solidarity.

2. The Textual Prehistory

As is the case for the prescript concerning the sabbatical year, the regulation concerning the interest prohibition in Leviticus 25 was not invented by the Levitical lawmaker. The "Book of the Covenant" already mentions it in Exodus 22:25. In this pericope, the interest prohibition is, it is true, only valid with regard to poor compatriots: "If you lend money to my people, to the poor among you, you shall not deal with them as a creditor; you shall not exact interest from them."

Whereas, according to Exodus 22, the rules surrounding the system of credit must of course apply to Israelites who were not poor, the Deuteronomic law broadened this rule to include all compatriots without exception (Deuteronomy 23:19-20):

> [19]"You shall not charge interest on loans to another Israelite, interest on money, interest on provisions, interest on anything that is lent. [20]On loans to a foreigner you may charge interest, but on loans to another Israelite you may not charge interest, so that the Lord your God may bless you in all your undertakings in the land that you are about to enter and possess."

By including all compatriots, the author shows that he is aware of the fact that "usury capitalism" can pose a threat to society as a whole. For this reason, demanding interest from people who are not Israelites is still tolerated. Demanding interest makes the borrower extremely dependent upon (the will of) the lender, and a gulf between rich creditors and impoverished debtors can develop. This can mean that a large part of the population becomes more and more impoverished. Although it is emphasised that the wealthy — wealth was considered a sign of God's blessing (Deuteronomy 28:44) — must help impoverished countrymen, they may nevertheless secure the loan by asking for something as a pledge. However, both the "Book of the Covenant" and the Deuteronomic law place limits on taking goods as a pledge: one may not touch the bare minimum that a person needs to survive. In Deuteronomy 24:6, this is made more concrete by specifically referring to a millstone. In Exodus 22:26-27 (and in Deuteronomy 24:12-13),

clothing represents these basic necessities: "If you take your neighbour's cloak in pawn, you shall restore it before the sun goes down;
for it may be your neighbour's only clothing to use as cover; in
what else shall that person sleep? And if your neighbour cries out
to me, I will listen, for I am compassionate."

By emphasising the interest prohibition, the authors of the Old
Testament collections of laws distance themselves from a purely
economic order. Regulations such as the interest prohibition are
indeed only possible if people rise above the commercial economy.
For Ancient Israel, faith in God contributed to this. Standing up for
the poor is a direct consequence of Israel's belief in a liberating
God. And, as we can see from the so-called "small historical
creed" in Deuteronomy 26:5-9, the faith experience of being liberated by God from slavery in Egypt was of overriding importance
in this regard: "When the Egyptians treated us harshly and afflicted
us, by imposing hard labour on us, we cried to the Lord, the God
of our ancestors; the Lord heard our voice and saw our affliction,
our toil, and our oppression. The Lord brought us out of Egypt with
a mighty hand and an outstretched arm, with a terrifying display
of power, and with signs and wonders; and he brought us into this
place and gave us this land, a land flowing with milk and honey."

Against this background we can also include the instructions to
release property after a period of time has passed and to free people
who are in bondage, and all the theologically motivated concerns
to ensure a balance between self-interest and the common good.

d. *Property is Released (Leviticus 25:13-34)*

1. Text and Context

Following the introduction to the "sabbatical year" in Leviticus
25:1-7, verses 8-12 summarise in a nutshell what the "jubilee

year" stands for: after seven sabbatical years have past — a year every seven years in which the land can rest "for YaHWeH" — the fiftieth year shall be a year of liberty for property and people. Against this background, the release of property forms the primary focus of verses 13-17 and 23-34:

> [13]In this year of jubilee you shall return, every one of you, to your property. [14]When you make a sale to your neighbour or buy from your neighbour, you shall not cheat one another. [15]When you buy from your neighbour, you shall pay only for the number of years since the jubilee; the seller shall charge you only for the remaining crop-years. [16]If the years are more, you shall increase the price, and if the years are fewer, you shall diminish the price; for it is a certain number of harvests that are being sold to you. [17]You shall not cheat one another, but you shall fear your God; for I am the Lord your God. (...)

> [23]The land shall not be sold in perpetuity, for the land is mine; with me you are but aliens and tenants. [24]Throughout the land that you hold, you shall provide for the redemption of the land. [25]If anyone of your kin falls into difficulty and sells a piece of property, then the next-of-kin shall come and redeem what the relative has sold. [26]If the person has no one to redeem it, but then prospers and finds sufficient means to do so, [27]the years since its sale shall be computed and the difference shall be refunded to the person to whom it was sold, and the property shall be returned. [28]But if there are not sufficient means to recover it, what was sold shall remain with the purchaser until the year of jubilee; in the jubilee it shall be released, and the property shall be returned. [29]If anyone sells a dwelling-house in a walled city, it may be redeemed until a year has elapsed since its sale; the right of redemption shall be for one year. [30]If it is not redeemed before a full year has elapsed, a house that is in a walled city shall pass in perpetuity to the purchaser, throughout the generations; it shall not be released in the jubilee. [31]But houses in villages that have no walls around them shall be classed as open country; they may be redeemed, and they shall be released in the jubilee. [32]As for the cities of the Levites, the Levites shall for ever have the right of redemption of the

houses in the cities belonging to them. [33]Such property as may be redeemed from the Levites — houses sold in a city belonging to them — shall be released in the jubilee; because the houses in the cities of the Levites are their possession among the people of Israel. [34]But the open land around their cities may not be sold; for that is their possession for all time.

As a general rule, Leviticus 25:13 states that, on the occasion of the "jubilee year," everyone must return to their original properties. If someone could not pay back his debts, then, according to the prevailing credit law, the creditor was permitted to attach the debtor's property. This had, as already mentioned, the consequence that a large portion of the land came under the control of wealthy elite.

2. The Radical Option for the Poor in Leviticus 25

Although Deuteronomy demands the cancellation of debt, we find that Leviticus 25 introduces two important reforms. First, the latter text stipulates that debts must be forgiven every fifty years instead of after seven years as in the Deutoronomic law. At first sight, this appears to be a weakening of the older law. But appearances can be deceiving. The prescripts of Leviticus 25 in fact seek at all costs to make sure that nobody ever loses their property. After all, in the context of the discussion of the interest prohibition we have already seen, from the central position that it is given, how they sought to prevent people from sliding into poverty. Furthermore, Leviticus 25 once more emphasises that land may not be sold. If one, through debt, must surrender one's property, then only the right to make use of it — the "usufruct" — falls to the creditor. The "naked property" is not transferable. This is again legitimised on religious grounds in verse 23: the land itself belongs to YaHWeH; the Israelites are only there as guests.

Next, Leviticus 25 stipulates that the debtor can get his property back earlier. To do this, he first and foremost makes an appeal to the obligations of family solidarity. Next-of-kin have the duty to buy back a piece of land that a family member has to sell out of necessity. However, the one who has lost the right of ownership can also acquire his lost property again if things have been going well for him for a while. Here too, the Priestly reformers (who composed the book of Leviticus) wish to protect the weak. They do this by means of the principle of degressive debt repayment: if a person must relinquish a piece of land shortly after a "jubilee year," but after twenty-five years acquires the means to buy it back, then the person must only pay half the original price. After all, over the previous twenty-five years, the creditor would have been able to profit from the plot of land.

It is only when a debtor has no one who can redeem his property and he himself fails to get it back that it is, without exception, released in the "jubilee year." This is, indeed, the only alternative that remains to break out of the downward spiral of poverty in which people, despite all possible preventative measures — interest prohibition, family solidarity and the right to redeem one's property — can nevertheless still find themselves.

With the introduction of the "jubilee year," they totally and utterly turn their backs on the economic order. From a strictly economic point of view, the release of land in the "jubilee year" is unjustifiable. As a believer, however, one cannot but do otherwise. After all, the religious experience of Israel taught the nation that it had no absolute right of ownership to the Promised Land. Israel realised all too well that it received its land as a gift from God.

e. People are Set Free (Leviticus 25:39-55)

The second part of Leviticus 25 deals with the liberation of people. As in the case of the regulations regarding the cancellation of debts, the central position of the interest prohibition underlines how they wanted to prevent, at all costs, people from falling into slavery. In order to be able to fully assess the value of the prescripts in Leviticus 25:39-55, in which the liberation of people in bondage is treated, a few precepts from the "Book of the Covenant" and the Deuteronomic Law must once again be scrutinised. These concern the complicated question of slavery. Unlike in contemporary Western society, in which trade in human beings as slaves is deemed abominable, neither the Old Testament nor the New Testament explicitly protests against the generally accepted practice of slavery.

1. The Textual Prehistory and the Attitude Regarding Slavery

Exodus 21:1-11 is probably the oldest Old Testament legal text that sets out rules with regard to slavery:

> [1]These are the ordinances that you shall set before them: [2]When you buy a male Hebrew slave, he shall serve for six years, but in the seventh he shall go out a free person, without debt. [3]If he comes in single, he shall go out single; if he comes in married, then his wife shall go out with him. [4]If his master gives him a wife and she bears him sons or daughters, the wife and her children shall be her master's and he shall go out alone. [5]But if the slave declares, 'I love my master, my wife, and my children; I will not go out a free person', [6]then his master shall bring him before God. He shall be brought to the door or the doorpost; and his master shall pierce his ear with an awl; and he shall serve him for life. [7]When a man sells his daughter as a slave, she shall not go out as the male slaves do. [8]If she does not please her master, who designated her for himself, then he shall let her be redeemed; he shall have no right to sell her to a foreign

people, since he has dealt unfairly with her. [9]If he designates her for his son, he shall deal with her as with a daughter. [10]If he takes another wife to himself, he shall not diminish the food, clothing, or marital rights of the first wife. [11]And if he does not do these three things for her, she shall go out without debt, without payment of money.

Although prisoners of war were still doomed to slavery in Ancient Israel, and this was thus a common form of slavery, the regulations in Exodus 21:1-11 very specifically deal with debt slavery. This term refers to people who, because of their inability to pay off their debts, end up in slavery. An account from the Second Book of Kings (4:1-7) illustrates this. It concerns the story of a widow who enlists the help of the prophet Elisha when the creditor comes around to take her two children as slaves. But, thanks to Elisha's miraculous intervention, she receives an abundance of oil that she can sell. She can pay the creditor with the proceeds. The widow's fear was not unfounded. When someone became a slave they were reduced to a piece of property. The fact that various Old Testament texts list slaves in the same breath as sheep, cattle, donkeys and camels says a lot (see for example Genesis 12:16).

Perhaps for the first time in history, in this pericope, the regulations of the "Book of the Convenant" limit debt slavery to six years, whatever the debts may amount to. As with the agricultural practice of leaving the land to lie fallow for a year after every six years, slaves may only remain in service for six years. It should be noted that this prescription applies exclusively to Israelite slaves. Foreigners cannot benefit from this rule. Moreover, the law is apparently only valid for male slaves. A female slave does not receive her freedom after six years of service. Yet, the passage does address the question of the wife of a slave. Here, the assumption is that, in conformity with the patriarchal culture, the wife is the property of her husband (and is thus also the last possession taken before the man himself becomes a slave). If a man is already married at the time he is taken into slavery, then he has the oldest right to his wife. For this reason, she will be set free together with her husband after six years. If, however, the male slave is given a wife by his master, then the master has the oldest right to the woman and so she and her children remain the property of the master. In this case, the released slave must leave his family behind. If, however, the man has become devoted to his master and to his family, then he can renounce his acquired freedom and choose to remain a slave for the rest of his life. He must, however, first publicly declare that he waives his right to freedom. So, by means of a ritual, his choice to stay in lifelong bondage is confirmed with a visible mark. The master must bring his slave before the "gods."[58] This is probably a remnant of the folk religion referring to the household gods or family gods. The piercing of the ear against the door(post) — this may refer to the door of the master's house — emphasises the attachment of the slave to his master. The whole ritual symbolically expresses the idea that the slave will obey his master.[59]

The text in Exodus 21:7-11 concerns a special situation. Here, the question of a father who sells his daughter as a concubine is addressed. It is not certain whether this action has something to do with paying off a debt. Indeed, the Hebrew term that is translated as "sell" can also be rendered as "transfer." Such female slaves remain concubines for life.

---

[58] Although the Hebrew term אלהים (elohim) is a plural form, this word is frequently used in the Old Testament to refer to the one God YaHWeH, which is apparent from the use of the singular verb. Exodus 21:6, however, appears to be an exception. Indeed, the use of the term in this verse corresponds to its use in Exodus 22:7-8, where the noun functions as the subject of a plural verb. The NRSV seemingly takes into account that plural verb in translating more freely with "the judges."

[59] See Cornelis Houtman, Exodus. Vol. 3, 122-127.

The difference between male and female slaves described above is dispensed with in Deuteronomy 15:12-18:

> [12]If a member of your community, whether a Hebrew man or a Hebrew woman, is sold to you and works for you for six years, in the seventh year you shall set that person free. [13]And when you send a male slave out from you a free person, you shall not send him out empty-handed. [14]Provide liberally out of your flock, your threshing-floor, and your wine press, thus giving to him some of the bounty with which the Lord your God has blessed you. [15]Remember that you were a slave in the land of Egypt, and the Lord your God redeemed you; for this reason I lay this command upon you today. [16]But if he says to you, 'I will not go out from you', because he loves you and your household, since he is well off with you, [17]then you shall take an awl and thrust it through his earlobe into the door, and he shall be your slave for ever. You shall do the same with regard to your female slave. [18]Do not consider it a hardship when you send them out from you free persons, because for six years they have given you services worth the wages of hired labourers; and the Lord your God will bless you in all that you do.

According to this passage, the female as well as the male slaves must be set free after six years of service. Moreover, the opportunities for the freed slaves to make a new start are fundamentally improved. The master is obliged to provide them with a sort of start-up capital. Although this rule in no sense abolishes debt slavery, it still, to some extent, undermines its principles. After all, slaves no longer work exclusively to pay off their debts, but must, at the same time, receive — albeit small — a wage for their work.

The Deuteronomic lawgiver wants to make this law, which is perhaps difficult for the wealthy, upper classes to accept, more acceptable in two ways. Firstly, he appeals to the economic sense of the master. After all, despite the obligatory freeing of slaves after six years of work, working with debt slaves is more advantageous than employing day labourers (verse 18). Secondly, the author puts forward religious arguments. He motivates the setting free of slaves by promising God's blessing (verses 14 and 18) and by referring to the Exodus event. In this respect, God's liberating actions function as an example for human behaviour. As a member of the people of Israel, the master is reminded that he was once a slave in Egypt and, thanks to God's intervention, was freed. Mindful of this religious conviction, the master must, when the time comes, set the slaves in his service free.

2. The Elaboration in Leviticus 25

As in the case of the cancellation of debts, it appears as if the Priestly authors of Leviticus 25 take a step backwards with regard to debt slavery:

> [39]If any who are dependent on you become so impoverished that they sell themselves to you, you shall not make them serve as slaves. [40]They shall remain with you as hired or bound labourers. They shall serve with you until the year of the jubilee. [41]Then they and their children with them shall be free from your authority; they shall go back to their own family and return to their ancestral property. [42]For they are my servants, whom I brought out of the land of Egypt; they shall not be sold as slaves are sold. [43]You shall not rule over them with harshness, but shall fear your God. [44]As for the male and female slaves whom you may have, it is from the nations around you that you may acquire male and female slaves. [45]You may also acquire them from among the aliens residing with you, and from their families that are with you, who have been born in your land; and they may be your property. [46]You may keep them as a possession for your children after you, for them to inherit as property. These you may treat as slaves, but as for your fellow Israelites, no one shall rule over the other with harshness. [47]If resident aliens among you prosper, and if any of your kin fall into difficulty with one of them and sell themselves to an alien, or to a branch of the alien's family, [48]after they have sold themselves they shall have the right of redemption; one of

their brothers may redeem them, [49]or their uncle or their uncle's son may redeem them, or anyone of their family who is of their own flesh may redeem them; or if they prosper they may redeem themselves. [50]They shall compute with the purchaser the total from the year when they sold themselves to the alien until the jubilee year; the price of the sale shall be applied to the number of years: the time they were with the owner shall be rated as the time of a hired labourer. [51]If many years remain, they shall pay for their redemption in proportion to the purchase price; [52]and if few years remain until the jubilee year, they shall compute thus: according to the years involved they shall make payment for their redemption. [53]As a labourer hired by the year they shall be under the alien's authority, who shall not, however, rule with harshness over them in your sight. [54]And if they have not been redeemed in any of these ways, they and their children with them shall go free in the jubilee year. [55]For to me the people of Israel are servants; they are my servants whom I brought out from the land of Egypt: I am the Lord your God.

First of all, Leviticus distances itself from the Deuteronomic obligation to free slaves after six years. Instead of six years, Leviticus prescribes a service period of forty-nine years. The starting capital that should be given by the master is also no longer mentioned. Here too, however, the first impression is deceiving. Leviticus 25 is in fact much more radical than Deuteronomy 15. As mentioned above, the intention of the interest prohibition was to stop Israelites from becoming impoverished. If it should still occur, then the impoverished brother may no longer be viewed as a slave, or harshly treated, at all (verses 43 and 46). He is no longer a slave. He becomes a hired labourer who must be paid for his work. As such, this rule is a guarantee that the impoverished Israelite will be able to benefit from an income until the next "jubilee year." Moreover, because he is remunerated for the work done, he can potentially buy back the lost usufruct of his land. While Israelites in the service of other Israelites remain day labourers until the jubilee year, this does not apply to Israelites who, due to unpaid debts, serve non-Israelites, who are also obliged to treat Israelites as day labourers and to pay them for their work. In this instance, however, an appeal can be made to family solidarity and the Israelite also has the possibility of buying his freedom himself. In the event that an Israelite out of sheer necessity has to go into the service of a non-Israelite, then the jubilee year is obviously, in this case too, a last resort.

Just like the rest of the regulations concerning the "jubilee year," this abolition of slavery, even before the term existed, is grounded upon religious arguments. Seeing that Israel was freed, by God, from slavery in Egypt, and acknowledging him as Lord and Master, every Israelite is now God's slave. Therefore, Israelites cannot and may not treat each other as slaves. Foreigners are in a different position. They can actually still be doomed to slavery (verses 44-46).

This double standard has various roots. Firstly, the particularism of Israel as the chosen people is central to the whole of the Old Testament. Foreigners, after all, did not share in God's liberating actions with regard to Israel. Secondly, the enslavement of foreigners poses no threat to the harmony of Israelite society, which the jubilee year ordinances were intended to preserve.

f. Historical Background to the Jubilee Year

Concerning the question of the age of the "jubilee year" laws, opinion is strongly divided. According to some scholars, the prescriptions are very old and they in fact go back to the Mosaic period. However, there are several elements that suggest that the text of Leviticus 25, as we now have it, should be dated much later. Indeed, the law on the "sabbatical year," upon which the jubilee year is built, presupposes a historical situation in which the Sabbath has already become central to the religious life of Ancient

Israel. This may only have been true since the Babylonian exile. In the centuries preceding the Babylonian Exile and the associated destruction of Jerusalem and its temple — *the* sanctuary in honour of YaHWeH — the Sabbath did not yet play a central role in the religious understanding of Ancient Israel. This is apparent from Exodus 23:12 and 34:21 where every seventh day is a day of rest — and "to rest" has the Hebrew term שבת (*sjabbat*) as its equivalent.

In addition, there are compositional data that suggest that Leviticus 25 should be dated as post-exilic. The chapter forms a diptych with Leviticus 23. In both chapters, the institutions of the Sabbath and the "Day of Atonement" — on which, according to Leviticus 25, the "jubilee year" begins — as well as the numbers forty-nine and fifty, are important. According to Leviticus 23:23, one must offer the first fruits of the new harvest to YaHWeH on the fiftieth day, i.e., after seven times seven days. This presupposes the rebuilding of the temple, which was only completed in 515 BC.

This post-exilic period, in which Leviticus was compiled, was anything but one of peace and harmony. The prophets had promised the exiles a glorious return to the homeland. The reality was, however, completely different. At their return, they found that their land had changed hands. The matter of ownership rights to previously owned properties thus became a burning issue. It was simply no longer possible for them to return to their former properties. The non-exiled part of the population was, furthermore, not prepared to return the rights of inheritance to the returning original owners. Moreover, post-exilic Judea was in social crisis. In Nehemia 5:1-5 we read how a large number of Judean farmers, possibly under the burden of Persian tax, are forced to pledge, first, their children — the workforce — and then also their fields and homes — the means of production. Finally, they must sell themselves as slaves. Consequently, the issue of lost land and the oppressive debt burden in the anything but rosy situation of post-exilic Israel is once again

central. The regulations concerning the "jubilee year" possibly
came about as an answer to the prevailing social abuses. This later
dating of Leviticus 25, nevertheless, takes nothing away from the
fact that a number of ideas in the chapter may have already taken
shape at an earlier stage in Israelite history. The text as it now
stands, however, is of another order.

g. *Reality or Utopia?*

The previous section makes it clear that the regulations concerning
the jubilee year were probably formulated with a view to actually
putting them into practice. Nonetheless, in the Old Testament,
there is not a single testimony to the actual application of the commandment to proclaim the fiftieth year a jubilee year. In Judaism,
non-observance of the law is connected with the fact that the conditions necessary for the fulfilment of the law are not present. After
all, in Leviticus 25 we read that the prescripts apply to all inhabitants of the land. However, since the Babylonian exile, the land had
not been in the possession of the Jewish people as a whole. The
law of the "sabbatical year," on the other hand, has indeed been
observed in some devout circles of Judaism over the course of history. Flavius Josephus, for example, tells of how Alexander the
Great and Julius Caesar exempted the Jews from the payment of
taxes during the sabbatical year. Today we still come across
attempts to observe a combination of the prescripts of Deuteronomy 15 (cancellation of debts) and Leviticus 25 (letting the land
lie fallow) in certain Jewish circles.

The fact that the biblical "jubilee year" was never put into practice, does not however mean that its underlying concerns were
completely ignored. On the contrary, Leviticus 25 became important in the eschatological, endtime expectations of early Judaism.
An important text in this evolution is Isaiah 61:1-3. Third Isaiah,

the post-exilic author of this pericope, is addressing the returning exiles. They feel they have been deceived by Second Isaiah's promises[60] that God would soon lead them in a triumphal march through the desert back to their land and that Jerusalem would be rebuilt as a city of never-before-seen glory. In practice, none of this comes about. Only a few are willing or able to wander out of Babylon; Jerusalem still lies in ruins and the reconstruction of the temple gets underway with difficulty. In the midst of this situation, Third Isaiah proclaims an enormous turnaround. YAHWEH will intervene in history and, soon, the deep sorrow and disillusionment will give way to joy and jubilation: "he has sent me to bring good news to the oppressed, to bind up the broken-hearted, to proclaim liberty to the captives, and release to the prisoners; to proclaim the year of the Lord's favour..."

But this great turnaround also fails to occur. As a result, Isaiah 61:1-3 also comes under the influence of the general tendency to apply prophetic promises to the end of time, as the basis of hope in an eschatological liberation of Israel brought about by the Messiah. We encounter this view in, among others, a text from the community of Qumran. In a manuscript named after its main character, 11QMelchizedek (first century BC), Melchizedek, by making reference to the passage from Isaiah, is presented as a Messianic, endtime liberator. At the same time, 11QMelchizedek connects Leviticus 25 with eschatological events. The forgiveness of (material) debt is therefore viewed as an essential element of the final and definitive deliverance.[61]

---

[60] Second Isaiah refers to Chapters 40–55 of the Book of Isaiah, while Third Isaiah refers to the last part of the book, namely chapters 56–66.

[61] For more background and an English translation of this document, see Florentino García Martínez and Eibert J. C. Tigchelaar, *The Dead Sea Scrolls. Study Edition, Vol. 2 (4Q274-11Q31)* (Leiden/Grand Rapids, MI: Brill /Eerdmans, 2000) 1206-1208.

One should probably also understand Jesus' appearance in the synagogue in Nazareth, which Luke 4:16-19 narrates, against this background. According to the evangelist, the promise of Isaiah 61:1-3 is fulfilled in Jesus. Luke however does not just copy the passage. He adds, among other things, a part of a verse from Isaiah 58:6 ("to let the oppressed go free"). In so doing, Luke introduces a text that plainly takes sides with the poor against the rich, whose religious piety is at variance with their social conduct. Yet Luke presents Jesus, right from the beginning of his gospel, not only as the one who definitively fulfils Isaiah's eschatologically interpreted promises, but, in the light of Isaiah 58:6, as the one who actually stands up for the poor and the oppressed. There are numerous texts in the rest of Luke's gospel in which Jesus resolutely takes the side of begging invalids. As such, Jesus' behaviour is completely in line with the concerns of the Old Testament "jubilee year." But Jesus transcends the particularism of the Old Testament. It is no longer about those who mourn in Zion. He argues in favour of the poor *tout court*.

h. *And Then? Reception History and Contemporary Application*

Over the course of history in general, and church history in particular, Leviticus has played an important role. However, improvement in the lot of the poor was most often not the aim in these cases. White church communities in South Africa misused Leviticus 25 to legitimise black slave labour. After all, verses 44-45 indeed state that one should acquire slaves from the surrounding nations. Within European Christendom it is primarily since 1300 that Leviticus 25 has often been referred to. In that year, Pope Boniface VIII proclaimed a jubilee year for the first time. However, the central idea of "freedom," which, as demonstrated, has everything to do with striving for a religiously grounded balance between self-interest and the common good, has since then been almost always interpreted spiritually as remission of penalty. This is, after all, the crux of the "indulgence," which has been considered an essential element of the ecclesiastical jubilee year. The fact that a large part of Christendom has, since the sixteenth century, looked upon the jubilee year — also called the holy year since the fifteenth century — with suspicion, is undoubtedly connected to the abuses that characterised the practice of indulgences.

In the last ecclesiastical jubilee year (2000), the jubilee indulgence was a key feature according to the papal bull *Incarnationis Mysterium* (28 November 1998). However, the bull also calls for social action. Pope John Paul II appealed for a new culture of international solidarity and cooperation. This can be realised via the quest for an economic model that benefits everybody in the world and by which the unbearable burden of debt no longer has a stranglehold on the poorest countries.

During the discussion of the creation poem in Genesis 1:1–2:4, it became clear that the Old Testament texts seem to proclaim how it should be rather than relate how it really was in the time of Ancient Israel. This is done because of a belief in a God who is believed to have revealed Himself in history as a liberating and loving God. The Old Testament social ordinances should also be read from this perspective. Starting from faith in God — here translated as: the land ultimately belongs not to people but to God, and one cannot make a slave of one's fellow human being because one believes that God is the only "lord" — one takes a stand for a humane society in which self-interest and the common good are kept in balance. This is perhaps an ideal that, due to the unrelenting harshness of the economic mechanisms against which it is reacting, is seldom if ever achieved in practice. Nonetheless, this fact should not be allowed to detract from the value of this ideal. After all,

Jesus' commandment to love one's enemies (Matthew 5:44) does not become worthless just because, over two millennia, the Christian church may have never actually succeeded in ending a war or hastening its conclusion. Although the Old Testament can in no way be used as an ethical recipe book for the solution of contemporary social problems, it can indeed, from the perspective of an ideal, be a source of inspiration for believers in the twenty-first century.

First of all, the Old Testament prescripts handed down in the "Book of the Covenant," the Deuteronomic law and the "Holiness Code" (Leviticus), confront us with one of the most essential features of divine worship and religion, namely with the need to adapt oneself to changing social circumstances while still remaining true to oneself. When religious institutions fail to meet the demands of new social realities, then a lively faith must be strong enough to reinvigorate and renew itself. After all, a religion that does not take new situations that confront it into account is doomed.

Furthermore, the Old Testament social prescripts emphasise the radical nature of faith in God. Building on the prophetic protest against abuses, the ordinances concerning the jubilee year make it clear that authentic faith in God demands tangible initiatives. As an attempt to overcome social crises, the jubilee year was, after all, a consequence of Israel's belief in YaHWeH as a liberating God. Therefore, the jubilee year confronts us with the inescapable interplay between theology and praxis. The social responsibility of the faithful is rooted in obedience to God. Understood thus, religion or faith in God is anything but opium for and/or of the masses. The Old Testament social prescripts demonstrate that faith in God can and should be radical and dynamic and that in an unjust society, religion should be far from satisfied with the status quo.

Conclusion

In this chapter, we first considered the Decalogue in Exodus 20:1-17 against the backdrop of biblical thought on achieving human coexistence. The second section raised the Old Testament legislation surrounding the sabbatical year and the jubilee year, situating these in the context of an authentic concern for social justice. In both examples, it doubtless became clear that these Old Testament texts should never be uncritically applied based on a literal reading of the biblical text. However, approached in a critical and nuanced way, they provide invaluable pointers along the way to a more dignified coexistence in authentic solidarity.

CHAPTER FOUR

GOD AND THE FORTUNES OF HUMANKIND

Introduction

In this fourth and final chapter, we shall examine the ways in which biblical narratives interpret human fortunes. In other words, we shall demonstrate how the biblical tradition implicates God himself in the daily experiences of human beings. Concretely, from the perspective of three different, illustrative issues, namely (divine) violence, suffering and love, we shall demonstrate how intensely familiar the Old Testament tradition is with the fundamental, existential human emotions that, to this day, and perhaps sometimes more so than we would like, essentially determine the course of our lives.

After all, it would be absurdly short-sighted to think that human life was wholly and utterly determined by rational engagement and intentional planning. Notwithstanding the strong emphasis that modernity places on rationality, believing it to be sacrosanct, we have indeed already shown in the first chapter of this book that this outlook is grossly inadequate. Very fundamentally, if we get right down to it, we sometimes have absolutely nothing to plan. Many fundamental things "overcome" us: getting us with our backs to the wall in crippling powerlessness, laying waste — sometimes in only an instant — to the greatest dreams, and changing in the blink of an eye all that we intended to achieve. Pain and loss belong to life; they are an intrinsic part of it. We feel this and learn it during childhood; we know it; we even find it completely normal. In this regard, the following anecdote says a great deal. Some time ago, we were driving to the city with our children. It began to rain very softly, a few drops on the car's windscreen. Our oldest son, seven year old Matthias, noticed it and said, purely as an observation, "It is starting to rain," whereupon the youngest, three year old Ruben, replied, "No, those are just a few tears from the clouds." Our five year old daughter, Elke, could only echo this sentiment: "Clouds can be sad." Tears are part of it all, for a child of three; for a person of eighty. Grief, pain, and violence too, make up part of the reality in which we grow up. Nevertheless, love is just as much a fundamentally characteristic fact of life that not only moulds and gives shape to our lives but that can also completely fill it, "full-fill" it with a majesty that we could not have imagined beforehand. Love opens up new vistas, throws another light on reality, makes reality a "shared" reality, fashions the future, and clears new paths.

This chapter deals with human emotions. The people of the Bible were also familiar with sorrow and pain, undeserved suffering, powerlessness and despair. But they also came to know a transcendent love that lifts people up, making the divine almost tangible. Against this background, the first section will focus on a particular problem that is often held against the Old Testament. Human life, in a broader social context, and sadly often also in the personal context, is characterised by the presence of violence. This was no different in the world of Ancient Israel. Remarkably, God himself is sometimes — perhaps even often and almost indiscriminately — connected to violence. This problem is addressed in the light of various illustrative Old Testament narratives and in particular the story of the exodus in Exodus 1–15. In the second section we turn our attention to undeserved suffering. Pain and suffering, in all their senselessness, raise many pressing questions, raise feelings of opposition and rebellion, and raise the question of God's responsibility. This was no different for the people in the Bible. This issue is addressed using the book of Job. Finally, the third section will take a closer look at love. A book about the Bible, about a God who accompanies humankind and repeatedly says to them, "I love you," must also put this most all-encompassing and transformative of human emotions under its lens. This will be based on the "Song of Songs," the book of Canticles, of which the Jewish rabbi Akiba has written: "The world had neither value nor meaning before the Song of songs was given to Israel."[1]

1. God: Terrific or Terrifying?

a. *The Old Testament: A Book Full of Violence?*

The heading above and the issue that it raises, namely the violence that sometimes accompanies God's appearances,[2] is at the heart of the problems that many of today's Christian's struggle with when the Old Testament comes up for discussion.[3] Very concretely, the

---

[1] Rabbi Akiba, quoted here on the basis of André Chouraqui, *La Bible* (Paris: Desclée de Brouwer, 2003) in his introduction to the book of Canticles.

[2] This title is taken from Bénédicte Lemmelijn, "God, geweldig of gewelddadig? Het 'Plagenverhaal' in Exodus 7–11," *Kerk en Leven* 50 (1999), a contribution that is elaborated on in Bénédicte Lemmelijn, "God, geweldig of gewelddadig? Het 'Plagenverhaal' in Exodus 7–11," *Wordt verteld: Levende geloofsverhalen*, ed. Peter De Mey and Luc Devisscher (Antwerpen: Halewijn, 2000) 18-26. Various ideas developed in the scope of these contributions are integrated into this section. See also Bénédicte Lemmelijn, "'Zoals het nog nooit geweest was en ook nooit meer zou zijn' (Ex.11,6): De 'plagen van Egypte' volgens Ex. 7–11: historiciteit en theologie," *Tijdschrift voor Theologie* 36 (1996) 115-131, and in particular 128-130 but more recently also Bénédicte Lemmelijn, "Not Fact, Yet True: Historicity versus Theology in the 'Plague Narrative' (Ex. 7–11)", *Old Testament Essays* 20 (2007) 395-417, especially 410-412.

[3] The literature concerning violence in the Old Testament is extensive. By way of example, see, Norbert Lohfink (ed.), *Gewalt und Gewaltlosigkeit im Alten Testament*, Quaestiones Disputatae, 96 (Freiburg: Herder, 1983); Robert Oberforcher, "Verkündet das Alte Testament einen gewalttätigen Gott?

violent nature of many passages is undoubtedly the most severe reproach aimed at the Old Testament. One often hears it said that the God described in the historical books, whose message the prophets proclaim, who is worshipped or cursed in the Psalms, and upon whom the wisdom literature is founded, is a different God to the God of Jesus in the New Testament. The God that the Old Testament speaks of is a cruel, vengeful and violent God who stands in stark contrast to the peace-loving and merciful God that is spoken of in the New Testament. Often, scholarly and popular publications highlight the inferiority of the Old Testament, precisely due to its violent nature. From feminist theology, moreover, comes the critique that the God of the Old Testament is a patriarchal God and that this image of God seeks to legitimise male violence against women.

Of course, one cannot deny that many Old Testament stories are full of violence. Texts such as those about the conquering of the Promised Land in the book of Joshua, whereby the Israelites raze entire cities, brutally slaughter men and women and finally claim their possessions as the spoils of war, for example, shed light on human violence. In addition, in the Old Testament there is also a

Fundamentalistische Relikte im Umgang mit gewalttätigen Zugen im biblischen Gottesbild," *Eindeutige Antworten? Fundamentalistische Versuchung in Religion und Gesellschaft,* ed. Jozef Niewiadomski (Thaur: Österreichischer Kulturverlag, 1988) 133-158; Marc Vervenne, "'Smeed uw ploegscharen om tot zwaarden' (Joël 4,10): Verkenningen rond geweld en oorlog in het Oude Testament," *Strijden op de weg van Jahweh, God, Allah!? De heilige oorlog in jodendom, christendom en islam,* Cahiers voor vredestheologie, 2, ed. Roger Burggraeve and Johan De Tavernier (Leuven: Peeters, 1989) 23-68; and the revision thereof in Marc Vervenne, "'Satanic Verses'? Violence and War in the Bible," *Swords into Plowshares: Theological Reflections on Peace,* ed. Roger Burggraeve and Marc Vervenne, Louvain Theological & Pastoral Monographs, 8 (Leuven: Peeters, 1991) 65-126 (including a brief but significant bibliography on war and violence in the Bible).

lot of divine violence. It is horrifying to read how God completely devastates the Egyptians with one plague after the next because they would not let the Israelites go, and then finally, in a gruesome fashion, allows them to die as they try to cross the sea (Exodus 13–14). In this regard, we could also refer to numerous texts in the book of Numbers that tell of how God even inflicts harsh punishments on the Israelites themselves, how he causes the earth to open and swallow up the rebels, Korah, Dathan and Abiram (Numbers 16), how he condemns a whole generation to death because of their unbelief (Numbers 14:26-35), and even sentences his own messenger, Moses, to a premature death, just because he doubted God's promises (Numbers 20).

Those who, on the basis of such violent texts, would like to discard the Old Testament entirely are, of course, approaching these problems as consummate fundamentalists. After all, the violent character of the texts mentioned, in which not only the Israelites but God too come across as being extremely cruel, can only be understood in their immediate and surrounding literary contexts. Moreover, the issue of violence in the Old Testament cannot be simply and unequivocally solved. The Old Testament deals with violence from various perspectives. First, it should be noted that the historical core of the biblical accounts of violence, the exodus from Egypt as well as the fate of whole generations of Israelites during their wanderings through the desert and the extremely violent conquest of the Promised Land, is exceptionally small, if not non-existent. After all, the Old Testament does not record history. It is anything but an objective account of what actually happened back then. On the contrary, it aims to bear witness to experiences that are, moreover, religious experiences. Experiences are, of course, by definition subjective. The realisation that all the violence perpetrated by the Israelites or God in the Old Testament did not actually take place is also the first requirement necessary to be able to assess the violent texts found in the first part of the Christian Bible. These texts are first and foremost "stories" that reflect the faith and hope of their authors and their contemporaries. An example will illustrate this.

b. *Horrified by God's Violence: A Question of Perspective?*

The books of Exodus, Numbers and Joshua are undoubtedly the most violent books in the Old Testament. They primarily tell of Israel's exodus from Egypt, the dangerous travels through the desert and the brutal occupation of the land, in which the original inhabitants of the land promised by God are simply massacred en masse without too many qualms. Against this background we zoom in on Exodus 7–15, the so-called "Plague Narrative" and its account of the actual exodus of Israel from Egypt. In these narratives too, violence, and particularly violence perpetrated by God, is the order of the day. This fact is difficult to handle for "sensitive readers." The violence raises a whole series of questions and doubts. However, the way in which it can be interpreted is illustrative.

Who can remain unmoved by the scene in the animated film *Prince of Egypt* (Dreamworks) in which the queen of Egypt, the pharaoh's wife, enters after the tenth plague has struck with the lifeless body of a little boy in her arms? How can a god who loves people do something like this? What sort of a god is that? Is that the god of love who whispers to us that every hair on our heads has been counted, the father we can rely on? How can a "loving" god do something like that to Egypt? Are the children of the enemy not also just children? In the context of the Cold War, in which the then Soviet Union was thought by the West to be the personification of evil, Sting sung: "The Russians love their children too...." Or Willem Vermandere, who upon seeing the countless graves of the war dead — Germans and Allies — said: "always someone's father, always someone's child." What reasonable person can suppress his horror at a god who, in Exodus 9:14-16 says to Pharaoh:

> For this time I will send all my plagues upon you yourself, and upon your officials, and upon your people, so that you may know that there is no one like me in all the earth. For by now I could have stretched out my hand and struck you and your people with pestilence, and you would have been cut off from the earth. But this is why I have let you live: to show you my power, and to make my name resound through all the earth.

Is this the kind of recognition God wants? Recognition by totally defeated people who finally acknowledge the power that he, in such a harsh tone, proclaims? A bitter victory, as in every war. Are the plagues in Exodus 7–11 not just expressions of the capricious behaviour of a tyrannical divinity? And, above all, what answer can one formulate to such questions? Should exegetes defend God with a few eloquent excuses in order to iron out the flaws in his image? Perhaps we can plead mitigating circumstances?

The answer is, "Definitely not." Smoothing over any problems in the biblical text whatsoever only testifies to uncritical (and fundamentalistic) attitudes. Instead, we must search for the correct interpretation, while still doing justice to the text and taking seriously the events related. However, a nuanced answer to the problems mentioned is not self-evident. Nonetheless, in what follows, we shall try to formulate a careful and direction giving proposal that may contribute toward an explanation.

If we return to the account of the exodus, and more generally to the whole book of Exodus, which, together with Numbers and Joshua, was earlier characterised as being violent, then it must be said that the implications of these texts can be correctly appreciated only in the light of the first chapters of the book of Exodus. Here, we are confronted by the perspective from which these texts are written. If we leave aside the historicity of the text (as mentioned above), Exodus 1 confronts us with a people who suffered enormously under the Egyptians, who exploited them as forced labour. Moreover, when Pharaoh realises that the Israelites are becoming more numerous and may thereby potentially undermine his rule, he orders all newborns to be killed. In what must have been an intolerable situation for the Israelites, God calls Moses to be their saviour. In the call narrative of Moses, in which God speaks to Moses from a burning bush, God speaks directly for the first time since the Israelites have been in Egypt. And it is precisely herein that we find the key to understanding the texts of violence. God is a God who hears the lamentations and the plea for help of the slaves (Exodus 2:23), who keeps His promises (Exodus 2:24), and who sympathises with the oppressed (Exodus 3:7). This is the lens through which we should interpret God's violent appearances during the course of the exodus and occupation of the Promised Land. God is not just a violent God who takes pleasure in making people's lives hell. He simply can't allow the Israelites to suffer. God is not neutral when it comes to injustice.

With regard to our own disgust at the violence that occurs, the same principle applies. Perhaps one could also say that, here, the perspective and existential situation of the individual reader/listener will to a great extent determine how the depiction of God's radically violent actions is experienced. In our pretty comfortable lives in the context of western Europe, we only worry about the violence that Egypt, as oppressor, must undergo in this narrative because we are looking at it disapprovingly from our "luxury position" of prosperity, safety and freedom. If we ourselves were oppressed, if we had no rights and day in and day out didn't know if their would even be a tomorrow, would we not instead rejoice or at least be relieved to see the downfall of the oppressor in this narrative? An example will illustrate how the position in which we find ourselves always fundamentally influences how we perceive the facts. Let us first consider a typical weekend film in which the classic "good vs. evil" scenario is played out, for example, a weak woman is repeatedly beaten by her husband. In this case, we who have taken the side of the woman, seem to have no problem, and are even thrilled, when, at the end of the film, the violent man is himself killed, and so receives his "just desserts." We even call this a "happy ending," even though, just as for Egypt in the Exodus story, it is not such a "happy ending" for the man in question. However, we take up a specific position — choosing the side of the victim — and from this perspective, we judge the situation. In other words, this perspective determines the way we look at things, the choices that we make and the emotions that arise in us.

In the Exodus narrative, it is no different. The writers and the original recipients did not find themselves in the comfortable position that we are in now. They experienced, most likely in the context of the Babylonian exile, real oppression and fear. In this threatening situation, they chose in favour of the oppressed people of Israel against the overwhelming might of Egypt. The fact that Exodus tells us that God took their side and showed that his might was greater than that of the oppressor made it a comforting and encouraging story for these needy people. A story of relief, a breath of fresh air in the midst of their anxiety. That is why people who still live under oppression today find strength and reassurance in this narrative. Marc Vervenne puts it this way in the context of the "Sea Narrative" (the demise of the Egyptians in the Sea in Exodus 13:17–14:31): "For people who must live with uncertainty, threats and oppression, the 'violent' Sea Narrative can indeed find resonance. Paralysed by the power of the 'the strong', they recognise, in this tale of old, their own powerlessness *and* the hope that God will give them a way out."[4] The accounts of violence are, in other words, a message of hope for the oppressed and at the same time a call to the oppressors to change their ways. The perspective from which the violence is related is therefore extremely important. For the powerless and the weak, God's violent actions are a message of hope. The pericopes in which God's cruel behaviour is depicted are not the propaganda of the powerful but rather represent hope to people who live under devastating oppression. The texts are written from the belief and hope that God takes the side of the weak. The mighty Pharaoh, ultimately, does not have the final say. While God makes a stand for the oppressed, he judges the oppressors and repays them for the injustices they have perpetrated. This is not irrational revenge, but an attempt to repair a situation gone awry. And so, the violence in the Old Testament should not just be explained away with smooth talk and overly spiritual interpretations. On the contrary, even if the Old Testament violence is often difficult for us to accept, for the original recipients of the biblical texts, it had an essential meaning. Moreover, most of the political and military conflicts that the Israelites engaged in according to the Old Testament were forced upon them. Indeed, throughout their entire history, Israel was the plaything of the great powers like Egypt, Assyria and Babylon. The biblical Israel endured these wars and frequently reflected on their lot. Within these reflections, a particular theology of war, in which God takes the side of Israel and enters the fray, found its place. It is written from Israel's perspective and, from that perspective, it can also be reasonably understood.

[4] Translated from the Dutch: see Marc Vervenne, "'Zij stelden vertrouwen in Jahwe en in Mozes zijn dienaar': Kanttekeningen bij het Zeeverhaal (Ex 13,17–14,31)," *Exodus: Verhaal en leidmotief*, ed. Marc Vervenne (Leuven: Vlaamse Bijbelstichting, 1989) 102-120, especially 120.

c. *The Essence of God or a Human Image of God?*

Closely associated with this, there is the fundamental question of
the realisation that the Old Testament narratives are, first of all,
stories, that is to say that they are written by and for people and
that this thus essentially influences and limits them. Concretely,
this means that even the Bible cannot tell us who or what God is
in essence. It is always a story of people, for people, about a God
who no one individual can actually comprehend. It is absolutely
impossible for a single person to write down or to proclaim who
or what God actually is. Putting a person into one or other cate-
gory, objectifying a person by means of a particular "label," testifies to enormous disrespect for the range of personality traits that
constitute a person. *A fortiori*, no individual can pretend to have a
monopoly on the absolute truth about who God is. You can't put
God in a box. This insight fits in with, for example, the prohibition
on the making of images of God in Ancient Israel. If one makes
an image of someone — human or divine — then one captures him
in one particular moment, in one particular facial expression or
mood that can never be an integral rendering of the person's whole
essence. Everything that people know or think they know, everything that they have ever written about God is the result of cautious
conjecture and well thought-out, deeply reflected upon experience.
Moreover, this has always come about on the basis of analogies
with (inter-)human existence, just as any other fantasy always demonstrates points of contact with reality. It never concerns an absolutely all-encompassing definition of being.

The Old Testament also contains no statements about God *in se*.
It is always about God insofar as he enters into relations with the
world and with people. Only against this background can certain
characteristics that the Bible ascribes to him be understood. It is
thus also not about seeing "wrath and violence" as typical of the

Old Testament God and in opposition to the "love" that is supposed to be characteristic of the New Testament God. Firstly, the God of the Old Testament is characterised by at least as much, if not much more so, faithful love (*chesed*) and justice (*tsedaqa*) as by violence. Secondly, both the "wrath" and the "love" are always attributes of one and the same God, in the New Testament as well as the Old. This fact will be illustrated in what follows.

The Old Testament creation narratives in Genesis, which in fact function as narrative theology, offer a nice example of the way in which both wrath and love are characteristics of God, but also of the fact that God's love always triumphs. In the second creation narrative, the so-called "Paradise Narrative" about "Adam" and "Eve," God has only just created human beings as man and woman in their own, custom made, luxury paradise, when he is confronted by an endless series of disappointments. Human beings greedily and violently take possession of everything that they set their hearts on. Even their banishment from their five star oasis, in the hope that the hard labour of being farmers would make human beings more peace loving and humble, made no impact. On the contrary, God must resignedly watch as people kill each other — immediately after the Paradise Narrative comes the pericope about Cain who murders his brother Abel (Genesis 4:1-16). The more human beings increase in number, the more violent they become. It is, of course, true that God is not as lonely any more since he created people, but his worries have also risen exponentially. How long does he have to stand by and watch these ungrateful creatures deal shamelessly and violently not only with each other and his beloved Earth, but with God himself? Genesis 6:5–6:11-13 put it as follows:

> The Lord saw that the wickedness of humankind was great in the earth, and that every inclination of the thoughts of their hearts was only evil continually. And the Lord was sorry that he had made

humankind on the earth, and it grieved him to his heart. (…) Now the earth was corrupt in God's sight, and the earth was filled with violence. And God saw that the earth was corrupt; for all flesh had corrupted its ways upon the earth. And God said to Noah, 'I have determined to make an end of all flesh, for the earth is filled with violence because of them; now I am going to destroy them along with the earth.

For God, it was anything but a pleasant experience to realise that his experiment had failed and that his greatest expectations, which Genesis 1:1–2:4 tell us about by describing a world free of violence, had not been met. Was it not therefore logical or understandable that God wanted to put a premature end to his experiment and that he should regret having created human beings? Is his decision not in any way comprehendible? God sends an enormous flood to cover the Earth in order to destroy it all. He reacts in a way that has been typical of all rulers and for all time: he punishes and destroys. God answers violence with violence.

The motif of a divine deluge that frees the divinity of burdensome people was not thought up by Israel. They probably relied on much older Babylonian texts. In this regard, consider the Atrahasis epic and the eleventh tablet of the Gilgamesh epic (second half of the second millennium BC).[5] In both texts, the flood is the result of a conflict. Human beings who — unlike in the biblical creation narrative — are created by the gods to serve them as slaves, make so much noise that they disturb the gods' rest. In reaction, the god Enlil wants to wipe out humanity with a flood. No other god dares to protest against Enlil's decision. Even the mother goddess (in the Gilgamesh epic she is called Ishtar; in the Atrahasis epic she is Nintu) agrees, though, let it be said, with an aching heart. But when

---

[5] For the texts of these works see William W. Hallo, *The Context of Scripture*, 3 vols. (Leiden/Boston/Cologne: Brill, 1997-2002).

the flood actually begins, it is said that she wept and moaned.[6] In the figure of the mother goddess in these extra-biblical texts, we encounter the contradictory nature of divine violence. Othmar Keel words it as follows: "Es ist wie die Erfahrung einer Mutter, die das, was sie unter Mühen und Schmerzen geboren hat, unter keinen Umständen vernichtet sehen will."[7] Consequently, she is overjoyed when she discovers at the end of the flood that at least one person has survived the catastrophe. In the Gilgamesh epic, this human survivor is called Utnapishtim, in the Atrahasis epic it is Atrahasis. Out of gratitude for being rescued, he builds an altar and brings offerings. When the smoke reaches the gods, the mother goddess swears that she will always remember this day.

The various divine characteristics that the Mesopotamian tradition divides among different gods (Enlil = rage; Ishtar = mercy), are attributed to one and the same God in the biblical Flood Narrative, namely YAHWEH. The God of the biblical Flood Narrative is a different God at the end of it. If he displays the characteristics of Enlil at the beginning, his destructive fury, then by the end of the story he is much more like Ishtar, the goddess of motherly love. When YAHWEH smells Noah's burnt offering in Genesis 8:21-22, He solemnly proclaims, "I will never again curse the ground because of humankind, for the inclination of the human heart is evil from youth; nor will I ever again destroy every living creature as I have done."

---

[6] See, for a critical edition of the Ancient Near East textual material, William W. Hallo, *The Context of Scripture: Canonical Compositions: Monumental Inscriptions and Archival Documents from the Biblical World*, 3 vols. (Leiden/New York/Cologne: Brill, resp. 1997, 2000 and 2002). For a Dutch translation, specifically of the Gilgamesh story, see Franz Marius Theodor de Liagre Böhl, *Het Gilgamesj epos: Vertaald en toegelicht* (Brussel/Den Haag: Manteau, 1978 [= ³1958]).

[7] Cf. Othmar Keel, "Jahweh in der Rolle der Muttergottheit," *Orientierung* 53 (1989) 90.

After the flood, God sees people differently. Erich Zenger puts it thus: "Es sind doch seine Kinder, die er bedingungslos lieben und zu denen er halten will, nicht nur in guten, sondern vor allem in bösen Tagen. Nachdem er sich auf die Menschen eingelassen hat, will er sich *voll* auf sie einlassen — nicht mit der kalten Logik von law and order, sondern mit der großzügigen Liebe einer Mutter, die immer noch zu ihren Kindern Hält und ihnen hilft, wenn niemand mehr helfen will."[8] Herein lies the meaning of the rainbow that God places in the clouds and at the same time says (Genesis 9:14-15), "When I bring clouds over the earth and the bow is seen in the clouds, I will remember my covenant that is between me and you and every living creature of all flesh; and the waters shall never again become a flood to destroy all flesh."

This is then also the final divine word in the biblical "prehistory" (Genesis 1–11). Thereafter, the Bible begins, with the story of Abraham, to relate the "history," the time in which we live. It is important to realise this. The Flood Narrative is not about an actual event that really happened in history, when a furious God struck the Earth with a gigantic catastrophe. What Genesis 6–9 wants to say is just the opposite: even if God, who created everything, really *ought* to flood the Earth again because people are so wicked, He will *never* do it. Thus, God's last word is one of patient and saving love. Or, as the book of Wisdom put it (Wisdom 11:24-26): "For you love all things that exist, and detest none of the things that you have made, for you would not have made anything if you had hated it. How would anything have endured if you had not willed it? Or how would anything not called forth by you have been preserved? You spare all things, for they are yours, O Lord, you who love the living."

---

[8] Erich Zenger, *Das Erste Testament*, 76.

d. *Conclusion*

Against this background, it may have become clear that the confrontation with violence, whether between people or perpetrated by God, appears in the Old Testament narratives due to their intrinsic connection with daily realities. However, we have demonstrated that this fact is, first and foremost, a literary one, and therefore it makes no claim to be historical reality. In addition, we have illustrated the way in which both the fact that the biblical person had no problem with divine violence and the fact that the contemporary reader may well be disturbed by it are largely determined by the perspective that one reads the text from. Finally we have emphasised that, no matter which biblical narrative one reads, it is never about an absolute representation of God's essence. Rather, it is about the image of God, partly constituted by the different characteristics of wrath and love, and they are all essentially part of one and the same divinity found in both the Old and the New Testament.

At the end of this section, we would like to once again emphasise that for all these reasons, one cannot and may not simply push the Old Testament aside as a violent book. Seen in its entirety, the Old Testament is, after all, not violent; it only becomes violent when one reads it in a fragmented way. Indeed, alongside texts in which brutal violence seems to have the upper hand, God, according to other texts, categorically turns away from violence and sabre rattling. Many Old Testament texts present an explicit protest against every form of violence and allow us to catch a glimpse, from an idealistic perspective perhaps, of a time of complete harmony and peace in which there is absolutely no war any more.[9]

The God of the Old Testament is in fact also and above all a loving father, who journeys alongside his people, day after day, who wants to bless the lives of his people with everything that

---

[9] Cf. the discussion of the development of the Decalogue above.

makes people happy, and who, like a mother, always worries about her child: "As a mother comforts her child, so I will comfort you" (Isaiah 66:13).

2. God and Suffering

Another issue that confronts people with the finiteness and the limitedness of existence is that of undeserved suffering. Suffering that comes over people, breaking into existence like a thief, turning everything upside down. When suffering strikes — setbacks, sickness or death — then the question, "Why?" invariably raises its head. Why did I get cancer? Why was our child run over by a drunk driver? For believers, there is yet another dimension: Where, in God's name, is God in all this suffering? Why did God let it happen that our child should be run over on her way to sing in the church choir on a beautiful Sunday morning?

These are eternal questions. Thus, the Old Testament is also unable to escape them. And although these questions and the laments that often accompany them seem to appear all over the Bible, the issue is mainly addressed in the so-called wisdom literature. To the wisdom literature belong, among others, the books of Psalms, Ecclesiastes, Ecclesiasticus and Proverbs. However, there is one book from the wisdom literature that is exemplary in the way that it deals with the issue of the suffering of the just — the book of Job.

The book of Job grapples with the question, "Why?," with the issue of God's part in suffering, and above all with the lack of a definitive answer. In this regard, it should be pointed out that the character Job is not in any way a historical person. He is a literary character, a sort of Elckerlyc who represents all of us and who is valid for all time. This is, incidentally, typical of Old Testament wisdom literature.

a. *The Book of Job: Structure and Framework*

The book of Job is a well thought-out literary and theological work that reflects on a most pressing existential question, namely, the suffering of a "good" and "just" person.[10] In the book of Job, two major subdivisions can be identified. The framework (chapters 1–2 and 42:7-17) is written in prose. The body of the work (3:1–42:6) is poetic literature. Although both parts are related to one another and essentially inseparable in the final text, they nevertheless reflect the evolution of the piece; it is widely accepted that the framework contains the oldest material. In any case, the framework and the body show different visions of Job's suffering and the relationship between suffering and God.

1. The Prologue (Job 1–2)

At the beginning of the framework the central character, Job, after whom the book is named, is introduced as a righteous and faithful man: "That man was blameless and upright, one who feared God and turned away from evil." These verses also imply that the irreproachable Job has not experienced too many problems in life: "There were born to him seven sons and three daughters. He had seven thousand sheep, three thousand camels, five hundred yoke

---

[10] A few excellent and accessible works on Job are: Walter Vogels, *Job*, Belichting van het bijbelboek (Boxtel/Leuven/Brugge: Katholieke Bijbelstichting, 1989); Ellen van Wolde, *Meneer en mevrouw Job: Job in gesprek met zijn vrouw, zijn vrienden en God* (Baarn: Ten Have, 1991). For this introduction to the book of Job, we have made use of the above works and, in addition, those of Willem A. M. Beuken (ed.), *The Book of Job*, Bibliotheca Ephemeridum Theologicarum Lovaniensium, 114 (Leuven: Leuven University Press, 1994); and Ludger Schwienhorst-Schönberger, "Das Buch Ijob," *Einleitung in das Alte Testament*, ed. Erich Zenger, Kohlhammer Studienbücher Theologie, 1/1 (Stuttgart: Kohlhammer, [5]2004) 335-347.

of oxen, five hundred donkeys, and very many servants; so that this man was the greatest of all the people of the east" (Job 1:2-3). By making a connection between Job's righteousness and his prosperity, voice is given to the accepted wisdom of the time: The good are rewarded. One also regularly encounters this "doctrine of reward" in other wisdom literature in the Old Testament. Conversely, this view, however, implies that those who experience suffering and misfortune, have their own incorrect, or in religious terms, sinful conduct to thank for it. Moreover, people were also convinced that the wrongdoings of parents could have repercussions for the children. For example, the prophet Ezekiel quotes an Old Testament proverb: "The parents have eaten sour grapes, and the children's teeth are set on edge" (Ezekiel 18:2). The story of the healing of the man who was born blind in the New Testament Gospel of John again reflects this belief. When they see a man born blind, the disciples ask Jesus, "Rabbi, who sinned, this man or his parents, that he was born blind?" (John 9:2). Job is clearly flying high. However, soon Job's adversary appears: "Satan." Literally, this term means "the adversary," and the use of an article in the Hebrew suggests that this is not a personal name but a noun. He is thus also not the "devil." He assumes the role of "devil's advocate" so to speak, who, according to Job 1:6, is part of God's heavenly court. In accordance with his character, the satan calls the integrity of Job's righteousness and respect for God into question: "Does Job fear God for nothing?" (Job 1:9). In other words, is Job's behaviour and faith not simply the consequence of self-interest? The satan even makes a bet with God: if Job loses his possessions, then it will not be long before he curses God. The satan then receives God's permission to target Job's possessions. Job loses his livestock, and then even all his children die. Despite these severe losses, Job remains firmly devout. The Job of the prologue reacts to his suffering in accordance with the traditional rules. He tears his clothes, shaves his head, and falls to the ground. And, possibly with traditional expressions of faith, he spontaneously responds, "Naked I came from my mother's womb, and naked shall I return there; the LORD gave, and the LORD has taken away," and then he even adds, "blessed be the name of the LORD" (1:21). Here, Job is employing the language of popular religion.

But the satan approaches God again. He drives his point home. This time he proposes that he be allowed to strike Job himself, betting that Job will then definitely curse God. And Job is covered from head to toe in angry sores. Job's response is now somewhat less infused with the expressions typical of popular religion. He no longer blesses God, but instead only emphasises his acceptance of his suffering: "Shall we receive the good at the hand of God, and not receive the bad?" (Job 2:10).

Job's attitude in the prologue leaves us with the impression that, for a believer, the correct attitude with regard to suffering consists of resigned and stoical acceptance of it. The Christian tradition has, among other things, seen in this presentation of Job as devout and resigned to his fate the archetypical example of the suffering person. One should best resign oneself to the human suffering orchestrated by God. Typical of this is, for example, the exhortation given by the founder of the Opus Dei, who was canonised by Pope John Paul II, José Escrivá de Balaguer: "Are things going against you? Are you going through a rough time? Say very slowly, as if relishing it, this powerful and manly prayer: 'May the most just and most lovable will of God be done, be fulfilled, be praised and eternally exalted above all things. Amen, Amen.' I assure you that you will find peace."[11]

---

[11] Translated from the Dutch, see Josemaria Escrivá de Balaguer, *De Weg* (Amsterdam/Brussel: De boog, ²1972) 180.

Nonetheless, in the prologue of the book of Job, an entirely different attitude with regard to human suffering is found in the reaction of Job's wife. She only speaks once in the whole book, when she says to Job, "Do you still persist in your integrity? Curse God, and die." By telling Job to turn away from God, Job's wife seems to represent the other extreme when it comes to dealing with suffering. This reaction of turning away from God is frequently found among people confronted by suffering, whether they believe in God or not. Because, if God existed, surely he would not allow such misery? And how can one still believe in God when one is confronted with such suffering?

2. The Epilogue (Job 42:7-17)

If Job's faithful resignation seems to be central to the prologue of the book, then the epilogue (42:7-17) seems to suggest that Job's attitude with regard to suffering ultimately bears fruit. Indeed, the final verses give us the impression that, in the end, Job is rewarded by God for his patient, faithful and resigned acceptance of his suffering:

> The LORD blessed the latter days of Job more than his beginning; and he had fourteen thousand sheep, six thousand camels, a thousand yoke of oxen, and a thousand donkeys. He also had seven sons and three daughters. (…) In all the land there were no women so beautiful as Job's daughters; and their father gave them an inheritance along with their brothers. After this Job lived for one hundred and forty years, and saw his children, and his children's children, four generations. And Job died, old and full of days. (Job 42:12-17)

Although these verses do not explicitly say that Job was given back his possessions because he always spoke of God in the correct way, they nevertheless leave one with the impression that one will ultimately be rewarded if one resigns oneself to one's suffering and one does not curse God for it. In so doing, one abides by the prevailing doctrine of reward — the good will be rewarded. Needless to say, this interpretation of the framework really makes people's suffering seem banal. Try explaining it this way to parents whose only child has been killed by a drunk driver!

b. *The Central Part of the Book: Job and his "Friends" Converse*

1. The Argumentation of the "Friends"

When evil strikes, one hears various answers as to why we suffer. In the prologue, Job uses the language of the popular religion, while Job's wife, confronted by suffering, renounces her faith in God. At the end of the prologue, three of Job's friends arrive on the scene. When Eliphaz, Bildad and Zophar learn of Job's misfortune, they come looking for him. Their first reaction when they see Job, covered in sores, is one of intense sympathy. In conformity with the accepted practice, they lament, tear their clothes and throw dust on their heads. The text goes on to say, "They sat with him on the ground for seven days and seven nights, and no one spoke a word to him, for they saw that his suffering was very great." In the third chapter, Job breaks this silence in very radical way: "After this Job opened his mouth and cursed the day of his birth."

The second part of the book (chapters 3–31) begins with an extended lament by Job (Job 3):

> Let the day perish on which I was born,
>> and the night that said,
>> "A man-child is conceived." (Job 3:3)

> Why did I not die at birth,
>> come forth from the womb and expire? (Job 3:11)

In reaction to Job's lament, his friends break their silence. Three rounds of discourse follow, in which Eliphaz, Bildad and Zophar speak in turn. Each attempts to explain and justify Job's suffering and to counter Job's lament. In doing so, they primarily raise the following elements with regard to Job's suffering.

First, Job's suffering is explained by referring to human contingency and insignificance. The fact that human beings are mortal "creatures" implies that he is also finite and imperfect:

> Even in his servants [God] puts no trust,
>   and his angels he charges with error;
> how much more those who live in houses of clay,
>   whose foundation is in the dust,
>   who are crushed like a moth.
> Between morning and evening they are destroyed;
>   they perish for ever without any regarding it.
> Their tent-cord is plucked up within them,
>   and they die devoid of wisdom." (4:18-21)

> What are mortals, that they can be clean?
>   Or those born of woman, that they can be righteous?

> God puts no trust even in his holy ones,
>   and the heavens are not clean in his sight;
> how much less one who is abominable and corrupt,
>   one who drinks iniquity like water! (15:14-16).

In addition to this reference to human creatureliness, the view of suffering as the consequence of human guilt — the traditional teaching of retribution, with its motto, "those who plough iniquity and sow trouble reap the same," (Job 4:8) — runs like a golden thread through the entire book:

> Surely the light of the wicked is put out,
>   and the flame of their fire does not shine.
> The light is dark in their tent,
>   and the lamp above them is put out.
> Their strong steps are shortened,
>   and their own schemes throw them down.

For they are thrust into a net by their own feet,
  and they walk into a pitfall.
A trap seizes them by the heel;
  a snare lays hold of them.
A rope is hid for them in the ground,
  a trap for them in the path.
Terrors frighten them on every side,
  and chase them at their heels.
Their strength is consumed by hunger,
  and calamity is ready for their stumbling. (18:5-12)

Moreover, Job is even accused of committing all sorts of wrongs that supposedly lie at the root of his suffering. Eliphaz puts it thus:

Is not your wickedness great?
  There is no end to your iniquities.
For you have exacted pledges from your family for no reason,
  and stripped the naked of their clothing.
You have given no water to the weary to drink,
  and you have withheld bread from the hungry.
The powerful possess the land,
  and the favoured live in it.
You have sent widows away empty-handed,
  and the arms of the orphans you have crushed.
Therefore snares are around you,
  and sudden terror overwhelms you.... (22:5-10).

2. Job's Protest

Job not only rebels against his suffering He refuses to accept the explanations that Eliphaz, Bildad and Zophar put forward concerning his suffering; and this is exactly what the book is about. In response to the reference made to human contingency, he argues that it was God himself who wanted to make him suffer: "or the arrows of the Almighty are in me; my spirit drinks their poison;

the terrors of God are arrayed against me" (6:4). Furthermore, Job
repeatedly stresses the righteousness of his conduct. Job even
cries out, "I am blameless" (9:21). This is very explicit in Job's
long monologue (29–31), which concludes the three rounds of
discourse:[12]

> Far be it from me to say that you are right;
>> until I die I will not put away my integrity from me.
> I hold fast my righteousness, and will not let it go;
>> my heart does not reproach me for any of my days. (27:5-6)

> I cry to you and you do not answer me;
>> I stand, and you merely look at me.
> You have turned cruel to me;
>> with the might of your hand you persecute me. (30:20-21)

In other words, after 31 chapters, Job's question remains unanswered. Thus, even the layout of the book already says something about the problem, or better yet, the enigma, of suffering.
Through the very long considerations of the friends — three rounds
of discourse —, and the even longer rebuttal by Job, the author
shows that there is in fact no final answer concerning the issue of
human suffering. There is no end to the debate on suffering. In
such discussions, some parties will usually just give up any hope
of reaching consensus, simply because such debates never come to
an end. The same is true for the book of Job. The third round of
discourse is of a very different nature to the first two. Bildad's
speech is very short and Zophar doesn't even speak. Only Job
keeps harping on. And so he is the gloomy party par excellence.
He cannot and will not resign himself to his situation. At the end

---

[12] Before Job begins his great monologue in chapter 29, he praises Wisdom in
Job 28. Here, Job stresses that true wisdom belongs only to God, and is thus inac-
cessable to human beings. As regards human beings, "Truly, the fear of the Lord,
that is wisdom; and to depart from evil is understanding" (Job 28:28).

of his concluding monologue, he once more puts the ball in God's court, and challenges God to answer him:

> O that I had one to hear me!
>   (Here is my signature! Let the Almighty answer me!)
>   O that I had the indictment written by my adversary! (31:35)

3. Elihu: God's Defence

Before God speaks, however, a fourth, as yet unnamed, character takes the stage, namely Elihu. According to Job 32:1-6, he had followed the discussion between Job and his friends, but he had not entered the debate. Since Eliphaz, Bildad and Zophar failed to make Job see the light, he decides to speak. But, he rounds on both Job and his friends. Elihu reproaches Job for thinking himself more righteous than God. He reproaches the three friends for failing to make Job see that there is a reason for his suffering. Elihu takes up God's defence. Unlike Eliphaz, Bildad and Zophar, he chiefly emphasises the divine purpose of suffering: suffering is a form of divine admonition that aims to lead wrongdoers back to the straight and narrow:

> In a dream, in a vision of the night,
>   when deep sleep falls on mortals,
>   while they slumber on their beds,
> then he opens their ears,
>   and terrifies them with warnings,
> that he may turn them aside from their deeds,
>   and keep them from pride,
> to spare their souls from the Pit,
>   their lives from traversing the River.
> They are also chastened with pain upon their beds,
>   and with continual strife in their bones,
> so that their lives loathe bread,
>   and their appetites dainty food.

> Their flesh is so wasted away that it cannot be seen;
>   and their bones, once invisible, now stick out.
> Their souls draw near the Pit,
>   and their lives to those who bring death. (Job 33:15-22)

By punishing people with suffering for the wrongs they have done, God "opens their ears to instruction, and commands that they return from iniquity" (36:10); he "opens their ear by adversity" (36:15). Even if the righteous are affected, this is, according to Elihu, how God "declares to them their work and their transgressions, that they are behaving arrogantly" (36:9). Elihu's attitude also reflects traditional wisdom. The following proverb taken from the Old Testament book of Proverbs (13:24) applies to his argument: "Those who spare the rod hate their children, but those who love them are diligent to discipline them." In this way, Elihu responds to Job's accusation that God is silent in suffering. God, in fact, speaks through suffering. And since God's ways are mysterious (36:27-29), the only appropriate attitude for people to have towards God is one of awe and respect (37:24).

c. *God Himself Speaks: At Last, an Answer?*

After Elihu's explanation, God himself finally speaks, in Job 38:1. God's speech consists of two parts (38:2–40:2 and 40:6–41:26). Job replies briefly to each part (40:3-5 and 42:1-6). In his discourses, God does not even think it worthwhile to address the arguments of the friends. God simply ignores the possibility that wrongdoings lie at the root of Job's suffering. And, in the epilogue of the book, God explicitly reprimands the three friends. God says to Eliphaz, "My wrath is kindled against you and against your two friends; for you have not spoken of me what is right" (42:7). But God is likewise silent regarding Job's actual suffering. Like all people who suffer, Job is ultimately left sitting with an unanswered question. All that God does in his two speeches is bring up the magnificence of Creation. In the first discourse, God speaks about Creation as a mystery. But He gives no answer regarding the issue of suffering. On the contrary, he bombards Job with one question after the other:

> Where were you when I laid the foundation of the earth?
>   Tell me, if you have understanding.
> Who determined its measurements – surely you know!
>   Or who stretched the line upon it?
> On what were its bases sunk,
>   or who laid its cornerstone
> when the morning stars sang together
>   and all the heavenly beings shouted for joy?
> Or who shut in the sea with doors
>   when it burst out from the womb?

While God puts the grandeur of Creation and her order in the spotlight in the first discourse, in the second he refers to the chaotic in Creation. This is especially so in the reference made to the primal monsters *Behemoth* and *Leviathan*, which, although they are of course reduced to creatures, still embody the powers of chaos in Creation.

God, in his creation plan, had a pure and perfect order in mind (see the passage about Genesis 1:1–2:4), in which the powers of chaos would be completely restrained and in which there would be no place for suffering and violence. However, in reality, the disruption of the intended order by chaos remains a possibility.

In this regard, there seems to be a remarkable parallel between the creation narrative in Genesis 1:1–2:4 and God's second discourse in Job. In the first narrative, God does not create out of nothing. It is not a *creatio ex nihilo*. On the contrary, chaos is the cosmic power that was initially present. It is precisely this chaos that God applies boundaries too by incorporating it into the rhythm of an ordered Creation. However, even in this context, the potentially menacing power of chaos still exists. In an analogous way, God's second discourse in Job, by referring to the two primal monsters *Behemoth* and *Leviathan*, seems to say that though these embodiments of chaos, as "creatures," are incorporated into the order of Creation, they nevertheless remain essentially chaotic or "evil." This seems to suggest that suffering is just part of the chaos. As a form of chaos, suffering consequently proves to be an inextricable part of Creation.

Nonetheless, it is noteworthy that God, in the same narrative tradition, was not the one who created chaos. God is not the origin of chaos. Chaos pre-existed. It was primordial to creation. Genesis 1:1 tells us that chaos and darkness was the original situation in which God began the process of creation. In other words, the suffering that is an intrinsic part of chaos was there before God brought about Creation. In the act of creation, God set limits to this chaos, but the chaos itself somehow continues to exist.

d. *Conclusion*

At the end of this section, we can, in other words, conclude that dogmatic or philosophical discussions about the incompatibility of God's omnipotence or goodness with suffering are thus not what the book of Job is about. Suffering is part of chaos. And so, the book of Job does not primarily examine the relationship between God and human suffering. In fact, particularly in the first thirty-seven chapters, it appears to be about the attitudes that people adopt towards God when they are confronted by suffering as a manifestation of chaos. These attitudes posed a problem for people living so many centuries ago… and not much has changed today. It remains a difficult question. The realisation that people in the Old Testament also struggled with this seems to prove, in any case, that biblical literature is fundamentally and existentially rooted in human life. Thus, though it may in many ways seem "strange," it can certainly never be "strange to life."

3. Love in the Bible: The Last Word?

A chapter on biblical language concerning human fortunes and emotions would not be complete without reference to perhaps the most intense of all human emotions, love. Love can make a fundamental mark on human life, moulding it and giving it shape, completely filling it and "full-filling" it. Love comes over (and overcomes) people unexpectedly and often also undeservedly, breaking into their lives, transforming and sometimes dominating them, transforming the future and opening up new vistas and new roads, to finally raise people above themselves, up to the almost tangible presence of the transcendent and the divine.

In what follows, this love is discussed within the framework of the literature of the Old Testament. Here, it is about love in the full sense of the word, not a pale reflection, not some spiritualised form, but indeed the real, lived, intense — even bodily — love. In addition to the countless sayings in the books of Ecclesiastes and Ecclesiasticus, which praise the love between a man and a woman as well as the ideal of a harmonious marriage and family life, the beautiful story of Tobit and the famous book of Canticles point to the full appreciation of human love in all its aspects. This section discusses love from the perspective of the book of Canticles. Notably, this book, free of the institutional aspect of marriage and also not primarily out of a concern, so prominent elsewhere, for the generation of offspring, sings the praises of the (erotic) love between a man and a woman, and does so in an exceptional way that is in contrast to the other abovementioned books — namely it does so from the perspective of the woman.[13]

---

[13] Cf. Hans Ausloos and Bénédicte Lemmelijn, "Man en vrouw schiep hij hen (Gn 1,27): Het bijbelse concept van het huwelijk en zijn receptie in de conciliaire documenten van Vaticanum II," *Levensrituelen: Het Huwelijk*, ed. Roger Burggraeve, Michel Cloet, Karel Dobbelaere and Lambert Leijssen, Kadoc-studies, 24 (Leuven: Universitaire pers Leuven, 2000) 164-178, especially 170.

a. *A Love Poem in an Anti-Erotic Tradition?*

One of the reproaches most often heard with regard to the Judeo-Christian tradition concerns its disparaging attitude to love and sexuality. Without doubt, this is rooted in a limited and very old-fashioned reading of the so-called second creation narrative (Genesis 2–3). This text tells of how the man and his wife ("Adam and Eve") eat from the "tree of knowledge of good and evil" (Genesis 3:1-6). This story has long been interpreted as referring to the "fall" of humankind, whereby the author supposedly wanted to explain how, because of humankind — a woman at that! — evil entered the world. Moreover, by making a connection between the notion of "knowledge" and the biblical, sexual "knowing," a link was soon made between sin and sexuality. Indeed, in Hebrew, the verb ידע (*jada'*) can as easily refer to knowledge in terms of understanding or experience as it can to knowing one another sexually (sexual intercourse). And so, Genesis 4:1, the verse that immediately follows the story of their banishment from paradise, tells us that the man ("Adam") "knew" his wife, at which she fell pregnant and gave birth to Cain.

This connection between "sin" and sexuality has absolutely no basis in the text. In the Paradise Narrative, sexual "knowledge" is in no way what is meant. "Good and evil" function as a merism that refers to all knowledge. Nevertheless, the abovementioned (incorrect) interpretation has fundamentally left its mark on the history of Judaism and Christianity. Note, this is about a particular interpretation, not about the Bible text itself. However, if one interprets the biblical creation narrative in this way and at the same time makes it *the* biblical vision of sexuality, one unavoidably comes up against serious problems when one looks at the Old Testament book of Canticles, in which a besotted young man and an equally besotted girl declare their love for one another, in no

238

THE BIBLE: A BOOK OF LIFE

way shying away from using erotic language either.[14] A few
excerpts will illustrate this.

In Canticles 2:2, the young man sings of the uniqueness of his
girl using imagery from nature:

> As a lily among brambles,
> so is my love among maidens.

The girl replies in Canticles 2:3-4:

> As an apple tree among the trees of the wood,
> so is my beloved among young men.
> With great delight I sat in his shadow,
> and his fruit was sweet to my taste.
> He brought me to the banqueting house,
> and his intention towards me was love.

In Canticles 4:1-7, the young man rejoices over the beauty of his
girl:

> How beautiful you are, my love,
> how very beautiful!
> Your eyes are doves
> behind your veil.
> Your hair is like a flock of goats,
> moving down the slopes of Gilead.
> Your teeth are like a flock of shorn ewes
> that have come up from the washing,

---

[14] See among others Jan Fokkelman, "Liefdespoëzie: Het Hooglied," *Dichtkunst in de bijbel: Een handleiding bij literair lezen*, ed. Jan Fokkelman (Zoetermeer: Meinema, 2000) 212-231; Jan Fokkelman, "Hooglied," *De bijbel literair: Opbouw en gedachtegang van de bijbelse geschriften en hun onderlinge relaties*, ed. Jan Fokkelman and Wim Weren (Zoetermeer/Kapellen: Meinema, 2003) 377-388; Ludger Schwienhorst-Schönberger, "Das Hohelied," *Einleitung in das Alte Testament*, ed. Erich Zenger, Kohlhammer Studienbücher Theologie, 1/1 (Stuttgart: Kohlhammer, [5]2004) 389-395. In the latter contribution one can find a bibliographical overview of the most important recent commentaries and studies concerning Canticles.

all of which bear twins,
    and not one among them is bereaved.
Your lips are like a crimson thread,
    and your mouth is lovely.
Your cheeks are like halves of a pomegranate
    behind your veil.
Your neck is like the tower of David,
    built in courses;
on it hang a thousand bucklers,
    all of them shields of warriors.
Your two breasts are like two fawns,
    twins of a gazelle,
    that feed among the lilies.
Until the day breathes
    and the shadows flee,
I will hasten to the mountain of myrrh
    and the hill of frankincense.

The last four lines are a very literal translation that fully expresses the bearing of this text. They make it clear that the whole love scene takes place at night.

In Canticles 7:2-9, the young man admires his girl while she dances. Note that the reader in this passage follows the young man's gaze from bottom to top:

How graceful are your feet in sandals,
    O queenly maiden!
Your rounded thighs are like jewels,
    the work of a master hand.
Your navel is a rounded bowl
    that never lacks mixed wine.
Your belly is a heap of wheat,
    encircled with lilies.
Your two breasts are like two fawns,
    twins of a gazelle.
Your neck is like an ivory tower.

Your eyes are pools in Heshbon,
by the gate of Bath-rabbim.
Your nose is like a tower of Lebanon,
overlooking Damascus.
Your head crowns you like Carmel,
and your flowing locks are like purple;
a king is held captive in the tresses.

How fair and pleasant you are,
O loved one, delectable maiden!
You are stately as a palm tree,
and your breasts are like its clusters.
I say I will climb the palm tree
and lay hold of its branches.
O may your breasts be like clusters of the vine,
and the scent of your breath like apples,
and your kisses like the best wine
that goes down smoothly,
gliding over lips and teeth.

It is not only the young man who praises the girl. She too is
delighted by her boy. In contrast to the above passage, her description goes from top to bottom. Here is what she says in Canticles
5:10-16.

My beloved is all radiant and ruddy,
distinguished among ten thousand.
His head is the finest gold;
his locks are wavy,
black as a raven.
His eyes are like doves
beside springs of water,
bathed in milk,
fitly set.
His cheeks are like beds of spices,
yielding fragrance.
His lips are lilies,
distilling liquid myrrh.

His arms are rounded gold,
   set with jewels.
His body is ivory work,
   encrusted with sapphires.
His legs are alabaster columns,
   set upon bases of gold.
His appearance is like Lebanon,
   choice as the cedars.
His speech is most sweet,
   and he is altogether desirable.
This is my beloved and this is my friend,
   O daughters of Jerusalem.

b. *Origin and Interpretation of the Book of Canticles*

Although the book of Canticles — literally Song of Songs — is traditionally ascribed to King Solomon, the final redaction thereof possibly dates from the fourth or third century BC. People have always had difficulties with the text, as is patently obvious from the very heated discussions that continued to take place in Judaism until the first century AD and in Christianity until the sixth century AD over the question of whether this work should be given a place in the Bible or not. After all, it is striking that there is no evident mention of God. Only in Canticles 8:6 does one possibly encounter an explicit reference to God. The last two consonants of the Hebrew word שלהבתיה (*sjalhevetjah*) may be a possible abbreviation of the name YaHWeH. The NRSV translates this Hebrew *hapax legomenon* (a word that only appears once in the Bible) as follows: love is "a raging flame." Yet, if one translates it thus, then there is not a single explicit reference to God in the entire book. In addition, the fact that Canticles appears to be pure love poetry, in which erotic language is anything but avoided, certainly opens the way to doubting its canonicity — its eligibility to belong to the biblical canon. Whatever the case may be, the fact is that both Judaism and

Christianity ultimately consider Canticles to be part of the Holy Scriptures.

For a long time, it was accepted that the reason why Canticles was accorded a place by both Jews and Christians in the official list of biblical writings had to do with the allegorical manner in which the work was read[15]. Within Judaism, the boy and the girl were read as metaphors for God and Israel and their mutual relationship. Christianity built on this and viewed the lovers as representative of Christ and the Church or Mary. One of the reasons why they thought that Canticles should be read allegorically can perhaps be found in the place that the book ascribes to the motif of the vineyard. After all, in various Old Testament texts — one thinks of the song of the vineyard in Isaiah 5 — the vineyard functions as a metaphor for the people of Israel. Moreover, they referred to the prophetic literature, in which the marriage between two people, as well as the potential problems encountered in a marital relationship, is seen as representing the relationship between God and Israel.[16] In order to confront Israel with her unfaithfulness, God orders the prophet Hosea to become a symbol

[15] See also Hans Ausloos and Bénédicte Lemmelijn, "Canticles as Allegory? Textual Criticism and Literary Criticism in Dialogue", *Florilegium Lovaniense. Studies in Septuagint and Textual Criticism in Honour of Florentino García Martínez*, ed. Hans Ausloos, Bénédicte Lemmelijn, Marc Vervenne, Bibliotheca Ephemeridum Theologicarum Lovaniensium, 224 (Leuven/Paris/Dudley, MA: Peeters, 2008) 35-48. Cf. also Hans Ausloos and Bénédicte Lemmelijn, "Eine Neue Interpretation des Hoheliedes 8,5ab," *Zeitschrift für die alttestamentliche Wissenschaft* 119 (2007) 556-563.

[16] In this regard see Hans Ausloos and Bénédicte Lemmelijn, translated from the Dutch: "It is remarkable that the biblical, and in particular the Old Testament, language does not put forward the relationship between God and Israel as the model for marriage, but rather the other way around, using the human and social reality of marriage with all its joys, but also with all its possible problems, as the methaphor to characterise the relationship between God and his people." *Man en vrouw schiep hij hen (Gn 1,27)*, 175.

of it by marrying a prostitute, "for the land commits great whore-dom by forsaking the LORD" (Hosea 1:2). The fact that the theme of the wedding also comes up here and there in Canticles, they then took to mean that the relationship between the boy and the girl should also be interpreted as a metaphor for the relationship between God and Israel. Furthermore, the references to marriage in Canticles also led people to make an explicit connection with marriage. This is most apparent in the older Bible Translations, such as the Dutch Willibrord translation of 1978, in which the speakers are indicated as the "bride" and "bridegroom." However, in the Hebrew original, this indication of who is speaking is not present. They are the comments made by the translators. In Hebrew, one has to determine oneself who is speaking, based on the idiom. Usually this works, because, among other things, one can discern whether the speaker is male or female based on the form of the verb in Hebrew.

Although the metaphorical reading of Canticles can be a valua-ble approach, the original meaning and function has, nevertheless, been emphasised again since the seventeenth century. By analogy with Egyptian and Greek parallels, Canticles was originally an anthology of profane love songs that sung the praises of erotic love and in which, in all probability, there was an absence of any refer-ence to God. Canticles is erotic poetry in which, with similes and metaphors, the full range of sensual love is praised. On the one hand, this insight is an achievement of biblical research that one can hardly ignore. However, on the other hand, the fact that Can-ticles now makes up an integral part of the Bible as the "Holy Scriptures" obliges us to view the book as part of the Bible, thereby making it something more than just profane love poetry. Whether, and in which ways, Canticles has something to say to people in the twenty-first century as part of the Judeo-Christian Bible will be briefly addressed in the next section.

c. *Meaning and Function: "Divine" Love between Humans*

Above all, due to the fact that a biblical book sings the praises of human love, it is impossible to maintain that the foundation of the Judeo-Christian tradition — perhaps otherwise than its later elaboration — viewed erotic-sexual love as bad or sinful.

Its inclusion in the Bible accordingly demonstrates that Canticles — even though it clearly makes no reference to God — is in no way untheological. Especially in recent exegetical literature, people have tried to assess the true value of the theology in Canticles without falling into the old allegorical interpretation.[17] Various elements in Canticles make it plausible that, according to the book, the erotic-sexual love between a man and a woman is interpreted as a return to "paradise." This can be clearly seen in a number of striking similarities between Canticles and the abovementioned Paradise Narrative in Genesis 2–3. For example, Canticles 4:13 uses a Hebrew transcription of the Greek word παράδεισος (*paradeisos* – "paradise"). We come across this term thirteen times in the Greek version of Genesis 2–3, where the original Hebrew reads גן (*gan* – "garden"). Moreover, the motif of the garden plays a very important role in Canticles. The Paradise Narrative in Genesis 2–3 ends as follows:

> … therefore the Lord God sent him forth from the garden of Eden, to till the ground from which he was taken. He drove out the man; and at the east of the garden of Eden he placed the cherubim, and a sword flaming and turning to guard the way to the tree of life (Genesis 3:23-24).

At the end of the Paradise Narrative, the luxurious oasis that God had prepared for people has become a *"paradise lost."* Canticles

[17] The ideas that follow are primarily borrowed from Othmar Keel, *Das Hohelied,* Zürcher Bibel Kommentare, 18 (Zurich: Theologischer Verlag, 1986).

4:12-15 seems to envision the rediscovery of this lost paradise when the young man says of his lover:

> A garden locked is my sister, my bride,
>   a garden locked, a fountain sealed.
> Your channel is an orchard of pomegranates
>   with all choicest fruits,
>   henna with nard,
> nard and saffron, calamus and cinnamon,
>   with all trees of frankincense,
> myrrh and aloes,
>   with all chief spices –
> a garden fountain, a well of living water,
>   and flowing streams from Lebanon.

Furthermore, Canticles 7:10 could also be key to the interpretation that this book addresses the love that makes the restoration of the lost paradise possible. Here, the girl calls out, "I am my beloved's, and his desire is for me." With this, the author appears to echo Genesis 3:16. This verse is part of the divine "punishment" for the humans' transgression of God's prohibition that they may not eat from the tree of knowledge of good and evil. After God has condemned the snake to forever creep on its belly, God says to the woman, "I will greatly increase your pangs in childbearing; in pain you shall bring forth children, yet your desire shall be for your husband, and he shall rule over you." In her longing for children, the woman will pursue the love of the man. However, the man shall misuse this by making the woman into an object of his dominion. Well, Canticles 7:10 stands in stark contrast to this judgement by God in Genesis 3:16; Canticles 7:10 eliminates this inequality between man and woman, which had served as the basis for the oppression of women by men — common practice in the context in which the biblical writings came about. Just as the girl longs for the boy (Genesis 3:16) so the boy longs for the girl (Canticles 7:10). In this way, the disparity between man and woman that arose following "the fall" is undone, and a return is made to the original vision of creation: God made humankind as male and female. As an aside, the fact that the girl speaks most in Canticles is, in the context of the patriarchal society in which it was written, anything but normal. Moreover, she has the first (Canticles 1:2-4) and the last word (Canticles 8:14)!

Even if one denies that Canticles makes any explicit reference to God, love itself is viewed as divine. Pius Drijvers and Jan Renkman have rendered this beautifully in their Dutch translation (here translated again into English) of 8:6, mentioned earlier, in which the girl talks about her love for the boy:[18]

> Wear me as a seal upon your heart,
> as a ring on your finger.
> Because strong as death
> is love,
> relentless as the netherworld
> is passion.
> Her flames, flames of fire,
> a *divine* blaze.

With this, Canticles testifies to the fact that bodily-sexual love is "transcendent," or at least that it can be. It surpasses the human being. Canticles is convinced that love between people stems from a "divine" power that overcomes death and chaos and that is manifested in the uniqueness of the couple. So it is that the young man can cry out in 6:8-9:

> There are sixty queens and eighty concubines,
>   and maidens without number.
> My dove, my perfect one, is the only one...

---

[18] "Draag mij als een zegel op je hart, als een ring aan je vinger. Want sterk als de dood is de liefde, onverbiddelijk als het dodenrijk is de hartstocht. Haar vlammen, vlammen van vuur, een *goddelijke* gloed." Pius Drijvers and Jan Renkema, *Hooglied: Vertaald en van commentaar voorzien* (Baarn/Leuven: Davidsfonds, 2003) 29-31.

In this way, Canticles makes a case for personal love and against soulless sexuality. However, just like the rest of the Old Testament, the author of Canticles is also not naïve about life. On the one hand, he praises the beauty of the love between the boy and the girl and calls on them to enjoy their love to the full: "... drink, and be drunk with love" (Canticles 5:1). Yet, on the other hand he is himself aware of the many perils that lie in wait. This is not only apparent from the fact that the love scenes in Canticles, as already mentioned, mostly take place at night. It is also formally expressed in an ingenious way in the so-called Springtime Rhapsody (Canticles 2:8-17). In a very balanced literary composition, the young man and woman, using language that calls springtime to mind, evoke their love for each other. But this composition is interrupted, both in its form and its content, by an intermezzo in verse 15 in which the couple together ask for their garden of love to be defended against attackers:

> Catch us the foxes,
>   the little foxes,
> that ruin the vineyards –
>   for our vineyards are in blossom.

Thanks to Canticles, erotic-sexual love, as a manifestation of "divine" love, not only receives a place in the Bible, but also in the Judeo-Christian tradition. Love and sexuality are not sinful and bad. Canticles instead testifies to the firm conviction that, thanks to sexuality, the lost paradise can be regained, that which is most deeply human can find expression and the divine can become "tangibly" present in our reality.

Conclusion

At the end of the fourth chapter, it should by now be clear that the deepest human emotions are also echoed in the Bible's Old

Testament literature. People always begin to write and think from the perspective of who they are, what they see and feel, and what they experience. When people write about God and his involvement in our human existence, they also write in this way, in images, from the points of contact with us. One can, of course, only talk about something and think about something insofar as it is not completely alien to one. The same is true for the Bible. Of God and his influence on people, or perhaps rather of us and our experience of God, the Bible shares stories and poems that each, in their own way, bring other aspects of God and our reality to light. In doing so, it appeals to familiar experiences. How could one imagine that God looks with favour on human beings, if one does not know what it means "to love?"

Against this background, the above discussion has shown that the Old Testament literature is in no way naïve or otherworldly. On the contrary, it turns out to be intrinsically rooted in the human condition, the daily life and work of people who search and yearn, who know pain and suffering, but who are also just as capable of surpassing themselves in all-filling, almost transcendent love. And maybe that is something worth pondering: perhaps love does indeed have the last word.

CONCLUSION TO PART III

In the third part of this book, an attempt was made to illustrate the positive response to the disenchantment that was described in the second part, and which we argued was in a position to achieve a critical treatment of biblical texts, by applying it to a number of concrete examples. With this in mind, an introductory chapter first focused on the relationship between the Old and New Testaments. In the second chapter the question of the origin and purpose of humanity was dealt with against the background of a critical discussion of the Creation Narrative in Genesis 1:1–2:4. The third chapter focused on the way in which the Old Testament literature raises the issue of the realisation of human co-existence. Concretely we did this in two ways. First, we addressed interpersonal relationships and the fundamental respect for life in the context of a discussion of the so-called Decalogue in Exodus 20:1-17. Then we turned our attention to the theme of social justice in a discussion of the Old Testament concept of the jubilee year. Finally, in the fourth chapter, we looked at the issue of God and his relationship to human fortunes. More concretely, we focused on the three fundamental human emotions and experiences that define both the experience of and the reflection upon day to day existence, namely violence, suffering and love. Against this background, it was demonstrated that the Old Testament literature is existentially interwoven with all that occupies people, their desires and concerns, their work and leisure, their pain and joy. By using true-to-life realities, the Bible descries traces of the transcendent. That is where we experience God.

It should now be clear that when the Bible is approached and read in a critical, nuanced way, i.e. keeping in mind both the original, "strange" context in which it was composed and the deep significance of the concerns that are reflected upon and put into words, it can indeed reliably provide valuable insights that endow human life with more depth — even in this day and age.

GENERAL CONCLUSION

The aim of this book was to stimulate critical reflection on faith and the meaning and purpose of life in the context of our contemporary social climate in Western society based on a dialogue with biblical, and particularly with Old Testament, literature. With this in mind, the first part, "From Mystery to Disenchantment," presented the point of departure for this reflection. The "crisis" with which religion, faith and Christianity was confronted was interpreted against the backdrop of the cultural-historical evolution from pre-modernity, via modernity, to post-modernity on the one hand (chapter one), and the "strange" character of biblical literature, which serves as the foundation of faith and Christianity, on the other (chapter two).

Under the heading "Response to the Disenchantment," the second part outlined the possible reactions to this crisis. In two chapters, the negative and positive responses were describe and explained. The negative response was characterised as upheaval and resistance arising from a desire to protect "truth" and "reality," whether by trying to historicise the biblical stories, or, shifting hither and thither between literal and symbolic readings, by trying to fundamentalistically interpret and apply them. This approach was illustrated using the biblical fundamentalism of the Jehovah's Witnesses. The positive response was characterised as "Enrichment in Critical Relationship," which effortlessly rises above the disenchantment of modernity. In this context, the Bible was first critically related to questions such as historicity and archaeology. Then, attention was paid to the rise and value of historical-critical exegesis, which presents and interprets the biblical

texts as literature that has evolved over time. Finally, the more
recent evolution from diachronic to synchronic approaches to biblical texts was examined.

Against this, more theoretical, background, the third part, which
carries the title of this book, concretely sought to demonstrate the
way in which this critical, enriching interaction with biblical texts
can still mean a great deal for people today. After an introductory
first chapter, various fundamental, existential questions were raised
that still occupy people to this day, and that apparently also occupied them so many ages ago. In the second chapter, using the
Creation Narrative in Genesis 1:1–2:4, the origin and purpose of
human life is addressed. The third chapter zoomed in on the
achievement of human coexistence from the perspective of interpersonal relationships and respect for life on one hand, focussing
on the so-called Decalogue in Exodus 20:1-17, and on the other
hand, shed light on the issue of social justice using the Old Testament concept of the jubilee year as its point of departure. The
fourth and final chapter considered God's involvement in the highs
and lows of human existence. Focussing on three themes that
people, both then as now, have to deal with and are indeed fasci-
nated by — violence, suffering, and love — this chapter demonstrated how the Old Testament literature is intrinsically and realistically bound up with human existence and its enigmas.

We hope that we have thus made it clear that the core of biblical
literature concerns human existence and that it is directly associated with both the organisation of a liveable, dignified society, and
the way in which we relate to our fellow human beings and to
the transcendent that we sense or suspect in life. This suspicion,
this experience, and our reflection upon it, is what the biblical
person attempted to give expression to in narratives and in poetry.
The ancient literature that puts this into words may seem somewhat "strange" and surely it is so, but at its heart lies always the

relationship between human beings and God, between people and the reality of life which transcends them. In this sense, the essential question is always on the agenda, the so-called "meaning-giving" question.[1] This search for meaning seems to be an essentially human question, to the extent that it transcends the present moment. Thus, this question is then also intrinsically connected to our perception of time. People, perhaps now more than ever, are occupied with the future, even to the extent that the present is sometimes reduced to the preparation for the future and the road to be trodden is a road with a goal. They look towards where they would like to end up. In other words, the question is posed as to what purpose the "now" serves, or put differently, what the meaning of our lives is. This fact, on account of a one-sided, linear orientation, runs the risk of just becoming a continuous reaching out for what is to come. The consequence of this is that the present flies lightly by without one even wondering whether that is in fact a good thing. This is exactly what the Old Testament book of Ecclesiastes (or Qoheleth) is referring to when it says that "All is vanity" (1:2-4):

> Vanity of vanities, says the Teacher,
>   vanity of vanities! All is vanity.
> What do people gain from all the toil
>   at which they toil under the sun?
> A generation goes, and a generation comes,
>   but the earth remains for ever.

---

[1] The ideas elaborated upon in this conclusion were originally developed in the scope of a response to an argument put forward by Erik Borgman in the context of the Postacademische Vorming K.U.Leuven, Faculteit Godgeleerdheid, Vliebergh-Sencieleergangen, 2004. The publication thereof has appeared in Bénédicte Lemmelijn, "Bijbelse verhalen: Van mensen voor mensen, over een God die geen mens ooit vatten kan," *Toekomst voor verhalen en rituelen? Op het snijpunt van bijbel en geloofscommunicatie*, ed. Paul Kevers and Joke Maex (Leuven: Acco, 2005) 61-74.

Ecclesiastes' conclusion laconically tells us that it is better to enjoy the good things in life *now*. Incidentally, this is advice that is not uncommonly heard in today's social circumstances, perhaps precisely because it is a reaction to, and an expression of dissatisfaction with an all too strongly unequivocal linear orientation towards the accomplishment of tasks and assignments, or in religious terms, striving for fulfilment.

In contrast to a strong linear orientation, there is the concrete reality of nature and the world. In reality, a number of cyclical elements also turn out to be definitive. Incidentally, these recurring events were originally of great importance in the Judeo-Christian religion. The great liturgical feasts were and are celebrated to honour recurring moments in the rhythm of the seasons and nature. However, as long as people are only busy striving for and realising "projects" with important objectives, the days will indeed fly by, all seeming much the same. Nevertheless, when one, for example together with children, once again pays attention to the dawning of springtime, the feast of Easter, the summer holidays, the autumn and the winter with the feast of Saint Nicholas and Christmas, then one quickly realises that concrete reality is actually not at all linear, but rather cyclical. If people today were to once more have an eye for these things, and were not always doggedly pursuing their own goals, and indeed being mostly only interested in the completion of these goals, then perhaps the path of life that we travel would no longer just be a path with a destination, but rather a path that really becomes a path, because we consciously and deliberately walk it, step by step, here and now.

This reflection likewise raises the following question. Is it possible that precisely this linear orientation toward the future is at least partly responsible for the persistence with which people today still ask for "meaning and purpose" in life? The "meaning-giving question" attempts to discover what the meaning of something is.

In other words, the term "meaning" is here identified with the purpose or significance of the future. It is remarkable that this often seems to imply that things don't *have* meaning but that instead one has to *give* meaning to something.

In contrast to this way of thinking and living, the Old Testament wisdom literature, which was discussed in the last chapter of this book, presents an entirely different perception of reality. The Old Testament wisdom is, namely, oriented towards the realisation of a "blessed" existence in the present. The aim is to achieve a "full" life, here and now. The blessing of God means a happy, "fruitful" life, without harming one's fellow human beings. This blessing of God can be described as everything that brings people their deepest sense of happiness and fulfilment. It is, incidentally, also paired with "peace" in the broad, biblical sense of the word: inner harmony, peace with one's neighbour and peace with God. Against this background, this obviously seems to be talking about "worth," rather than about "meaning and purpose," with the connotations that these terms have. Not everything seems to make sense, to have meaning, as part of some grand scheme or perspective. Nevertheless, most things do indeed have "worth" in themselves. Ordinary, sincere living in the now, calmly experiencing all ordinary things, caring for a child and really teaching it everything, changing the sheets, doing the washing and ironing, cooking what they don't really like ... again. These are all undeniably things that mean little or nothing to the "grand future." However, in life in the here and now — and that is ultimately still the only time that one actually lives — they make life pleasant and "worth-while." Perhaps this is really about "diakonia" or a willingness to help. Ordinary life, with all its little and big day to day cares and worries, is all too often made to seem banal. Nonetheless, it is there that life actually plays itself out. This is life. All the rest — status, success, the goals that drive us, all that seems often so important to us — is only possible if we first live ordinary life. Is that then "meaning-less?" Maybe. But whatever the case may be, it seems "worth-full" to us. And perhaps we should, in the light of biblical literature, take that perspective a little further. If we start from the fact that all good things have "worth," then we could perhaps also say that they acquire "meaning" in the one perspective that supports "meaning," namely love. And this is precisely the horizon that both the Old and the New Testaments emphasise when they give equal weight to the two central tenets: Love God and love your neighbour.

In grateful memory of his lectures, we conclude this book with a saying of Prof. Em. Dr. Herman-Emiel Mertens. At the end of your life, it is perhaps not so important whether you were a "good Catholic," maybe it is a bit more important whether you were a "good Christian," but what it is ultimately about is whether you have been a "good person."[2] Towards the realisation of this ideal, the Judeo-Christian tradition and in particular its biblical foundation can, in our opinion, make an essential contribution. If this book, and the course "Religion, Finding Meaning and Philosophies of Life" on which it is based, can help to spread this insight, then our thought and writing has been both a "worth-full" and a "meaning-full" undertaking.

---

[2] Cf., about Herman-Emiel Mertens, also Marijke Verduyn, *De grote woorden voorbij: Een generatie theologen over God, werk en leven* (Zoetermeer: Meinema, 1998) 130.

PRINTED ON PERMANENT PAPER • IMPRIME SUR PAPIER PERMANENT • GEDRUKT OP DUURZAAM PAPIER - ISO 9706

N.V. PEETERS S.A., WAROTSTRAAT 50, B-3020 HERENT